Documentary
for the Small Screen

'This is how we see the world. We see it as being outside ourselves even though it is only a mental representation of what we experience on the inside.'
— René Magritte

'Life is very nice, but it lacks form. It is the aim of art to give it some.'
— David Puttnam
quoting Jean Anouilh

Documentary
for the Small Screen

Paul Kriwaczek

OXFORD AMSTERDAM BOSTON LONDON NEW YORK PARIS
SAN DIEGO SAN FRANCISCO SINGAPORE SYDNEY TOKYO

Focal Press
An imprint of Elsevier Science
Linacre House, Jordan Hill, Oxford OX2 8DP
200 Wheeler Road, Burlington MA 01803

First published 1997
Transferred to digital printing 2003

British Library Cataloguing in Publication Data
A catalogue record for this book is available from the British Library

Library of Congress Cataloguing in Publication Data
A catalogue record for this book is available from the Library of Congress

ISBN 0 240 51472 6

For information on all Focal Press publications
visit our website at www.focalpress.com

Printed and bound in Great Britain by Antony Rowe Ltd, Eastbourne

Contents

Contents

Preface

Why this book?

Until recently, film, video and television, both fiction and documentary, have been devised and created by specialized craft workers, using specialized knowledge and training. But now that is changing—and changing very fast.

That is not to say that professional film and video programme-makers are disappearing from the scene. Quite the reverse in fact. Britain, for example, has at the time of writing just under a thousand independent television film and video production companies—perhaps between two to three thousand directors and producers—mostly working in documentary, and all vying with each other to gain commissions from the limited number of broadcasters in this country. The same pattern is repeated on the continent of Europe, in Asia, Africa and the Americas. The number of programme-makers is growing all the time world wide.

What is new is that knowing something about film and video documentaries is rapidly evolving from being a difficult and complicated speciality, better left to the experts, to being a skill—or at least an understanding—now demanded from a large number of people in many different fields of work. The cost of video shooting and editing equipment has been falling for some time and is coming within reach of the general public. Its technical operation becomes ever simpler. Abstruse and arcane knowledge of electronic engineering is no longer a requirement. Unlike film, video does not have to be developed and printed; what has been shot can be seen and judged immediately.

As a result, a grasp of documentary film and video production, an understanding of how documentaries work and how they are made, is increasingly becoming part of the general literacy demanded of many walks of life. Of writers and journalists, of course, but also of teachers, public relations consultants, managers, university students, personnel officers—the list is a long one. And as older engineering industries are replaced by the new enterprises of the information age, it gets ever longer.

Film and video are becoming as central to communicating ideas and experiences in our late twentieth century societies as books, newspapers, magazines, leaflets, brochures, business reports, even diaries. The preferred mode for that communication is the genre of documentary. Whatever a person's job or position, it is likely that at some time or other he or she will come into contact with a film or video documentary of some sort: either by being in one, by being responsible for one, by commissioning one, by being asked to come to a judgement about one, even by coming across a subject about which they wish to make one.

Most people have been educated to work and think in a written rather than a visual medium. We are all trained from an early age in the use of the written word. Success in teaching reading and writing are the first touchstones by which many judge the quality of schools. Later on we try to learn how best to express ourselves on the page. We read and analyse the work of great writers of the past. Later yet, we may buy one of the many available self-improvement books on writing stories, screenplays, newspaper articles, memoirs, business reports, even letters.

By comparison with the written word, the moving image is much less well understood. Even perceptive viewers of television may not be aware of the devices and techniques, not to say the tricks, used by programme-makers to persuade us of the reality of what we are watching. The programme-makers themselves may not fully understand how they are achieving their effects, relying instead on a mixture of routine formula, gut-instinct and occasional inspiration. Film-making grew up as a specialist craft, not as an intellectual exercise, and has traditionally been learned by a form of apprenticeship. In the great broadcasting organizations, to which most workers in the industry once belonged, film school training used to be rather frowned upon, as if breaching some kind of amateur code—except in the case of a very few high-profile film-makers who were licensed to pursue the documentary form's artistic dimension. In most cases craft training on the job—'sitting next to Nellie'—was deemed all that was necessary for a documentary producer's or director's professional development.

A would-be director or producer would spend years doing one of the lowlier jobs in production until one day given the big chance. You might have a double-first from Oxford University, but you've still got to do your stint as researcher and assistant producer first. When formal training was given—in Britain it was mostly by broadcasters like the BBC—it was aimed at those doing such apprenticeship service, and was intended more to stop them wasting money than to improving their art. Over the years there seemed little need to think about and systematize the basic principles on which the medium depends and no point at all in working out how these might be taught to a much wider group of the population.

Today, the situation is changing. Many people are now involved in making films and videos of all kinds: people who cannot be expected to spend years learning on the job, but who are nonetheless expected to deliver a workmanlike product. Others are called upon to judge television documentaries commissioned in the course of their work. Still others would like to know more about the provenance of the documentary programmes they watch on broadcast television.

A distillation of what has been learned about the small-screen documentary, since its beginnings some fifty years or so ago, would be helpful to the many people who need to know something of the documentary production process or even how to look at and judge the documentaries they see on television or at work: to help them understand the principles of putting moving images together; to help them recognize the differences between the variety of techniques used in documentary making; to help them know something of the different stages of the production process and recognize the different skills that are called upon in each.

Documentry for the Small Screen is intended to introduce some of this. It cannot be the whole story. Film-making can no more be learned from an instruction manual than can sculpture or music composition. Nor can this or will this be the last word. Documentary is a living form and changes all the time in accordance with developments in our technology, our tastes, our fashions, our whole view of the world. It is in the throes of particularly rapid change as we career towards the end of the century.

Yet there are, I believe, some fixed points by which to steer. Film-making, like other creative arts and crafts, ultimately depends on the psychology of human perception. Though narrative conventions may change, we respond to story-telling in much the same way as our parents' and our grandparents' generations. Though our expectations of speed, slickness and style of film-making may differ, we react to a succession of moving pictures almost exactly as they did too. The illusion, usually called Persistence of Vision, which invests a series of still images with movement and is the base on which the whole television enterprise is founded, is a function of the brain and not the intellect. In the same way, unchanging human responses may be the foundation of many other of the principles of small screen documentary making. The film-maker's task amounts to a constant experiment to distinguish the inbuilt from the acquired, the functional from the learned, the necessary from the arbitrary. This book is intended to help both the would-be documentarist and the working film-maker in their journey of discovery.

A note about words

I shall use the expression *television documentary* as a way of specifying a particular form, while avoiding commitment to a particular technology. The word *television* is important because a basic premise behind this book is that making films or videos for the small screen, designed to be viewed in an everyday domestic or working context, involves facing problems and finding solutions which are rather different from those which apply to the cinema screen, intended to be watched in a darkened theatre. So in this book the phrase *television documentary* will not necessarily mean a film intended to be broadcast. It will mean a production intended for the small rather than the large screen.

Another problem: it is very difficult to find a way to include both film and video in any statement without having pedantically to spell out the alternatives every time. This quickly becomes wearying. But there is simply no expression which properly includes both.

In spite of the fact that cinema features are today invariably broadcast over the air from taped copies, and that many people watch movies at home on video-cassettes hired from a video store, the word video is hard to use when meaning a documentary shot on film, and strangely wrong sounding even when applied to a documentary actually produced electronically. Of course all words change their meanings over time. The *camera* is no longer a room. The word *film* no longer refers just to the light-sensitive chemical coating which captures the image on a strip of celluloid.

I feel that the word *film* has by now extended its meaning far enough to permit me to stretch it just a little further to include work shot with an electronic camera and recorded on tape. In what follows, when I use the word film, it will be irrespective of the actual medium used to capture the images. Unless, of course, I write otherwise.

Part I

The Nature of
Television Documentary

Chapter 1

Introduction

Haven't I seen you on TV?

Television, in all its forms, is a dominant feature of today's world culture. From Baltimore to Buenos Aires to Beijing, from Malmö to Makhachkala to Mahabalipuram, television is in the home, in the office, in the factory, in the hospital, in the post office, in the hairdresser, in the bar-room. Everywhere where people are, there is television. It comes by transmission from terrestrial antennae, by cable, by satellite, by closed circuit wiring.

TV is the primary communications medium of our age. It is our entertainer, our informer, our educator, our transmitter of culture, our codifier of ideology. It sets the agenda for political debate, manipulates our attitudes to ourselves and others, suggests shared images, stereotypes and paradigms. TV programmes put in front of us role models powerful enough to alter the way we behave. Real police carry out real actions in the style of their representation on the small-screen; politicians take up catch phrases, gestures and mannerisms ascribed to them by television satires. We know how undertakers, soldiers, bricklayers, authors, airline pilots, rock stars, factory workers are supposed to behave because we—and they—have seen it on television.

Television is our favoured way of presenting ourselves to the world. Most youngsters would prefer to tell the wider community about their school in a co-operative video rather than a written essay. Most company marketing managers judge the publicity value of a promotional film well above that of a printed brochure. Most political pressure groups or charitable foundations know that the persuasive power of a single television appearance is worth hundreds of leaflets.

This preference results from a number of television's particular qualities. One is the illusion of transparent truth that film and video seem to offer. Another is the very familiarity and ubiquity of the medium. TV is such a part of everyday experience that its codes and conventions, its complications and craftsmanship go largely unnoticed. The process of making a television programme seems to the casual observer to need little more than common sense and an eye for a picture.

One important factor which gives television its special status is the fact that until now access to it by ordinary people has been severely restricted. In the capitalist as well as the former communist world, in the developing countries as among the new industrial tiger economies of the Far East, television has been under the exclusive control of a cultural, political, social, commercial or artistic élite—at face value, a wide enough spectrum of people, but an élite nonetheless. The selection criteria for admission to that élite differ from country to country and society to society, but wherever one looks, broadcast television programmes have been made by a privileged few, and those in control of broadcasting their works have been an oligarchy also. This might not be so important in fiction film-making, but in the field of documentary it has meant only the chosen few making films about the unchosen many. It has not been possible for ordinary people to present their own image of themselves; they were only ever to be seen through the others' eyes.

In consequence, television everywhere has come to fulfil an important validating role. To appear on television is as if to have one's existence officially acknowledged. Being allowed onto the box is a kind of formal recognition of a person or a group's presence in society. Back in the 1970s *Parosi*,[1] though not a documentary series but a drama serial set among the South Asian community of the British Midlands, and which included passages of dialogue in Hindi and Urdu, had at the time—according to a UN report—a notable effect on the self-image and self-confidence of British people of Asian origin. Even now if you ever appear on television, people who normally meet you every day of your life feel driven to approach you with an impressed and almost awestruck: 'Didn't I see you on TV yesterday?'

It is tempting to compare the status of television production with that of writing in the European Middle Ages before the development of printing. In fact there is a considerable difference. Writing may have been a skill restricted to the few and controlled, in mediæval Europe at any rate, by the Church, but the products of the literate labour of monks and clerks were, unlike the products of the television producer, only accessible to the tiny minority who could read them. It was that minority who held the power in their society. In our form of democracy, public opinion has power, and television has from quite early on been available to, indeed directed towards, the majority of the population either in their own homes or their places of relaxation and entertainment.

Thus until now television has had all the features of a typical twentieth century mass medium, with costs which are quite unbalanced between producer and consumer. Much like other cultural products of our mass age, pop music for example,

[1] BBC 1976

television has everywhere been centrally tightly controlled by large corporations or government bureaucracies. It has been expensive to produce and distribute. At the same time it has been relatively easy to acquire and cheap to consume. Power, for good or ill, was largely in the hands of the producers. The consumer's choice was to answer a multiple choice question, to select between a small number of predetermined responses: to buy this record, that one or neither, to watch this channel, that one or switch off the television altogether.

Today, as we look towards the beginning of a new century, this imbalance has already begun to change. The unstoppable development of technology is starting to render the previous dispensation quite out of date.

Smaller, faster, better, cheaper...

Exactly where technology will lead is hard to determine. The notion that the development of technology is the major driving force in history is a shallow one. But so is the idea that the scientific agenda is set purely by social forces. Many people once imagined the future of telephones and radio quite wrongly, believing that radio would be used for point-to-point communications, while the telephone would relay music from the concert hall to the private home. However, of some things we can be reasonably sure, for as the technology of production continues its development— smaller, faster, better, cheaper was always the motto of the microchip—the pattern of the future is already becoming visible.

On the production side, electronics has almost completed its conquest over film. Video cameras are getting cheaper and better every day. Though at the time of writing, there is still an observable difference between the quality of image created by the consumer video camera and that provided by professional video-recording equipment, the gap is narrowing rapidly. The Sony BETA format, at present the standard professional recording format for location shooting, is related to a failed attempt to capture the consumer market.

In stills photography, the professional and the amateur have long had access to identical cameras. The equipment used to take holiday snaps is the very same as is used to produce the pictures which illustrate newspapers and magazines. As the television commercials suggest, anybody can now possess exactly the same still camera with which the most famous and successful professional photographers are equipped. It is *how* the camera is used, rather than *which* camera is used that makes the difference. The same will surely soon apply to video shooting.

At the same time, a rapid increase in the speed and memory capacity of computers is stimulating the migration of sound and video editing from very expensive high-precision tape technology to the computer hard disk. This gives video-editing, until recently a rather crude process, the flexibility of old-style film-editing, without the disadvantages of working with an unwieldy and fragile physical material. Much the same is happening in the medium of sound, where mixing and mastering on computer is becoming the new norm. As a result we are approaching a situation in which many people with neither great wealth nor specially privileged access to technology are able to shoot and edit their own video productions, in their own styles, expressing their own thoughts and values.

Taken by itself, this might not mean very much. It is one thing to produce your own film, quite another to ensure that it is seen by an audience. Distribution rather than production is the key to getting your work in front of the public. But distribution is subject to the very same technological trends as production: lower cost, smaller, more powerful and much cleverer equipment. Technology is combining with other social, political and economic forces to change the pattern of television quite radically. As cable now first complements and then maybe replaces broadcasting from ground-based aerials altogether, the number of channels available to select from is increasing all the time. Add to that the channels beamed down directly from satellites and the number becomes very large indeed. These new channels are ravenous for material to broadcast. There is also the ever-growing market in pre-recorded video-cassettes for sale or rent. It is no longer possible for a select and approved few to control the proliferation of pathways through to the public.

And waiting in the wings is a change that may yet make all our conceptions of broadcasting and broadcasters obsolete. Digital electronics is in the process of taking over all media. Every kind of information, all pictures and sounds, can be represented by, or converted to, digital codes which can then be manipulated by computers. In coded form, music, speech and video can be copied and passed from one computer to another with virtually no loss.

The linking up of computers in offices, factories, homes, even eating places into a vast global network, today's Internet, offers the possibility of an entirely new kind of distribution system for all manner of creative, scholarly and informational works. Music, video, text and many other materials already pass continually to and fro across the globe on what is to become the so-called 'information super-highway'. The process and the network itself cannot but continue to grow as more and more people link themselves to it. The result is likely to be that control of all electronic media by the few will be consigned to history.

Television is in the throes of being radically democratized—access to the medium is becoming available and accessible to all. Yet the tradition of documentary film-making has a long and distinguished history that is rooted in a very different world: a world of scarcity, of restricted access, of control by a small number of powerful institutions, of a society divided in rather different ways from those of our own. The documentary forms which we mostly take for granted were developed to satisfy needs which may no longer be relevant to a new era.

A heady time

There is no inevitability to the pattern of broadcasting that has grown up through the twentieth century. The mass media belong to the century of the masses, but it is not commanded by any law that television should exclusively be divided between a small number of makers and a mass of viewers. As technology spreads the use of the television medium from the few to the many, the pattern of the next hundred years begins to look very different.

Of course, there will always be a market for escapism, for entertainment and for production values greater the individual can afford. There will surely always be a place for the hundred-million dollar movie or for the five episodes a week soap opera, just as there is for the best-selling thriller novel. But in the same way as the vast majority of books published—some 80,000 in Britain in 1994—are non-fiction titles, so most of the films and videos produced now and in the future are and will always be factual. Of those, a large proportion will be documentaries, though precisely what kind of production the word documentary implies may be different in the future from what it has meant in the past.

The style of factual television with which we are familiar today has a long history. So much so that many people take it for granted that the current way of making films is the only way possible, inherent perhaps in the medium itself. Or, it is said, productions are as they are, simply in response to the audience's demands, no more no less. In reality the styles and formats of today are the result of a very large number of factors: yes, there is the logic of the medium itself, yes, there are the preferences of viewers, but there are also the needs of the producing organizations, the economics of film production and broadcasting, the ideology of the society in which they work, the aesthetic assumptions of those who make the programmes.

Regular evolution of these parameters over time makes the style of non-fiction television seem to change much faster than that of TV and film drama. Fiction from the early days of television shows its age far less than do documentary productions of the same period. One reason may be that the world of the drama, for all its apparent naturalism, is actually highly stylized, and may have been as far from the reality of its own times as it is from ours. Another is that fiction generally explores the film-maker's interior world, which changes far less over the years than the wider social world addressed by the documentarist.

Some aspects of film-making are forever fixed. Film and video will always depend on showing a sequence of still pictures at a speed which makes the eye perceive them as moving. Human psychology will always search for meaning when presented with sequences of events. But some of the other limitations on documentary style are anything but unalterable. And the rapid technological revolution taking place in our time, with its radical consequences for television broadcasting ownership and access, is already having an impact on the way television documentaries are made.

The television aesthetic is changing noticeably fast in the 1990s. Techniques and devices which were once considered impossible or unacceptable are commonplace today. The great debate over how to make the documentary live up to its claim of truth looks set to be abandoned, as a new generation of documentary makers, who recognize that there is never only a single truth, enjoy overtly manipulating the camera's images as if to emphasize their nature as interpretative icons rather than as mappings of reality. Today, the opportunities for original, ground-breaking and challenging work are once again as great as they were in the early days of film, at the time of the introduction of synchronous sound, or during the development of television as a medium. Indeed we are witnessing something of a golden age of television documentary at present, as broadcasters again attract sizeable audiences to new non-fiction productions. In Britain many documentary strands feature in peak-time hours, underlining the interest and entertainment value of ordinary people's extraordinary experiences. Even in the United States, with its very different television culture, major networks now commission documentary 'network specials' for mid-evening viewing hours. A heady time indeed.

A time to question the accepted way of doing things. The late writer and chemist Primo Levi described hearing after many years about a paint factory of which he was once the manager. To his astonishment, he discovered that the workers were still incorporating into the mix an ingredient he himself had once prescribed simply to neutralize a defect in a particular batch of raw material. The need for this ingredient had long gone and its purpose had been long forgotten, yet the workers were still faithfully putting it in. One wonders how many tired conventions and over-used clichés of the television documentary are also responses to needs long since passed away?

Though it is important to apply a critical, perhaps even cynical, eye to the ways and means, styles and formats used by film-makers up to now, the maker of documentaries need not abandon everything from the past and start again with an empty slate— and an empty mind. Today's documentarist needs to distinguish between those processes and procedures dependent on the psychology of vision, those intrinsic to the medium of moving pictures, those demanded specifically by the small screen, and those brought to bear by outdated social, political, structural or economic constraints. The successful documentary film-maker will remember the way things have been done in the past, but will also seek out new and original ways of applying the underlying logic of film and television to the communication process—and will write his or her own artistic signature over all.

Chapter 2

What is a Television Documentary?

'... TELEVISION PROGRAMME PRESENTING AN ACTIVITY OF REAL LIFE WITH IMAGINATION BUT WITHOUT FICTIONAL COLOURING...'
—*Fowler's Modern English Usage*[1]

The definition of precisely what constitutes a television documentary is still, nearly fifty years on, a matter of debate. For some, the word refers only to a form of narrative film made in a specific ideological tradition: the Documentary Movement. For others, documentaries are more general in their style of execution, but are still limited in their subjects to stories about people and society, particularly if made from a radical point of view. In popular usage, as Fowler attests, the word is given the widest meaning of all, referring to almost any non-fiction production which aims to say something about the real world. Fowler even goes on to suggest that documentaries may or may not involve actors.

For many people non-fiction and documentary are nearly synonymous terms. When a word is in common use it seems perverse to insist on placing only a limited interpretation on it, but there must be some agreed boundary if the category is not to be so wide as to be worthless. Of course words are given their meanings by the people who speak and write them, dictionary definitions are only a record of common usage. But film-makers generally find it more appropriate to reserve the word documentary for non-fiction productions which aim to present, or 'document', some aspect of real life by actually showing it on the screen.

Though the public may use *documentary* to include far more varieties of television production than many film-makers would, they do nonetheless mean something specific by the word. Its use, or at least its equivalent in French, to describe a non-fiction film goes back a hundred years to the very beginnings of the film medium. Today the word retains historical associations and implications which are important in influencing the audience's assumptions. The word *documentary* carries with it suggestions of objectivity and evidence. In addition, the medium of film or video, of photography itself, has a special place in the representation of truth.

Unlike a written description or an artist's impression, we take

[1] Second edition 1965

it for granted that a camera is a device which records the image of
what is put in front of it without intervention or interpretation.
Though we cannot know how a film's subject came to be in front
of the camera, we do assume that whatever the camera recorded
did actually take place. Even fiction films are, in this sense,
documentary records of actors' real performances. And even
though most people know full well that photographs and film
sequences can be manipulated and changed by today's technology,
the idea that the camera does not lie is deeply entrenched in our
culture. Trust in the truth of the photographic image is reinforced
every time a horse race is decided by a photo-finish, a football
referee's decision is called into question by a televised action replay,
or a suspected criminal is identified from the records of a
surveillance video camera.

Yet many films which the general public call documentaries
use techniques which having nothing to do with the unmediated
capture of real world events. Many of the features of standard
television non-fiction—the use of voice-over commentary or a
presenter, the inclusion of graphics and stills, of sections
dramatized with actors—are not concerned with the direct
representation of the real. Other elements, such as interviews and
discussions, are events specifically organized for the purpose of
filming. While these are real events as recorded by the camera,
their world is that of the television medium and not that of day to
day reality. They belong to a kind of semi-, or television reality,
whose artificiality is drawn to our attention only when something
goes wrong. The shock value of an interviewee bursting into tears
or pleading for the filming to stop, being overcome by emotion or
getting up and walking out, is in the way it breaks the interview
convention. At that instant the interview jumps from
mere television reality into the directly real, out of the control of
the film-maker.

Showing not telling

To avoid confusion, a useful distinction is to separate the idea of a
documentary, the very general term which can mean so many things,
from the concept of *documentary technique*, to which we can give a
specific and restricted meaning. A *documentary sequence* uses the
documentary technique of *showing* the viewers rather than *telling*
them—playing out the story in front of the audience rather than
reporting it at second hand. This is what makes the technique
different from other ways of communicating about the real world
on television. Explanations to camera, descriptions and accounts
by experts, are not part of the documentary technique, nor is it

used in cookery demonstrations, most party political broadcasts, celebrity interviews or DIY shows.

The primary use of the documentary technique is to present evidence, since film is believed to be a record of objective truth. This impression is strongly enhanced by the fact that human intervention in the process, particularly when skilfully done, is not noticeable to most viewers. In actual fact the objective truth delivered by the documentary technique is less than it may seem. Though the camera captures what is in front of it by a purely physical process without human intervention, the claim to an unmediated record of reality can apply only to a single shot from a single stationary and randomly positioned camera. Even pointing the camera towards a particular part of the scene and switching it on at a particular moment are the result of a conscious human decision to influence what the audience sees.

But documentary sequences almost invariably consist of more than a single static shot. Shots must be linked together to built up sequences. To do this, the documentary technique uses precisely the same methods of montage and assembly of material as do fiction films. The similarity goes further than editing. Playing out a story in front of the viewers uses the same narrative methods, the same time compression, the same ways of showing cause and effect, the same encouragement to identify with the characters who appear on the screen. Fiction and the documentary technique constantly cross-fertilize each other, feature films borrowing the hand-held camera look from the documentary technique to give sequences an added verisimilitude, documentary makers making use of editing conventions learned by the audience from cinema movies.

Like the fiction film, the documentary technique aims to encourage the audience to experience what is shown *as if they themselves were there.* So, paradoxically, even though the premise of the documentary technique is that it represents a picture of the truth, it requires from the viewer a similar suspension of disbelief to that demanded by a fiction. In fact there is no way of discovering from the construction of a sequence whether it is documentary or drama. The difference will only be in its context and the film-maker's stated intention and procedure.

Of course it is true that sequences made by the documentary technique will generally look and sound very different from those which are dramatized with actors. This has nothing to do with the way that the shots were taken or the sequence assembled and everything to do with the style conventions of television drama. Though dramatists and directors may strive for what they think of as naturalism, screen acting style is actually highly conventionalized and stylized, particularly when delivering dialogue. Actors speaking lines, even if improvized, usually stand out as noticeably artificial and mannered when combined with real world characters performing as themselves.

Thus the documentary technique creates sequences which have their own particular character: fictional in shape and construction—film grammar as some call it—but recognizably different in manner and style. Audiences have by now become so familiar with the convention that they rarely question the artifice by which such sequences have been created.

The melting pot

Though combining documentary and non-documentary elements within the same sequence is rarely successful, most television productions happily link whole documentary sequences with a variety other kinds of materials. In fact films which adhere exclusively to the ideal of presenting an image of reality on the screen unmediated by other non-documentary elements, are relatively rare. Most subjects cannot be fully presented by documentary technique alone. Even in fiction, voice-over commentary has often been used to include otherwise inaccessible aspects of the wider environment, as in many examples of the 'Film Noir', which make use of the laconic 'hard-boiled' manner of detective speech developed by Dashiel Hammett and Raymond Chandler. Here the stylistic impact of the spoken text adds not just information but attitude. Documentary film-makers, particularly those working in a journalistic style, often use commentary to the same end. And not just commentary, of course, but many other kinds of different visual and sound techniques.

Thus a documentary or documentary film in its widest, popular sense, can be defined as a production which tells a story about, or describes something in, the real world, using the documentary technique to provide evidence and to forge a link with reality.

Most factual programmes on television are not pure examples of any genre. Television is a melting pot, using a mixture of techniques: exposition, description and analysis, as well as documentary sequences. Many productions which are actually billed as documentaries have the documentary technique as only one weapon in their armoury of effects. And many productions which do not claim documentary status at all nonetheless use documentary sequences as an integral part of their presentation method. For the documentary technique has become a standard way of displaying on the television screen evidence about events, characters, relationships or almost any other aspect of the real world.

Documentary scenes turn up in many different kinds of television productions: about people and about society of course, but also about science and the arts, about history and geography, as well as educational and promotional films, current affairs and religious programmes. Whenever the aim of the film-maker is to present the audience with an image of reality—an occasion, an event, a person or a group of people as they appear in real life—the documentary technique is the preferred choice.

The documentary technique can only provide an external, outsider's view. Without interviews or other non-documentary elements, it is very difficult to bring out the private thoughts and attitudes of the characters in the film. Unless thoughts are by chance expressed in dialogue, it is not often that people's public behaviour illuminates at all clearly what is going on in their minds. In pure documentary technique the favourite television question: 'how does that make you feel?', a question that interviewers believe (perhaps rightly) the audience most wants them to put, can be neither asked nor answered. Pure documentary is a play performed before an audience—it provides an external, one might say superficial, view only. There can be no explicit interpretation, no elaboration, no explanation. The documentary technique is the film equivalent of behaviourist psychology, which invests reality only in actual behaviour and ignores the significance of interior mental states. Of course film-makers strive energetically to find hints and indications of their subject's internal feelings in the details of their behaviour. But such details are not explicit—they can only be inferred. At the same time, because documentary technique restricts itself to the concrete and to the here-and-now, it is also limited in its ability to communicate more complex and wider-ranging phenomena: the Big Picture, in other words.

For many subjects, these limitations are a considerable disadvantage. Only certain kinds of topics can be handled this way, mostly matters relating to the specific, the personal and the individual. Any attempt to deal with subjects either not already familiar to the viewer, demanding an understanding of wider relationships and factors, or relating to the interior world of their subjects are not altogether suitable for pure documentary treatment.

57 different varieties

For reasons of corporate history and structural convenience, most television organizations divide their factual output into separate categories, usually relating to different subject areas. Actually of course, factual productions represent a continuum with no hard distinctions, belonging to rather more than 57 different varieties. But the need to process the output along a continuous assembly line—nothing is more terrifying to the television scheduler than the prospect of blankness and silence on the airwaves—and the recognition that packaging the product as predictably as cans of soup helps the audience to select from the bewildering array of material available to it—commissioning producers are given to saying things like: 'sorry but I don't really see this as a *Time and Tide*'—means that firm boundaries are usually drawn between productions dealing in different ways with different subject areas.

Thus separate departments may have been set up for— amongst other categories—'pure' documentaries, programmes about the arts, about the sciences, about history, about religion. This is convenient for the organization's permanent staff, since film-makers do develop expertise in a particular area of work. It is hard for someone who has always made, say, films about scientific subjects suddenly to switch to making religious documentaries. But as permanent staff decline in number and institutions move over to commissioning productions from independent documentarists, fewer and fewer film-makers will have the luxury of restricting themselves to a single thematic domain. This in itself may be no bad thing, both from the point of view of the audience and of the film-maker. Though perhaps uncomfortable for the documentarist, who is to say that a religious documentary would not benefit from the sensibility of an experienced science film-maker.

That is not to say that all television documentaries, whatever their subjects, are much the same. There are some real and clear distinctions to be made between different kinds of productions, though the differences are related not so much to the specific subject area as to the general purpose of the film.

The primary distinction to be drawn is between the kind of documentary where the subject appears directly on the screen, as opposed to the kind which uses the television medium to communicate ideas about something over and above the specific content of the images. Some films, in other words, are primarily about describing particular concrete subjects, others are principally about ideas, for which the screen images act as evidence, example or symbol. It is the difference between the literary sketch and the essay.

So for instance, *Volvo City*,[1] a film which painted an entertaining and informative picture of the community of orthodox Hasidic Jews in north London clearly belonged to the first category, which one may call pure or *observational documentary*. Though there were

[1] Channel 4 1991

inferences to be drawn and implications to be understood, the film was about the characters and situations which appeared on the screen. By contrast *The Last Exodus,*[1] a film about the last hundred years of Jewish history in Eastern Europe was not restricted to being about the people who appeared in it, but used them as indices or pointers to the larger story and larger idea, an example of what one may call the *essay documentary*.

No matter what the actual subjects, examples of the observational documentary—the literary sketch—have far more in common with each other than with the essay. Examples of the essay have more in common with each other than with the observational, even when there are wide differences in subject matter and content. Thus, though both productions were basically about groups of Jews, *Volvo City* shares its technique and style with a great variety of observational films dealing with subjects and characters very different from London Jews, while an essay such as *The Last Exodus* has much in common with productions about subjects as diverse as the discovery of the planet Pluto or the life of Picasso.

There is yet a third genre of film which is usually counted as a documentary form—in the widest sense of the word—though its inclusion is slightly problematic. These films are productions which have a purpose beyond that of description and narrative, whether about specific characters or general ideas—films with an ulterior motive, so to speak. Many film-makers would not call them documentaries at all, though they do fit in with the definition of the genre as films which describe something about the real world using the documentary technique to present evidence. In this category we find educational films and promotional videos.

The problem with such works is that their purpose may be so different from that of other documentaries that judging them by documentary standards is impossible. If a documentary is defined as a production which tells a story about, or provides a description of, the real world, then achievement or failure can be estimated by how far the production succeeds in telling the story or putting over the description. But educational or promotional productions may have other purposes altogether. They can only be classified together with documentaries insofar as their aims accord with those of the kinds of documentary considered so far.

All observational documentaries are essentially descriptive narratives and all make use of much the same film narrative techniques. Film essays all have much in common too, but the practical realization of the film essay depends much more on the subject of its basic theme. The primary task facing those working in the medium of the essay documentary is to find a way of converting the exposition of ideas into narrative and descriptive

[1] BBC 1991

form. The means by which this is done will be different in different subject areas. Science programmes usually bring to bear a rather different toolbox of effects from that used by films about the visual arts, documentaries about religion use rather different forms from those used by wild-life productions, music films have their own particular problems to overcome as do documentaries about history or geography.

That is not to say that there is never any cross-over. Clearly science and natural history share many characteristics—they may even be about the very same subjects—yet even so, audience expectations may ensure that the two varieties of documentary look rather different on the screen. In the same way, an arts documentary may cover much the same ground as a history film—indeed there have been many examples which certainly do—nevertheless the thrust of the work may be quite different and demand a different approach from the documentary maker. Making a famous painter's life into a filmically convincing story presents difficulties quite unlike those involved in turning an explanation of global warming into a workable documentary subject. Developing a critique of Wall Street into a satisfying film means using methods rather distinct from those involved in putting over an exploration of the beliefs of the Nation of Islam.

Though each particular subject faces the documentarist with a unique set of problems, the different subject areas mostly have a sufficiently long history to have accumulated a collective wisdom of a sort. The best way for a documentary maker to approach a new subject is to listen to the experiences of others who have worked in and faced the problems of that area before—and then make up his or her own mind. Most documentarists will want to put their own personal stamp on their filmic treatment. Here as elsewhere, excellence will be the result of a judicious combination of tradition with innovation, of the tried and tested with the novel and experimental. Art and craft usually advance most satisfactorily by small steps. Giant leaps may please the ego of the artist but may well leave the audience trailing far behind.

Chapter 3

How do we Start?

A documentary begins with an idea and the desire to communicate it to an audience. In this it is little different from the starting point of a fiction film. But the idea which begins a documentary is usually subtly different from the starting point of a fiction. Both arise from the real world—else there would be no contact point with the audience. But where the fiction film-maker turns inward to explore his or her internal world, putting imagined characters into an invented situation and following the consequences, the documentarist devotes him- or herself to the external world, the real world as we are forced to call it.

Both forms tell stories with which their creators hope to say something about life, the world and the human condition, but the documentary film-maker chooses a medium which, while less costly and easier to realize, is harder to excel in. Though there are vastly more workmanlike documentaries made than feature films, and many more good ones, great documentaries are as rare as, perhaps rarer than, great feature films. Both forms, like all films other than animations, depend on capturing a record of events which really happened in front of the camera. Here the two media divide. The fiction film-maker commands a world into existence to show to the audience. The documentarist must extract a world from the reality of life.

Believability is one of the judgements made about fiction. The fictional story must persuade its audience that the events could really have happened, that the characters could really have existed. Everybody knows that reality is sometimes just too unlikely to be convincing. Truth may not really very often be stranger than fiction, but it is frequently much less immediately convincing. Yet the documentary comes with a guarantee, not necessarily of truth, but of being grounded in reality. A documentary's authority depends on the explicit claim that what the film shows represents or corresponds to something in the real world. Though in fact the history of documentary is littered with examples of the faked and the phoney, the documentarist who cheats on the promise to present reality forfeits everything.

Audiences take the documentarist's honesty for granted. However, as they have become more discriminating over the years, viewers are perfectly well aware that film-makers only show a carefully selected part of the picture—the part that suits their argument. But though partiality is accepted, inconclusiveness is not. The documentarist's work is judged not so much on its content, but on its argument—how the content was presented. In the professional jargon: 'does the story stand up?'

In a feature film, story is everything. If there is an overt moral pay-off or a philosophical conclusion, that is a bonus; a fiction can do without them quite well enough. The audience responds to the way the story elements are handled and brought to a conclusion. But a documentary, because it makes a claim for reality, will inevitably do more than tell a story. Since the story is taken from reality its audience cannot but come to some judgement about it.

Much fiction is intended as entertainment and teaches us little. When fiction moves us, it is because something in its imaginary world corresponds to something in our real one; it takes considerable artistry by the fiction film-maker to persuade us to make the match. First we have to put the material through a complicated mental transfer from the film world to our own. In the case of a documentary production, the relationship between what is shown on screen and the reality which it records is not as simple as it may seem, but the distance between the two is nothing like as far as it is in fiction.

This is how we see the world

What is shown on the screen in a documentary are extracts from reality, presented in different ways, chosen to point up some meaning, some pattern in the real world. It could be a pattern of events, a pattern of relationships, a pattern of personalities, a pattern of facts. It may be expressly presented as a narrative, or by description, or by explanation. The aim of the documentary is to persuade the audience to see the same pattern as the film-maker. In this, the documentarist is engaged in a task which is absolutely fundamental to human understanding.

'Which is how we see the world,' said the surrealist painter René Magritte, in a lecture explaining his painting *La Condition Humaine*. 'We see it as being outside ourselves even though it is only a mental representation of what we experience on the inside.'[1]

All living creatures depend on the ability of their nervous systems, no matter how primitive, to impose order and meaning on the chaos of sensation. All are equipped with some kind of mechanism for pattern recognition. Even the simplest and most primitive living things, viruses and bacteria, are equipped to recognize, among the *tohu bohu* of the sub-microscopic world, the

[1] Magritte
—*La Ligne de la Vie* 1938

molecular patterns which spell substrate or food. More advanced creatures, including ourselves, depend on discriminating meaningful patterns from out of the apparently random signals constantly stimulating our senses. That is how we living creatures survive. But it is our brains that construct the images, not our eyes; our brains and not our ears that recreate for us the sounds we recognize; our brains not our eyes which build for us the image of friend's face or a yellow rush-woven chair, our brains not our ears which create in our minds the sound of a busker's violin above the traffic noise.

Discrimination begins early in life. The youngest baby is already primed to recognize the pattern of sight, sound, smell, taste and feel that means mother. Experiments have shown that such recognition even survives transmission by television. As we mature, our pattern recognition ability develops. We learn to read and write in words, sentences, paragraphs—patterns which become so tightly associated with our language that we cannot write without hearing the words inside our heads or speak the words without being affected by the way we write them. As functioning adults all our perceptions depend on the processing and matching of vast numbers of these memory patterns, the kind which lead us to recognize cousin Bill in the street from two hundred yards away by something about the way he walks.

So programmed are we to detect pattern in our environment that we almost invariably succeed—it is almost impossible not to see pattern even where there truly is none. Wherever and whenever human beings have looked up at the stars, they have seen patterns; though the patterns result from no more than chance lines of sight. But different people have seen different patterns, and the same pattern has been interpreted in many different ways. A cluster of seven points in the night sky have been seen as a Plough, as a Wain (wagon), as a Great Bear, even as a Big Dipper (ladle). Each image as valid as the next, but none expresses a real celestial relationship (Fig. 3.1).

Fig. 3.1 Seven stars can be seen as a plough, a wain, a bear or a dipper.

We apply pattern recognition not only to the input of our sense organs, we automatically look for patterns in all forms of information that enter our heads, even the purely abstract. And as with the stars, it is hard but useful work to distinguish the meaningful pattern from the accidental. The scientist looks for patterns in data; scientific method is then applied to find out if the patterns mean anything. The philosopher seeks out patterns in the world and tries by intellectual argument to establish how significant they are. The politician claims to discover patterns in the realm of society and politics; though not all politicians are keen to test if their observations correspond to any real underlying structure.

It is one thing to see the pattern yourself, it is quite another to cajole someone else into seeing it too. In some cases, a person's whole self-image and identity can be bound up in the everyday perception of, say, class struggle or God's handiwork. To persuade the really devout to relinquish the pattern they see in the world in favour of a new one is probably impossible, short of full scale brainwashing—which is the only known technique by which a victim can be forced to abandon long held mental patterns and replace them with new, approved, ones. We all hang on to our own view of things with pretty fierce tenacity. Changing one's perception is rather like the optical illusion in which one can switch depressions like craters on the moon from looking concave to convex: it takes some effort but once done, the impression sticks (Fig. 3.2). Patterns may at first be quite hard to make out, but once learned they are even harder to forget.

Fig. 3.2 Once seen as concave or convex, the perception is hard to change.

The documentary maker is a seeker and a pointer-out of patterns, often combining scientist, philosopher and politician in different measure, depending on the nature of the film. For the documentarist the patterns are sequences of events, combinations of characters, resonances in behaviour, connections between ideas. The documentary maker's work is to find ways of showing the audience an original and meaningful way of looking at things. Whatever it is about, whether it be a history of warfare, a video diary of a trip to the seaside, a record of a space mission, a story of an office power struggle, an ecological exploration of the Serengeti, a film is its maker's way of saying: notice the way that *this* relates to *that* and connects to yet something else.

So a documentary film is the result of sieving out from the real world those elements which best point up meaning. It is impossible to include all of them. The film's maker must select those cues, signs and details which tell the audience most. He or she is aided by the fact that human perception depends on a wide variety of sensory sources and great redundancy of information—the same content comes through to us in many different ways, reinforcing the security of our hold on the image. It is easier to hear someone in a noisy cocktail party if one can see the person's lips, even if we are not lip-readers; an ambiguous shadow is often resolved into a recognizable shape by its sound.

Because of this redundancy, one of the tasks of an artist in any field is to judge which clues are the most potent, the most evocative, and let go those which would merely add support or fill in unneeded detail. The task is not unlike that of the many optical illusions which depend on the brain's ability to pick up clues and fill in the rest. In a familiar optical illusion the white triangle varies from very indistinct, to clearer when the corners are marked by dots, and even clearer yet when the corner angles are supplied (Fig. 3.4). In no case is it explicitly drawn.

This optical illusion suggests a role for the artist in any medium. He or she will seek out just those details which enable the audience to supply the rest from their own mental resources. The more the audience contributes to the perception, the more satisfying is the resulting image—seeming to belong to them, rather than seeming an alien view foisted onto them less than willingly. To build up a picture in someone else's mind is to allow that person to contribute largely to it. So the search is always on to sum up as much as possible of the artist's argument with the simplest and most economical pointers possible. Give the audience too much, and they may have the feeling that they are being got at.

Great care must be taken to ensure that the details really do contribute to the pattern rather than distract from it. In the effect first demonstrated by Harmon (Fig. 3.3), spurious and irrelevant details—the edges of the blocks of tone—interfere with the brain's ability to make sense of the pattern. Only by screwing up the eyes or stepping well back so as to make the block edges less distinct, will most readers be readily able to make sense of the picture. This has been called the Abraham Lincon effect. How significant that so little information—hardly more than three hundred and fifty tonal squares—can generate such an immediately recognizable complex image.

Such considerations apply to artists working in all fields. A representational painter or designer depends for his or her success on providing the audience with just enough hints and clues to suggest three-dimensional form. And some cultures emphasize economy and subtlety above almost all other considerations: a Zen ideal is of a complete drawing made by a single stroke or gesture with the drawing brush. As Michael Caine has shown in his movie master classes, the art of the film actor depends largely on giving away only the most highly economical clues about the character's internal state. The audience is so attuned to reading such signs that anything more than a hint looks like over-acting.

Fig. 3.3 By screwing up the eyes or standing well back, most readers will be able to make sense of this picture.

Fig. 3.4 The white triangle varies from indistinct, to clearer when the corners are marked by dots, and even clearer when the angles on the corners are suggested.

The documentarist too is looking for economy and subtlety in presenting his or her vision of the world. One of the most important skills in the film-maker's repertoire is the ability to recognize which are the most significant, revealing moments, scenes, personalities, objects. And if any one such series of images can contribute pointers, clues and hints to more than one aspect of the overall pattern, then so much the better. Ambiguity is no problem. Allowing, encouraging the audience to make their own mental contribution to the film's meaning is not to short change them but to give them an active role in making sense of the film's world. And an activated audience is a satisfied audience, who will almost certainly ascribe to the skill of the film-maker what, in actual fact, they themselves have contributed to the meaning of the work. Sleight of hand? Maybe. But a factor on which the reputations of some of television's greatest documentarists have been founded.

Chapter 4

Telling the Story

Documentary is a form of story-telling. It can be nothing else. The reason is time.

Unlike other forms of visual art, paintings, photographs, sculptures, comic strips, installations, a television film is inevitably a traveller in time. It unrolls at a steady speed from start to finish. Like the writing of Omar Khayyam's moving finger: 'nor all thy piety nor wit shall lure it back to cancel half a line.' Time is built into the film as its basic premise. Event follows event in a pauseless flow.

Any description or presentation of events over time is a narrative of sorts. Whatever a film-maker puts on the television screen can only be presented as a story. Decisions about the order in which to put the materials are unavoidable and inescapable, no matter if each sequence in the film is intended by its maker to stand separate and equal. Even if it be the presentation of evidence about an arcane scientific hypothesis, the viewer cannot but receive each piece of information successively, spread out over time. What is seen first will inevitably inform and influence the viewer's response to what is seen later. Thus to the viewer too, a film will always be received as a story. The film-maker will wish it to be a good story, and will try to ensure that the story the viewer follows is the one that the film-maker wishes to tell. What cannot be done is to avoid telling a story at all.

Story is not plot. Plot is that chain of causal links—*this* action had *these* consequences—which connects the starting point of a drama through to its ending. All except the most avant garde and experimental fictions have plots. Audiences expect fictions to be invented. A cause-and-effect plot draws the audience in and, by harnessing the universal human instinct for detecting causality, helps to make the events of the imaginary fictional world believable and convincing. But documentaries get their authority not so much from their internal conviction but from the implicit claim that the events and actions they present are real and true. Thus though a documentary may well have a plot too, equally well it may not. But it will always have a story.

Documentary stories can be about anything: personal tales, accounts of history, predictions of the future, explanations, conflicts, cries of pain or shouts of joy; all share the quality of being stories, arrangements of events in time. And implicit in that quality is the natural response of the audience. Audiences follow stories. For them, the driving force of the story is the question: what happens next? What keeps them watching is desire to know how things turn out. The documentary maker must find in his or her subject those story elements which keep that question uppermost in the viewers' minds..

When the purpose of the film is simply to tell a tale which is already in story form, a history, a biography, an anecdote, this task is made relatively easy. The issue is one of compression—what do I show in order to tell the story as simply and effectively as possible in the time allowed? But many documentaries deal with materials that do not initially present themselves as stories at all. They may include accounts of concepts or ideas, descriptions of places or situations, summaries of knowledge or beliefs. Since there is no way to avoid the presentation of the material's elements successively through time, the documentarist has no choice but to make the succession a meaningful one—that is, to find a way through the material that tells a story. Such subjects thus demand that the documentarist's first and most important task to discover a narrative way of communicating the non-narrative material.

There are no universal means of performing this translation in a way guaranteed to succeed. Every case is unique. Though television has over the years developed a number of standard ways of presenting factual information, some more effective than others, many if not most of these devices have been devalued by familiarity and over-use. The documentarist will wish to study the subject until he or she finds within it that which lends itself best to a fresh and original treatment in story form.

How can that be done? Though we recognize that all arrangements of events over time are in some sense stories, we also know that not all are good ones. The video recordings of a surveillance camera also contain arrangements of events over time—a story of sorts—but they are not stories that anyone would be likely to find particularly appealing, nor wish to watch for their own sake. The fact that each event is neither related to the previous one nor connected to the next, that the characters shown change every few moments, that there is no underlying unity other than the location, all these factors quickly make watching such a recording a very boring experience. For a story to work, the events will usually relate to a single subject and follow a single theme, thread or line which runs right through, from a beginning to an ending. The theme will be revealed by means of these events.

The subject

In this context, the word *subject* is used more restrictively than usual. The subject of the documentary story means its principal figure. It is the answer to the question 'what is the story about?' It can be a person, an animal, an object, a concept, an idea, anything. Everyone can bring to mind countless documentary films on a limitless range of subjects: the life of the meerkat, the crisis in the London Zoo, the development of nanotechnology, the last days of an AIDS sufferer, the story of the ship *Golden Hind*, the world of the Khoi San people of South Africa, the true fate of Glenn Miller.

Subjects for documentary films share an important feature: they are not diffuse or indistinct ideas. Profound though its social impact may be, television is really not a very intense medium. Unlike the cinema screen, which immerses its audience in a total sensory environment to the exclusion of nearly every other stimulus, the television screen is small, fuzzy, limited in contrast, viewed in ordinary light among ordinary surroundings—a glowing postage stamp in the corner of the room. Television sound is of very much less than high fidelity. The set is often not even intended to be the sole focus of attention in the environment. A well-remembered survey of people's viewing habits, which placed cameras inside the sets of a sample of viewers, showed that for much of the time, much of the audience was engaged in doing something else while watching—a surprising range of activities, from wallpapering to sex.

To win the battle against the viewer's inattention using a medium with such limited presence, a documentary film's most important weapon is simplicity and clarity of concept. If the subject of a television film is too complex to be expressed in a phrase of a few words, it may well have to be re-thought and its focus narrowed before it can be expected to make a successful leap through the screen. The television set is an effective filter for woolly ideas, confused aims and pretentious complications. The television documentary maker must find a way of approaching the subject so as to see it with a simple, perhaps even innocent—though not, one hopes, na ve—eye.

That is not to suggest that difficult ideas must always be reduced to banalities. It does mean that thought and imagination must be applied to working out ways of presenting them in a suitable form for the medium. To this end, television documentaries very often use the classic rhetorical device technically known as *synecdoche*—letting a part of something stand in for the whole thing: a person for society at large, a tree for nature, a storm for weather, an individual crime for the notion of crime itself. The television image is after all not the thing itself, but a representation, a sign, which only stands for, rather than is, its counterpart in the real world. The symbolic use of reality is fundamental to television, which is good on down-to-earth detail and less good on the grand vision. As the art historian Warburg said of painting, God is in the details. On television too, truth is often better found in the details than in the generalization.

The presentation of a story by means of a limited selection of significant details is, as some film-makers have noted, not far from the technique of the nineteenth century naturalist novel. In his book *The New Journalism*, Tom Wolfe suggested that journalists should learn the lesson taught by such writers as Balzac, Dickens and Gogol. This lesson he characterized as the power of just four devices: 1—scene by scene construction, 2—the use of dialogue, 3—point-of-view, and 4—'the recording of everyday gestures, manners, habits, customs, styles of furniture, clothing, decoration, styles of travelling, eating, keeping house, modes of behaviour towards children, servants, superiors, inferiors, peers, plus the various looks, glances, poses, styles of walking and other symbolic details that might exist within a scene.'

Wolfe suggested that point-of-view and *status life*, his term for the content of device no. 4, are not achievable on film. Yet many film-makers would recognize in the above quotation exactly what they seek to represent in their work. Documentarists know well that the documentary technique provides a point-of-view and the singling out of such details as express a person's view of themselves and their place in the world. The camera must be placed somewhere, and wherever the camera stands, there stands the viewer. The camera must provide an image of something, and whatever it may be, that something will be invested by the viewer with significance. These factors do not draw attention to themselves. Audiences are mostly unaware of them. They are, as it were, the unobserved subtext of the film. Yet they give the film-maker powerful support in depicting the broad and complex sweep of reality, while using relatively modest and simple means.

The thread

A clear and simple subject is matched by a clear and simple thread. If the subject of a story is the answer to the question 'what is the story about?' then the thread, theme or line answers the question 'what route do we follow through the story?' The thread can be any which relates to the subject: the actions and experiences of a person, the survival or otherwise of an animal, the creation or destruction of an object, the history and consequences of a concept, the development or pursuit of an idea. Just as the television documentary form favours subjects which are easily grasped so it only welcomes threads which are easily followed. Yet documentary takes its themes from life and life is often very confusing. One of the first major interpretative acts a documentarist must make is to draw out of the confusions of reality a single strong, continuous and compelling thread.

In the course of following that thread, the story may well digress. It may occasionally proceed down side-paths. There might be explanations of phenomena, descriptions of events, background histories of people. The strength of the story will depend on the extent to which the digressions are related in the minds of the audience to the central theme. It is not enough that the digressions offer useful additions to the story. The viewers must be persuaded to expect them, want them and demand them. That is to say, the digressions must be motivated. The motivation for an explanatory digression is that it tells the viewers what they want to know, and no more than they want to know, just at the moment when they want to know it. The documentarist will strive to be an entertaining raconteur rather than a bore. No film-maker wishes to be thought of as given to long digressions, in a memorable phrase: 'beyond the speaker's competence and the listener's interest.' Afterwards the story will immediately return to its theme as it continues its journey onwards. If the story is the engine that pulls all the other materials in the film along in its train, then the thread represents the couplings that connect the wagons together.

Like the couplings on that train, each scene in the story links itself onto the end of the last one, and holds out a hook for the next to hang on to. Every passage answers the question 'what happens next?' and the answer itself—*this* does—contains the same question at its own end. The impetus of the story, like the pull of the locomotive, is passed on from scene to scene all the way through the film.

Change

The scenes of the documentary story are the records of events through which the story is told. *This* happened and then *that* occurred, *this* was learned, next *that* was researched; *this* was proposed, finally *that* was concluded. But it is still not quite enough for a story to be just a sequence of related events. A story has to have something to show for its journey through time and its passage through the viewer's consciousness—and the something that it must show is change.

J B Priestley, who was a fine story-teller, once wrote that we register time by noticing change. We tell the time that way too: the change in position of a clock's hands, the drip of water into a measuring container, the reduction in height of a marked candle. Without change there is no time. And without time there is no story. Stories involve change, are *about* change. And change has a direction: from before to afterwards. The direction of change is what reveals which way the pointer at the end of time's arrow is facing. The story follows the course of the subject through the change from before to afterwards.

Beginning and ending

Where does a television story begin? At the first moment of change. Where does it end? When the change is complete. That is easy to say, but choosing the moment is not always simple. Makers of cinema fiction are often advised to begin with the action already in progress, the later the better, film is an art of movement. The Roman poet Horace, in his *Art of Poetry*, gave the story teller a Latin tag to use: *in medias res, auditorem rapit* — he plunges the listener into the middle of things. But all stories, excepting perhaps the book of Genesis, start with a situation that is inherited from the past. Every story-teller has also to cope with the need to fill in the background of the tale, so that the audience can understand and appreciate the opening situation. The beginning of nearly every narrative work contains a résumé of what has gone before.

The successful story-teller will find a way to include the story's pre-history in the narrative in such a way as not to stop the forward movement of the story once it has started. Explanatory flashbacks and asides, if they appear at all, will move off from the main route only at a place where there is a natural pause in progress. Once back on course the story must pick up again in the middle of things, lest the story signals to the audience that common failing: a false, stuttering start and a second beginning.

Some story media have a simple start and the luxury of leisure to paint a picture of the status quo ante. A play begins with the rise of the curtain and a stage playwright knows that the audience is not going to get up and go home just because it takes five minutes of stage dialogue to establish who is who and what is what. Even cinema-goers will not leave their seats because the movie has a slow atmospheric start. Other media, the novel is one, need to get the story moving at once—how else to attract the bookshop browser?—but having done so can relax the pace in order to sketch in some needed history. The television documentary has a more difficult task. Because television is so uninvolving a medium, the story must start right off from the opening shot if the interest of the viewer is to be retained.

Furthermore, just as the nature of television demands simple treatment of subject and theme to compel the viewer's attention, so it also suggests that once the viewer's attention has been won it must be held onto. The documentary story will usually hit the screen running—and continue to run until the end. The need to persuade the audience to give their concentration is so strong that many television films—and not only those intended for broadcasting—no longer begin with an opening title sequence. The story is kicked off first, before the title, which is not introduced until the film-maker feels that the viewers' attention has been gained. The story itself gets going from the very first image, sometimes with a preview, at other times with a preamble.

The end of a film might seem to need less careful consideration than the beginning. After all, the audience must have remained attentive all the way, if the ending is being watched at all. Yet if the purpose of a documentary is more than just to fill time or offer a temporary diversion, the end needs as much care and attention as the beginning. The closing moments of the story will decide what the viewers take away with them from having watched the work. It is the place for the conclusion, the moral of the tale. And even if an explicit and overt moral message has little place in contemporary documentary, the viewer will expect, perhaps demand, to be left with some lasting impression, feeling or understanding, after the final image has faded from the screen. A Hollywood mogul is famously reputed to have said: 'If I want to send a message, I call Western Union.' That was disingenuous. Neither a fiction film nor a documentary film can avoid leaving its audience with a message, even if its maker and creator had no such explicit intention. The aim of the film-maker is to make sure that the message the audience receives is one he or she means to send.

The meaning of a film, like that of a person's life story, is never fully established until its end. It is established partly *by* its end. Yet in one sense, the events depicted in a documentary have no ending. The last scenes of a documentary are as tightly linked forward into the future as the beginning is connected back to the past. The world of a documentary is the real world, which has no ending. The final moments of any one story are always the first of another. Thus closure, the tying up of all loose threads and the sealing up of all opened accounts is not normally the way a documentary film can conclude its look at a subject. There are exceptions of course. Historical biography and obituary must both, after all, end in death. Yet even here, because we are watching the account of a person's life after its final completion, we know that afterwards the world went on its way. And in looking back from now to the past, hindsight can never be ignored. A biographical film will inevitably project the subject's shadow from its own time onto the present. Why else would one wish to watch the life story of a someone who has died, if not to learn something about his or her legacy to the world, his or her contribution to history, the consequences of his or her having once lived?

So just as to begin a documentary story is to merge the initial state into the ongoing change, to bring it to an end is to combine the final with the inconclusive. It is the relationship between the end result of change and the continuity of the world that gives the film its meaning. Whatever the subject, whatever the theme, the film-maker can never ignore the fact that the audience will always construct some final meaning to the story for themselves. The task is thus to make sure that the viewers has been left with the necessary materials from which to build their own conclusions.

The intention

One further factor, other than a single subject and continuous thread, makes a documentary story different from a mere sequence of events. A story is a shape placed on events by the interpretation of the human mind. It has no real concrete existence in the world of things. A story is a human concept and involves human emotion. The emotion is derived from the concept of intention.

The change with which the story starts creates a response from the subject. As the story begins, an aim or purpose emerges. In fiction, this is usually a human intention. The movement of the story through time and change is associated with an intention or desire on the part of to the subject of the story. The subject wishes to, aims to, intends to get to the desired goal or end from the given beginning. In fiction the intention is often quite simple, even stereotyped. A man wants to attract a woman, a detective wants to catch a crook, a singer wants to find stardom, a general wants to bask in glory, an artist wants to create a masterpiece. From the very starting point, the subject will form an idea of where he or she wishes to get to by the end. It is the film-maker's responsibility to communicate the subject's intention to the audience.

By contrast documentary films, being concerned with real people and real life, have no such easy options. Real human motives are, as often as not, complex and self-contradictory. And documentaries are frequently about inanimate objects or non-corporeal ideas to which intentions cannot be directly ascribed. But that does not relieve the film-maker from the task of establishing an intention of some sort. How can this be done? To solve this problem, the conventional idea of the nature of the intention, as propounded by makers of conventional fiction, must be taken rather further. For intention is actually not what it seems at first sight.

Examined more closely, it is clear that the intention of the story's protagonist is not itself the critical factor. It is there to generate similar feelings—identification—in the audience. When audiences identify with a character, they take on that character's intentions and respond emotionally to the snakes and ladders of that character's fortunes. The impetus to a story is not really given by the desires of the characters of the story themselves, but by the audience's emotions on their behalf. The subjects for whose emotions the audience stands proxy do not have to have intentions of their own at all, often they cannot have. Ivo Andric's great historical documentary novel *The Bridge Over The Drina*, certainly involves the audience in strong tension and emotion on behalf the bridge, even though the author never presents it as anything other than an unfeeling object, a stone construction. What the bridge comes to signify in the novel is, of course, far more than that. It comes to bear on its ancient piers the whole history of the little town which it created and in which it stands. The bridge is not personified by Andric at all, yet by the end the reader comes desperately to care about its fate. The intention which drives the book along is the desire to survive, to be permanently present. But it is actually felt, not by the bridge, but by the reader.

Andric's ability to make the reader feel for the bridge is the product of great artistry—he received the Nobel Prize for his work. But the task he set himself is not an uncommon one for the documentarist. The film-maker dealing with an object or an idea, and sometimes a person too, must always be looking for ways to engage the viewers' emotions in the story. One common, if obvious, solution is to present the material as told by an on-screen character, thus giving the audience a human subject to identify with. That screen character may even tell the story by addressing the camera directly, becoming in the process a presenter, whose aims and intentions can be written into the script.

Because the ability to address the camera in a natural way is not universal, film-makers wishing to use a presenter sometimes engage a professional to do the job. This is not always an ideal method. The degree to which an audience identifies with a professional presenter is likely to be less than the level of sympathy granted to someone whose real life is the subject of the film. And the constraint on the number of possible stories imposed by a professional presenter is a serious limitation. The presenter can really only tell one kind of story: this is where I went, these are the

people I met, these are the things I saw. In some contexts, this can
be a most effective narrative device, particularly if the presenter's
path is a rough one, and the resulting discoveries worthy of it. A
personal quest or exploration is a most natural purpose for a
presenter. The quest then becomes the subject of the film, its
progress and vicissitudes become the story, achievement of the
presenter's goal becomes the intention which drives the film along.
On the way, information can be collected, situations can be
described, exposition of ideas can be undertaken and the
presenter's own personal emotional responses explored. In some
contexts too, particularly on the US television channels, the
presenter's name in the title is what counts with the audience.
But there is an infinite number of different ways of telling the same
story and most film-makers will try to search out as original and
unexpected a way as they can.

The intention of the subject is the starting point of the story.
Tracking the fate of that intention gives the story its substance.
For a story is not just the account of one damned thing after
another. The progress of the subject in pursuance of the intention
will not be a smooth unhindered flow from start to finish. Stories
depend for their interest on some impediment to the flow of
movement. In a dramatic story, setbacks and resistance to the
leading characters' intentions are what gives the story its tension
and excitement. 'Will cop get robber, boy get girl, victim get
revenge?' and more generally, 'will they succeed in realising their
aims?' are the kinds of questions the audience is led to ask. The
uncertainty of the resolution is one of the major factors which gives
the story its edge.

There are others. Theatre audiences in classical Greece knew
very well the outcome of the stories and themes of their dramas.
No modern theatre-goer is surprised by the ending of Shakespeare's *Hamlet*. Every reader of Frederick Forsyth's *The Day of the
Jackal*, about an attempt on the life of President de Gaulle, must
know that in point of fact de Gaulle was not assassinated but died,
advanced in years, in his bed. And viewers of any episode of a
popular detective series know perfectly well that the detective
will somehow win in the end. And if the outcome of fiction is often
predetermined, how much more so in documentary work, which
so often pictures a world and a history already well known to the
viewers. Thus the question for the audience may not be: will the
subjects' intentions succeed? Instead they will ask: how will the
subjects behave along the way, how will they try to achieve their
purposes, what will happen to frustrate them, or even: what new
truths will tonight's performance reveal?

The ups and downs of the subject's intention: smooth success alternating with angry rebuff, is the stuff of which the story is built. The movement of a story is like that of a stalled motor car being pushed to start. It takes an effort to get it going; then it rolls a bit until it comes to some bumps in the road; after a struggle to overcome the bumps, the car finally accelerates until it has enough momentum for the engine to be started. The aim is to start the engine. The impediments are the bumps in the road. The ending is when the aim has been satisfied or has failed. The car drives off or is abandoned. Life goes on.

The subject's intention is not always fulfilled. Or the ending can be ambiguous. In fact in the documentary genre the outcome is not usually cut and dried. In *The Last Exodus*, the film about the emigration of Jews from the collapsing Soviet Union, the story tells of the Jews' attempts over the last 100 years to find a viable life for themselves in Russia. That intention is not realized. They fail. In the last scene of all, the arrival of a plane-full of Russian Jews in Israel, the story ends and the future begins in a mixture of grief and joy, hope and anxiety. We know, as perhaps they do not, that the security and peace that they yearn for, is unlikely to be found in their new home in the turbulent Middle East.

Every story one might wish to tell in a television documentary is shaped by the conflict between intention and obstruction. And all are likely to have an indeterminate end, for they are about real things which are never neatly concluded. 'They lived happily ever after,' may be a possible ending for a fairy tale, but life is not like that and documentaries reflect this fact. And the reverse is also true. An unhappy ending in the real world is not always necessarily for ever either. The convict condemned to life imprisonment may yet, one day, be released, or the executed felon may be granted a posthumous free pardon.

These uncertainties always influence the audience's reaction to the end of a film, even when the outcome seems absolutely cut and dried. Many documentaries about the history and origins of the Second World War have focused on the intentions of the leaders of Western European nations—to avoid war. A film might tell the story of how historical and social forces and events conspired, in the teeth of what the leaders thought were their best efforts, to send their nations into the bloodiest war in history. Here the audience may well identify not with the historical characters shown, but with the unseen millions who the audience know will perish at a time *after* that represented in the film. Yet though the intentions of the film's subjects are frustrated, the audience knows that, in the end, the Western Allies win. Tragedy and victory are intermingled.

The same considerations apply even to the comparatively

unemotional world of scientific research—not the researchers, who
are certainly not unemotional, but to the pursuit of understanding
itself. A film about the search for the W particle (an elementary
nuclear particle) was about the attempt to demonstrate the
existence of the particle in the face of the many obstacles constantly
thrown up by resistant nature. Here the identification of the
audience was directed, not so much towards the human
personalities doing the searching, but towards the very search
itself, an entirely abstract notion. Success or failure were, in a sense,
irrelevant. As the film ended, the audience had seen yet more
questions thrown up and knew full well that the search for
knowledge is never ending.

The film-maker is not always able to control the identification
of the viewers. In one episode of a technology series called *The
Limit*,[1] the story was told of the design problems and difficulties
involved in developing a super-airliner. The viewers were offered
a character—Hubert the French designer and father of the
project—to identify with. But the viewer's heart—and even that
of the commentary writer—were quickly stolen by the romance
and drama of the project itself, as one obstacle after another was
faced and overcome. Hubert's own personal story was rapidly
eclipsed. He was saying more than he knew when he summed up
both the aircraft project and the story's thread with the words:
'this programme is a jumping race.'

Film time

Just as much as in a fiction film, the audience for a documentary
hitches an emotional lift by identifying with the subject. The task
of the film-maker is to control the course of that ride, how exciting
or how sedate it is to be, where the bumps and the downhill runs
should come, by showing the audience a sequence of events over
time. The events are the moments of change in the story. To
determine how to lay them out needs an appreciation of the place
of time in the film. To do that, we must return to the subject of
time and examine it rather more closely.

Though time is the characteristic dimension of the film medium,
it is not all that it may seem. To be sure, a film is spread out over
time, but that time is not real time—'time of day,' as video
engineers call it. It may not even represent time at all, for it may
be used almost interchangeably in place of other dimensions and
other processes, and not just the progression of minutes, hours,
days and years.

Film time lends itself readily to conversion and translation. Just
as in the comic strip, time is represented by the arrangement of   [1] BBC 1996

the frames on the flat page, the readers moving through time as their eyes pass across it, so film time can represent space. The translation is easily made. It is a commonplace to follow Einstein in interpreting time as a kind of fourth spatial dimension. The 'journey through time' is a frequently used metaphor. To swap time for distance commits no assault on our concept of what a dimension is.

In a documentary about the river Nile, for example, the subject was the river itself and the film recorded its journey from its sources to the Mediterranean Sea. The course of the film was the course of the Nile. It seems fanciful to speak of a river having an aim, and that aim being impeded in some way. But even without explicitly personifying the world's longest river, it is not hard, as one stands at the headwaters flowing out of Lake Albert in Uganda, to think in terms of the destiny of the flow, easy to be swept up in the romance of the immense journey on which the waters are about to embark, plunging over waterfalls, passing through gorges, impeded by cataracts and slowed by reed marshes, flowing through ancient valleys and over the fields of the fellahin, to end four thousand miles away in the sea.

More symbolic, less concrete, is the use of time to represent the development in breadth of an idea or a concept. In one documentary looking at the current state of research into Hodgkin's disease, progress in time through the film was translated into progress in researching the disease. The aim of the subjects of the film, the researchers, was fully to collect together everything that was then known about it, believing that such a synthesis would reveal a new approach to treating the condition. The impediments to achieving that aim were to be found in the refractory nature of the biological world, the way in which underlying truths are hidden and evade the researchers' best efforts to tease them out with their experiments.

Film time can, of course, represent real time too. As when time itself is the subject of a story, for a good story does not have to be complicated. Such simplicity can, however, be overused. Perhaps too many natural history documentaries are based on the story of a day—sometimes a season or a year—in the life of a particular animal. The story is clear: the sun rises; the animal begins its day; later it has an adventure; it returns to its home; the sun sets. The story has a beginning, sunrise, and an ending, sunset. Like all true pictures of life and all true stories, it starts in the middle of things, *in medias res* as the classical author described it, and ends while the world goes on. The story has a structure—the day—which everybody understands. The aim of the subject of the film—the animal—is to get through the day and find its food without itself being eaten. The obstructions to its aims are the skill of the prey in evading its attacks and the threat of its own enemies. Yet though such a tale fulfils all the criteria for story-telling, its very familiarity makes it hard to come away without a feeling of 'so what?' The natural history film-makers, for all their skill, might have done better to discover in their subject a fresher and more original story.

A film such as 'A Day in the Life of...' does, however, demonstrate one very important point. Though the passage of time can itself be the theme of the story, film time is not real time. A day in the life of an animal is presented in thirty or fifty minutes of film time. The film is a compressed, a speeded-up, account of a day. Yet the moving pictures of which the film is composed—the shots themselves—happen in real time. A shot of a ten-second event must last ten seconds. Even when slowed down or speeded up, we perceive the film time as if it were real time. A time-lapse shot of a plant amazes us when a flower grows before our eyes from seed to maturity in thirty seconds.

In principle, the change of time could be expressed in film. The film could speed up, even reverse as it runs, as if searching through an endless video recording of reality. It might be an interesting technique for some purposes, but it is not a technique currently in use.

In the documentary convention, time in the film can only be manipulated during the invisible junctions between shots. A writer can span a century with a paragraph and leap back a thousand years within a sentence. But on film, change of time is inexpressible and unexpressed. A film-maker can never show, only imply, time switching tracks at the joints in the flow of the pictures and sounds.

Thus the way time is expressed in a documentary film is as what can be called *story time*. Control of the story time is one of the central tasks of the film story-teller. Balance, flow, a carefully calculated and appropriate pace, all are important features of the documentary medium. For the way in which events are distributed in the story time will not necessarily be even and regular. Events often follow each other in haste, give way to long gaps, and are then followed by another flurry of rapid activity. The density of the events in the story time will be related to the power of their impact on the story's thread. It will also be related to the viewers' ability to absorb what is going on. Too many events, composed too quickly, will overwhelm the audience. Too few will bore them.

A film story, therefore, consists of chosen moments, running in real time, linked so as to elide, to make invisible, the time-gaps between them. Much of the art of story-telling on film lies in the decisions on what to choose to show, what to leave out, and where to place the elements within the story time. Since stories are about change, the most significant moments in the story are by definition the moments of change. A documentary tells its story in terms of a chain of significant moments of change. The documentary maker selects the moments out of the seamless continuity of real life. The moments are expressed in images and sounds, pictures and words—the materials from which all documentaries are built.

Part II

Constructing a Television Documentary

Television documentaries can be looked at in two different ways. Both deal with the same primary building blocks from which films are put together—sounds, images, shots, sequences. The approaches differ in the way these materials are examined. If we think of film as a kind of language, we might see the distinction as similar to that between semantics—the study of the way words are used to create the meaning of a text—and syntax—the study of the rules governing the way the words are selected, adapted and connected together.

This is close to the familiar distinction between function and form. Film semantics gives us what can be called the functional approach: how do we use sounds, images, shots and sequences to tell the film's story? Film syntax, sometimes called film grammar, leads us to look at the forms themselves: how do we select and compose the images, and how do they connect together into shots and sequences?

As with most creative constructions, function comes first.

Section A

Building the Story

A view of the real world

The stories documentaries tell are different from other stories because they deal in a view taken of the real world. There are two principal means to this end. Some film-makers approach the task like a sculptor exploring a block of marble to find the sculpture hidden within. They shoot a great deal of material, usually over a long period of time, following many threads, and cultivating a sensitive instinct for knowing which thread to follow at any time. An hour-long story is then hewn out of perhaps fifty or sixty hours of shot material. Such filming can produce studies of great depth of detail and intimacy, perhaps the closest there is to representing the fine-grained texture of the real world—of course filtered through the film-maker's personality and opinions. It is also expensive.

Other film-makers choose a different way of working, more like a sculptor in clay adding material, piece by piece, to an armature. They devote most of their time not to filming but to informing themselves and learning about their subjects with the aim of distilling their understanding into the shooting of a relatively small number of significant and heightened scenes. Heightened, in the sense of being composed of only chosen moments, rather than the random disorder of the real world. While the stone sculptor is ultimately limited in scope by the size of the marble. The clay sculptor is not. Nor is there any limit to the breadth and sweep of a film made with the equivalent technique.

Once filming, the documentarist's task is to capture reality. Films—cinema and television, drama and documentary—are, with few exceptions, records of real events. That is to say: something actually happened in front of the camera and was photographed. If what happened was that paid actors performed to order, it is called fiction. If people appeared as themselves, improvising their own lives, perhaps even unconscious of being filmed, it is called documentary. But that distinction is somewhat false. Both fictional and factual films are records of performances. Indeed contributors to documentaries are often judged by their 'performance'. Do they become tongue-tied in front of the camera? Do they suddenly forget how to do the simplest tasks? Are they too knowing?

What is being asked is how good are they at acting—at acting as themselves.

In spite of its factual basis, the television documentary is a descendent of the theatrical presentation. It has a dramatic shape, and dramatic values inform the audience's response. Every attempt is usually made to avoid revealing the presence of the film crew and its equipment. Cameras, microphones, lights are usually studiously hidden from the viewer's awareness—even in news films. Contributors are discouraged from looking at the camera. Technical or artistic demands as well as equipment failures mean that contributors may be asked to repeat the same actions many times. People will be asked to do things for the shot rather than for themselves: walk along there, stop at that point, pick up that glass and drink, take your coat from the hook and put it on.

The justification, for those who use such filming techniques, is the attempt to recreate reality: to restage for the camera an event or an action that really has already happened. Some film-makers also allow themselves to include events that could reasonably be expected to have happened, even if they didn't. And of course there are documentary makers who include events which they merely wish had happened.

The stone sculptors adopt a different principle. In the interests of an honest depiction of reality, the camera team spend so long with the contributors that they become part of the everyday environment. The camera is hand-held and moves around the scene following developments as they happen. The crew does not interfere or often even speak. Nobody is asked to do anything for the camera. The contributors are intended in the end to forget the presence of the film crew—just as Greek audiences reputedly ignored the actors who froze like statues when not involved in a scene—and simply get on with their lives.

Even so, efforts are usually still made to hide the technology and its operators from the audience. Being part of the participants' unnoticed environment, they are deemed irrelevant to the scenes being shown. True, some documentarists make a feature of not denying the camera's presence at all. It becomes part of the action. The photographer or director allows him or herself to be addressed by the subjects of the film. Sometimes allowing his or her own voice to be heard asking questions, prompting responses, suggesting actions. The camera and its operator become part of the story.

The debate about which approach to documentary is the more honest and truthful has been going on a long time. Documentarists have always been concerned about how much their own presence distorts reality. The film equivalent of Heisenberg's principle surely operates here. Just as observing and measuring a physical particle or event cannot but influence its motion or position, so it is equally clear that the presence of a camera crew cannot avoid influencing any situation in which it finds itself. 'Fly on the wall' is a neat description, but a film crew comprising camera operator, sound recordist, perhaps director and even production assistant is some fly. Even without lights, a solo cine-photographer filming the proceedings hardly goes unnoticed in most company, though it only be nephew Albert with his new camcorder. On the other hand, experience suggests that if people are performing a task with which they are familiar and which is important to them, their occupational persona takes over, and this is usually considerably less affected by being observed than is their private self. In *The Young Offender,*[1] an improvised drama-documentary about a juvenile defendant, the staged interrogation by real police was rough enough to alarm press reviewers. It was clear to the director that the officer involved had quickly forgotten the fictional nature of the situation.

Where documentarists position themselves in the spectrum of non-interference principles will depend on many factors: their own personal predilections, the practicalities of the situation, the funding of their work. Making 'fly-on-the-wall' documentaries involves shooting a great deal of material, far more than when a film-maker decides in advance what story is to be told. Such a use of film-stock is expensive. Even on videotape, the amount of editing time needed, even only to view the recorded material, can make for a swollen budget.

What counts in the end is honesty. Every documentary film-maker must take a position on the truthfulness of his or her work. There is an implicit claim in every documentary that 'the following is true as I see it.' But there is no way that the viewer can tell whether the promise is fulfilled. It can only be a matter of trust. It is the implicit duty of every documentary maker to stand by the accuracy of the film's claim to truth.

But the people who appear in the film often also have their own agenda, quite irrespective of the film-maker's wishes. Nobody is completely natural in front of a camera because nobody is completely natural anywhere. We all have a self-image, or a series of self-images, that we try to project. As Goffman showed in *The Presentation of Self in Everyday Life*, all of life is a performance of one sort or another: to our relatives, to our friends, to our colleagues—we even perform to ourselves. And performing for the camera is just one particular way of presenting oneself, neither less nor more true than any other. Many people apply an artistry to that performance which may lead them to remould reality, while

[1] BBC 1974

it is actually happening, into a more artistically satisfying shape.

Barnardo's Children,[1] a series about adults who had been brought up in Dr Barnardo's homes for unwanted children, told the story of John Williams, a black man given away to Dr Barnardo's as a child by his white family many decades before. In one extraordinarily moving sequence, Williams meets the older brother he last saw with their mother, when she put him on the train to the children's home, sending him away from his family for ever. It was a scene to make—and really did make—many viewers cry, so powerful was it. Writing later about the experience, John remembers:

'Then suddenly he was there, walking down the stairs, a balding overweight white man dressed up in a smart suit and tie. "Is that you, John?" he called out and the waiting was over. He made as if to offer his hand but instead I embraced him. That's what I mentally rehearsed I would do. It would fit in with the rest of the film...   There were a few shared tears, some inconsequential conversation, then, taking charge, my brother placed his arm around my shoulder and said: "Come on, let's go home." I was taken by surprise and felt suddenly elated. I'd waited all my life for the relief of hearing such words.

'Out through the entrance hall and five yards down the steps my brother stopped, turned me round, and led me back inside... I immediately realized we shared one thing in common. We both aspired to be actors, and like a true professional, Brian had acted out his script. The journey home had only lasted for as long as we were in shot.'[2]

[1] BBC 1995

[2] *Guardian,*
   17 November 1995,
   quoting from 'Printer's Devil'

Chapter 5

The Building Blocks

Pictures and words

Thus far, the film-maker's raw material, what the film-maker is adding piece by piece to complete the work, has been assumed to be sequences of images moving in real time, joined one after another in a long line. It has been taken for granted that these shots will be accompanied by their own synchronous sounds, the natural sounds, that is, which were recorded at the same time as the pictures were captured. Some of these sounds will be effects: doors closing, cars starting, footsteps, telephones. Others will be the human sounds bound up with the images: coughs, yawns, laughs and above all, of course, speech.

Aside from the synchronous sounds, most documentaries have a further parallel element of equal importance. For in the final assembly of the film, words and music are usually laid alongside to accompany the shots or to link them together. This task is one of composition and arrangement and is another area within which the skill and artistry of the film-maker is put to the test. The analogy with sculpture is useful only in reflecting the overall approach of the documentarist. Sculptures are static, timeless, three dimensional. Films have, as we have seen, the important added dimension of time; the task of film-making is one of composing different elements in time.

Among all the arts, the problems of composition of a documentary out of sections of sound and vision is most related to the composition of a piece of music. Both consist of events artfully distributed in time. Both have an overall design, a shape, an architecture, which itself brings out a response in the audience. The way in which the various sections follow each other and fit together over the span of time occupied by the work, the changes of tempo, of modal colouring, of tension and resolution, contribute largely to the aesthetic impact. The inner quality of each passage in a film, and the way each leads on to the next, is arguably closer to the harmonic development of a piece of music than to any other form of artistic work.

The treatment of scale in both arts is similar too. There are great symphonic films, shot with a cast of thousands; there are concertos, designed to show off a particular star; there are smaller scale chamber works, more intense and less flashy without the full orchestra; there is even the occasional individual virtuoso tour-de-force.

The analogy between music and film fails with content, of course. Music's content is nothing else but musical, while the images of a documentary film signify items in a world other than their own. But a comparison with song can take us just a little further in exploring documentary architecture. For songs are made both of words and music, and they carry explicit meaning in the words. Documentaries are made of words as well as pictures. The visual sequences are combined with a written commentary.

In documentary film, vision usually takes the lead just as in most songs the music is the senior partner. Schubert's 'Die Forelle', the Trout, is surely remembered more for its music than for its text, as is the 'Ode to Joy' in Beethoven's Ninth Symphony. But there are songs in which music takes the lesser, supporting role. Most comic songs which survive do so because of their words: such British music hall songs as 'I'm 'enery the Eighth I am' and 'My Old Man's a Dustman.' Many of Noël Coward's works live on for the brilliance of lyrics like those of 'Mad Dogs and Englishmen' or 'Don't Put your Daughter on the Stage, Mrs Worthington.' Sometimes, though only in the best songs, words and music support each other and bring out the strengths of each to their best advantage; Blake's poem *Jerusalem* set to Parry's hymn tune comes to mind. Such a perfect combination is the aim of every composer and librettist or lyricist.

The documentary maker will also try to make word and image match to the benefit of both. The balance between words and pictures is a subject of constant concern. Cultural differences come into play here. In the United States, the verbal narration seems to play a much more important role in documentary making than on the other side of the Atlantic. In some cases, approval of a film by television network executives depends largely on the quality of the commentary. The images are chosen later to illustrate the text. To deliver excellence in such a project, however, the narration's wit and wisdom really does need to be of Noël Coward's standard. One would have thought that this is rarely achieved. It has been suggested the emphasis on the text in American television is because there documentaries are seen as an offshoot of news, which is largely word-driven.

Most film-makers however, particularly in Europe, think of themselves as visual artists first and of the visual elements of their work as paramount. Many would say that a film led by the commentary was not a film at all but mere radio with pictures. They would remind us that the medium of film began and flourished for many years without any sound at all. Pure film is an international, interlingual and intercultural medium. They would ask whether Charlie Chaplin would have become one of the most famous figures on earth if his work had been restricted by the use of sound and language to the English-speaking world.

Yet in reality some words are almost always necessary to accompany a television documentary. Without any words at all, documentary film is severely limited in the subjects which it can cover and in the manner in which it can cover them.

The application of words to film is not the same thing as the incorporation of the synchronous sound. The sound of a film shot belongs to that shot, is an integral part of the image. The commentary, the written words, of a documentary film belongs not to the film but to the literary medium. Commentary in the documentary ultimately derives from the written title cards in the silent film, used either to set a scene or to supply dialogue— either way they were an explicitly verbal rather than visual contribution. These cards were used sparingly and only where necessary for they interrupted the flow. In that sense the relationship of the commentary to the modern documentary still bears the same relationship as did the title card to the silent movie. Of course in today's documentaries the words 'only where necessary' may mean something rather different. Nonetheless, the best documentary films avoid the unnecessary use of words, and in particular the use of words when visual images are more suited to the task. Though everyone by now knows it is untrue to claim that the camera cannot lie, the conviction of a film and its impact on the viewer almost always depend far more on its filmic content, synchronous sound included, than on its text. Images are seen as primary evidence. Words are second-hand, merely hearsay. The film-maker's eternal watchword is: 'Don't tell me, show me.'

When words do count, they must be given space. Either words or pictures, only one can lead at any one time. For our response to words is quite different from our response to pictures. The meaning of a sentence is cumulative in time, one word after another. Images are absorbed as a whole. It takes much less time to grasp a picture than to understand a sentence. It is said that the blind live in a serial world, one stimulus after another; if sight is restored after a long time they find it almost impossible to make sense of the parallelism and simultaneity of vision. The visual sense is more powerful too; it can easily override the other senses. Film-makers recognize that busy visual sequences can so distract from the commentary that viewers fail to assimilate the words. As a result, it is usually the case, as many film-makers say, that 'one cannot watch and listen at the same time.' It seems as if the part of the brain responsible for decoding and understanding the meaning of the sound of the words is unavailable while we are watching images which grab our attention.

This is particularly an issue in documentaries influenced by what can be called the multi-media style, a style in which images, words, music and sometimes also text are combined together into a many-layered televisual confection. The possibilities and attractions of such an approach are often justified on the grounds that younger people are able to assimilate parallel information much more easily than the middle aged. There is actually little basis for this belief. Successful practitioners of the multi-media style are very careful to ensure that none of the elements they assemble are overwhelmingly demanding. Information science suggests that a communication channel like television is capable of transmitting only a set amount of information—the bandwidth. The more information one part of the signal carries, the less bandwidth is available for the other parts. Thus it seems likely that the sum of the information carried by the separate parts of a multi-media style documentary scene is no more than the information communicated by a single, but much more intense, live action film sequence.

The words of the commentary can perform a number of different tasks. They can be narrative, descriptive, explanatory. They can accompany the images, casting extra light on their meaning, or they can be links, helping the viewer to pass as smoothly as possible from one subject or scene or time to another. But the words of a commentary should not be thought of as a kind of film-maker's sticking plaster, applied to make up deficiencies in the visual content of the work. If the words are to be given their due importance, they must be selected and composed with as much care and attention and artistry as the images. Film-makers look for images which are able to stand alone and deliver their messages without having to lean on words for crutches. In turn, they expect words to bear their own meaning, and give their own aesthetic satisfaction, without needing help from the pictures.

In sections of a film where words are the principal player, the images are therefore usually played down, the preference being for shots and sequences which maintain movement without revealing new sights to be digested—long pans, slow zooms and smooth tracking shots. The viewer automatically estimates the time that a developing shot will take to reach a destination; the viewer's attention can therefore be relaxed and the words can be listened to while the shot gets on with its own business. In addition, developing shots can contribute an emotional charge to the words spoken over them. A zoom which speeds up as it nears its target is perceived almost as if it were another element of the speaker's tone of voice.

A memorable example was in the television drama series *I Claudius*.[1] The Roman Empress Livia is delivering a very long and difficult speech but we are not looking at her. We are looking at the Emperor Augustus lying on his couch, and we are slowly— very slowly—zooming in to a close-up of his face. Though we do not see her, the movement gives urgency to Livia's words, but it is not until she stops speaking and we have time to look closely at the image that we realize that Augustus has died—while we were watching. (The actress playing Livia was furious when she discovered how the scene had been edited. She said that she had only taken the part because of the opportunity of delivering that speech.)

In a scene from *Welcome to My World*,[2] a series about the future promised us by information technology, the subject is the future of war. The narration briefly becomes a verse lament for the vanished heroes, the soldiers and airmen made redundant by the brave new world of machine-to-machine battle. The words are accompanied by a shot tracking back endlessly along a line of empty, abandoned Tornado jet fighters. The shot continues throughout the entire poem. By the end of the shot, rejected aircraft seem to stretch from the foreground all the way to the horizon, adding their own desolate commentary to the irony of the text.

Thus voice and vision in documentary films are not separate channels to be separately constructed. Each has an effect upon the other. A changing image adds modulation to the words, the words add rhythm to a picture sequence. And like the warp and weft of a fabric, the words and the pictures help weave the documentary together into a seamless whole.

Acts and sections

The sequence of scenes and events, though integrated by vision and sound into a complete narrative structure, are actually not continuous and undifferentiated. A story told in that way would quickly become indigestible and unintelligible. Just as a book is broken into chapters to help the reader, so a film-maker needs to help the audience assimilate the material by structuring it, breaking it up into functional sections, to allow the audience to navigate its way through.

If the documentary maker's first major shaping of reality is to determine the thread of the film, its division into sections is another. Structuring the documentary as a series of acts is to put

[1] BBC 1976
[2] BBC 1987

up signposts along the track of the film, guiding the viewer and showing the way.

To structure a film is to decide how the film evidence is to be understood. The documentary maker who works like the sculptor in clay, adding chosen fragment to chosen fragment, will make the decisions in his or her imagination before actually shooting a frame. Those who work in the stone sculptor's way, with days of material to condense, will make the decisions on the basis of the shot footage. Either way the documentarist is again saying: 'look at the events this way.'

That is not to suggest that the film-maker will consciously try to predetermine the audience's response. Many documentarists claim to apply the Brechtian technique of putting the evidence in front of the audience and letting them be the judges of it. But it is impossible for a film not to reflect the views of its maker. The selection of one item over another, the structuring of the material this way rather than that way, can only be according to the film-maker's own vision. Making a documentary is a powerful way of confronting ourselves with our own, often unnoticed, attitudes and prejudices.

A film-maker gives the documentary a shape by dividing the work into sections, each containing one or more sequences. In terms of the film's content, the divisions are the equivalents of chapters in a book, each containing one or more paragraphs. In terms of the overall structure of the film, they are like the movements of a symphony, each with its introduction, its development and its finale. They are often called acts, as in a stage play.

Division into sections can also be demanded by the medium on which the documentary appears. Commercial broadcasting stations which must show advertisements in the course of a production's transmission sometimes specify at what point the breaks must come. This can be damaging to a film if it does not fall easily into the predetermined slices. A television programme maker will try to design the commercial breaks in from the very start, to make sure that the division into sections demanded by the material and the overall form of the film match the requirements of the broadcast channel.

The number of sections into which a documentary naturally falls depends on the subject, the story and the length of the film. Five sections or acts is a very common format. It is perhaps no coincidence that classic drama has much the same overall shape. Five acts allows a film-maker to vary the pace, tension, colour, visual interest and many other aspects of the work in a dynamic and interesting way. The acts do not all have to be the same

length. The duration of an act is just another parameter for the
film-maker to control.

So, for example, one documentary about the career of a well-
known popular musician was composed of five acts. The first,
full of excitement and optimism, dealt with his discovery and rise
to public notice; the second, slower paced, darker more downbeat,
followed his personal difficulties as he coped with the destructive
pressures of wealth and fame. In act three, superficially cheerful
but with an undertone of danger and an accelerating tempo, the
singer reacted to the conflicts in his life by suppressing them and
accepting the life of a hugely successful pop star; act four was a
dramatic slide from stability into the major crisis which was the
result of that suppression. The last act, rising in tone again, took
him from near breakdown through religious conversion to
spiritual contentment, calmness and peace.

The shape—the dynamic profile of each aspect of the film—is
a style of contour that is repeated at nearly every level. Just as the
film has an overall structure or architecture, so does each section.
It is a dynamic shape, with a beginning, a development and a
conclusion. And each sequence of which each section is
constructed has its own shape too, as does each shot which makes
up each sequence. These are not all the same shape of course. Yet
they all share similar characteristics. They are like the patterns in
music, where every bar has a pattern, as does the phrase of which
the bar is part, and the musical section to which the phrase
contributes, and the movement of which the section is part, and—
ultimately—the whole piece. As in music, so in film too it is the
interaction between the dynamic contours of the constituent
elements that gives the whole work its richness and texture.

Scenes and sequences

The sequences or scenes which the film-maker puts together to
make the sections may be classified into three different kinds:
narrative sequences, descriptive and explanatory sequences, and
formal sequences. Formal sequences are those required, not by
the content, but by the structure or format of the film. Descriptive
sequences are those in which nothing much happens, but are
included to set a scene, paint a portrait of a character, catch up on
the background to an event. Explanatory scenes are, self-evidently,
those whose function is to elaborate an idea, explain a concept or
make sense of what might not otherwise be understood. Of the
four categories, only the narrative sequences actually carry the
burden of telling the story. In practice, because of the essentially
narrative nature of the documentary, most film-makers will

usually try to find ways of converting exposition and description into story elements if at all possible, thus avoiding the need for descriptive or expository sequences altogether. If this is not done, there is a real danger that the film's onward movement, so essential to hold on to the viewer's interest and concentration, will grind to a halt during passages of explanation or scene-setting. The skill and imagination of the documentarist is much tested by the need for such conversions.

The narrative scene

Narrative scenes are the means by which the film-maker tells the film's story. They are the key scenes of the film. They depict actions and events which are the turning points of change. The choice of scenes by which to detail the narrative determines the meaning, the integrity and the persuasiveness of the film. Thus the question faced by every documentary maker is always: 'what events do I film to put over, as well as possible, what I want the film to say?' In the turbulent maelstrom of reality, it is sometimes difficult to decide on the selection of which particular elements are to be drawn from life. The real world is an extremely beguiling place. A film-maker is easily seduced by the unpredictably picturesque, the unexpectedly charming, the unforeseeably dramatic. A less than careful choice in the content of the scenes can take a documentary away from its planned path and into uncertainty and confusion. It is the film-maker's responsibility to select with great precision those and only those elements which combine to project the coherent narrative.

A documentary scene is the record of an event. It can be the raw documentary record of a real happening. It can be constructed from an artfully composed series of still images. It can even be dramatized with actors or depicted using animation. Whatever it is, it will, like the overall film and its separate sections, itself have a plan, a structure, with a start, a development and an end. It will run from immediately before the change it depicts, through the change, until immediately after the change. It will focus on the subject of the change—the person, the object, the situation, the concept that is changing.

Though most documentaries are most of the time composed of filmed records of real happenings, when the subject is not a person or even any other kind of living creature, or when the time span of the documentary is in the past or in the future and cannot therefore come before the film-maker's camera, the scenes which tell the story will necessarily be the products purely of the film-maker's imagination.

In one sense, almost all film making is done in this way—except for direct reportage. Much documentary filming of real subjects involves the repetition of actions already performed or of statements already made. The time between the event and its repetition for the camera may be very small. The subject does something which he or she is then asked to repeat, with the camera at another angle. The delay may also be much larger. The subject may be asked to role-play an event from yesterday or last year. At what point the scene loses its connection with reality and becomes no more than an acted performance is a matter for the film-maker's judgement—and perhaps conscience. It depends on how far the subject is reacting spontaneously and unconsciously under the influence of the remembered circumstances. To ask a subject to repeat an action without emotional overtones, like opening a door, is one thing. To ask him or her to open a door leading into a room where he or she will face a courtroom trial is quite another. Yet people differ. Some are so well able to bring back to mind feelings and emotions from the past, as to give their re-enactments considerable honesty and truth. Many even respond to the role-playing with authentic autonomic nervous responses like sweating, palpitations and tears.

Often, however, it is not possible to film the subject at all: the story may be about a concept or an idea which cannot be concretely visualized; it may be about a place or person at a time unreachably in the past. In cases like these the film-maker will have to use shots and sequences in a symbolic rather than a literal way.

This technique may be called the transferred context—the film equivalent of the literary device called the transferred epithet. The film-maker suggests, with a sequence of not directly related images, some aspect of change in the subject's fortunes that he or she is seeking to depict. The specifics of what the images record are not directly linked in a literal way to the subject's story. Rather they run in parallel, suggesting that the viewer transfer the ideas across from what appears on the screen to what the viewer knows is the real subject of the film.

The first episode of *Living Islam*,[1] a series about the origins, history and future of that religion, required a sequence outlining the religious and social atmosphere among the Arabian tribes of the seventh century, the time when the Prophet Muhammad brought them his Message. To suggest this inaccessible historic period, the film used the story of a *Marabout*, a 'living saint', in Mali, West Africa, as he went on a missionary expedition to convert a pagan village to Islam. The viewers were perfectly aware of the contemporary dimensions of what they were actually seeing. But, as the commentary went on to speak of the life of the Muslim   [1] BBC 1993

Prophet, the simple living conditions and heightened spiritual atmosphere of modern Africa were transferred in the viewers' minds to the historic Hejaz.

Transferred context can also include the use of non-documentary materials to add to the story. Archive materials, clips from old movies, commercials, music videos and many other kinds of footage all contribute to the documentarist's palette. The transfer is often of cultural associations, references which are believed to be part of the shared culture of both the documentarist and the viewers.

Such a film-maker must first be quite sure of which associations they are. Where the need is to communicate simple ideas, the problems that arise are those of working with clichés. Here, trains symbolize travel, clocks the passing of time and falling leaves the turning of the year. In a sense this is inevitable. Just as with words in a language, any symbol universally recognized must necessarily be well worn. Nonetheless film-makers will do their best to provide original symbols which will still be generally understood.

In putting over more complex matters, film-makers often have recourse to archive film: usually black and white, mostly documentary but sometimes even cinema fiction. Such a device can succeed, but can also be badly misleading. Representing mediæval times, for example, with stills or moving film from the end of the last century and the first decades of our own, is problematic. It is not clear what elements of the scenes could be usefully transferred. At other times, the use of archive film may be more justifiable. In *Living Islam*, a description of the antiquity of the pilgrimage route to Mecca was accompanied by very old film images of the Hajj. Though the 1930s motor truck was clearly anachronistic, the archive footage also showed travellers crossing the desert on camel-back, travellers whose experience would have been little different from that of their ancient counterparts. Use of old film avoided confusing the viewers with the gross infra-structure of modern mass transportation.

There is a limit to the possibilities of the transferred context. The further the scenes are from overt linkage to the subject, the greater the tension with the integrity of the story's thread. At some point, the connection may break and the viewers may begin to ask themselves: why am I watching this? Lamely to explain the connection in commentary is to admit to the failure of the technique.

An alternative to the transferred context is dramatization. The film-maker engages actors to perform according to an arranged script. If taken to its logical conclusion, a film made this way—a drama-documentary or docu-drama—is no longer documentary, but is rather more closely akin to the genre of fiction. In between the genres is the employment of actors to perform without words, in a way which is usually descriptive rather than narrative. The resulting scenes are sometimes known in the United States as 'sketch-tones'. In the series *Nautilus*,[1] a history of submarines, numerous underwater scenes were enacted by performers: navigators pored over charts, captains peered through periscopes, ratings rushed busily up and down companionways. All these scenes were shot with feature film gloss. The effect was quite different from what it would have been if the illustrations had been the grainy documentary record of real submariners. It is questionable whether the presumed purpose of these scenes— to give some indication of the reality of submarine life— was really achieved.

In the case of archive film the illustrations either directly support the commentary—insofar as they are authentic images of the time and the place—or transfer something of themselves into the film story's context. The audience knows that it is looking at the real thing. In the case of a cinematic performance, it knows full well that it is not. The effect is to distance the audience. Whether far enough for disbelief to creep back in depends on how specific the acted scenes are. In the case of *Nautilus* the filmed actions did at least help to give an idea of how cramped life is in a metal tube under the sea. *Galleons*,[2] a film about the history of the ships known by that name, featured shots of a man dressed in Elizabethan costume sitting on a rock staring out to sea, while the commentary told of Francis Drake. This was a rather more problematical example. There was nothing particular about the images which the audience could transfer to the real historic character. The idea of a man sitting on a rock hardly needed illustration.

At some point, however, it becomes impractical or impossible to provide images which contribute any further to telling the film's story. At that stage the film-maker has to fall back on using the images to communicate the story in words, either from a participant in the story—an interview—or from a presenter.

Description and exposition

Though sometimes necessary when words must be spoken and no pictures are to be found, the professional presenter is an ambiguous figure in a documentary production. He or she is both part of the story and equally not part of it. The presenter is a human personality with whom the viewer can identify but at the same time the viewer is well aware that the presenter's presence in the film is a matter of artifice. This is not the same as for a reporter.

[1] BBC 1995
[2] The History Channel 1996

The premise in journalism is that the reporter's first task is to collect the information. A journalist is judged on the ability to find things out. Communicating them to an audience with elegance and skill comes next. But a documentary presenter's main job is the communicating itself. Everyone is aware that a presenter is giving a professional performance and is served by an unseen army of support—researcher, director, producer, camera and sound crew. For this reason the presenter's presence in the scenes of a documentary story can be more difficult to justify and explain. For want of any other reason for the presenter's presence, audiences often assign to him or her a commanding role in the production. Even sophisticated viewers tend to ascribe to the presenter the sole authorship of the work. Perhaps the most honest presented scenes are those in which it really is the film-maker who personally appears on the screen.

Even then, the presence of a presenter on the screen radically alters the audience's relationship with the film. The commentary of a documentary speaks with the voice of the film-maker. When the commentary is spoken by an unseen narrator, the words—like all sounds—are perceived by the viewer as located in his or her own head. With no external anchor to which to attach the words, the commentary remains the viewer's private possession. But once associated with a character who appears on the screen, the commentary becomes objectified and externalized. The voice of the film is seen as merely belonging to a character on the screen. Thus, though the intention may be to help the audience to identify more closely with the subject of the film, the result may be just the opposite. A presenter who is trapped, as it were, within the screen, is merely part of the film world, not the real world.

In that world, by means of speaking directly to the viewer, the presenter, when on screen, can vie for attention with the subject of the film. The result may be that the film comes to have two subjects, an undesirable situation which divides the viewer's attention and interest. To avoid the confusion, documentary makers often go to great lengths to integrate their presenters into the action in some way. This is most easily done when the presenter is known to have some genuine personal interest or authority in the subject of the film and can genuinely participate.

The integration must of course be convincing and well thought through. In an effort to keep movement and action going, during what is effectively nothing more than the delivery of a long text, documentary directors sometimes get their presenters to speak while walking—usually, for practical reasons, towards the camera. This is hard to believe in if there has been no previous indication of where the presenter might be going and why. Just as in drama, unmotivated movement is mystifying and distracting to the audience.

On the other hand, a presenter can be used to help justify purely visual, non-story, elements of the work. Descriptive passages and images of scenes notable principally for their beauty, aesthetic or informative interest rather than their story content—always difficult to integrate into a story-led medium like documentary—can be made the location of a presenter's action. As long as there is a reason for the action, following the presenter's movements can be a successful way to include and develop what would otherwise be empty shots. This can contribute to the integrity of the work. In *Living Islam* the presenter's attempts in Central Asia to locate Muslim clergy who had hidden themselves away during the Communist era, allowed the audience a tour of the ancient and majestic city of Bokhara which would have been otherwise difficult to justify.

There are of course many examples of travel documentaries made more appealing and accessible by good selection and deployment of presenter scenes. In *Pole to Pole*,[1] a series of films about a journey from the North to the South Pole, presenter Michael Palin's adventures provided both the story for, as well as the illustrations of, what was in essence a geographical entertainment. As we have noted, presenters are restricted in the kinds of stories they can to tell. But original ideas have always been found. A live broadcast of the climbing of the great rock known as the Old Man of Hoy[2] on the island of Lewis, had Christopher Brasher and Ian McNaught Davis both as climbers and presenters. There was no question as to why they were there—to climb the rock. They were therefore able to give a running commentary on their progress, physical as well as emotional, which was itself the subject of the story. Such a device satisfied the part of us which says that first-hand accounts are always to be preferred to hearsay evidence and active participants to detached presenters.

The broadcast climbing of the Old Man of Hoy was not a documentary. But the same technique has been success-fully applied to true documentary films in which the central protagonist—or more than one—in the action also speaks through the camera directly to the viewer. In this case the presentation becomes part of the real action, so unifying the subject and countering the earlier suggestion that use of a presenter is not part of true documentary technique.

Not all protagonists are willing or able to address the camera with ease. Most people feel much more comfortable speaking to another person and answering specific questions rather

[1] BBC 1994
[2] BBC 1967

than having to construct their own agenda—in other words, being interviewed.

The interview

Because it provides personal testimony from an active participant, the interview has become a mainstay of the television documentarist's technique. With the interview, stories are told, rumours are passed on, beliefs are expressed, as well as opinions, conclusions, emotions: anything and everything.

Interviewees appear in documentary films as witnesses and the role of witnesses in a documentary is similar to that in law. Witnesses should be first-hand, not second-hand. Ideally they should only give direct evidence, not rumour or hearsay, unless the evidence be of the rumour itself. Most importantly, like witnesses in court, interviewees *are* facts, they are not a way to put facts across. They speak with authority only about what they feel, what they understand, what they know, from their own experience.

Clearly, there will be many cases where the view of facts as seen through the eyes of witnesses are the very substance itself of the film. *Shoah*, Claude Lanzmann's great film about the Jewish Holocaust, was entirely composed of interview, as was *Le Chagrin et la Pitié* (The Sorrow and the Pity), the film by Marcel Ophuls about French collaboration with the Nazi occupation. In both cases, the facts *were* the interviewees. Their memories, their reactions, their confusions, were what the films were about. In both these films also, the interviewer appeared in vision. This is not quite the same as being the presenter, though if a film has a presenter, he or she may well do the interviewing and be seen to do so. A presenter is master of a film, an interviewer is the servant.

Almost always, however, interview scenes will exclude the interviewer. By the standard convention, questions are removed, leaving only the interviewee's replies. This avoids the need to establish the identity of the interviewer—or, as often happens, interviewers—and concentrates attention on where it belongs: the interviewee.

The significance of the interview is that it really is unscripted. Earlier in film history, free unscripted speech was rarely used in documentaries; it was considered too dangerously uncontrollable—artistically as well as politically. Contributors were told what to say—and made to repeat it till they got it right. Today, such manipulation is considered unacceptable. In fact, there has been a swing in the opposite direction. So-called 'Vox Pops', random street interviews, are a commonly used device, supposed to gauge and represent the mood and opinions of the general public. The idea is, presumably, derived from the Roman saying: 'Vox populi, vox dei' (the voice of the people is the voice of God). Such 'evidence' is, however, fairly meaningless, as a small collection of individual and usually eccentric opinions can hardly stand in for the views of the entire public. Most serious documentarists avoid using Vox Pops, except for their potential entertainment value.

Practicalities, to be sure, demand that some preparation and management of the interview be undertaken. Indeed the conduct of an interview is an act of direction, as artful as directing actors, except that the direction is given non-verbally and within the conventions of the interview form. An interview is conducted by standing or sitting opposite the interviewee and directing him or her towards the desired performance with spoken questions and a constant flow of body language, looks and expressions. Many film-makers finish an interview with a face quite aching from all that communication. But honesty demands that the documentarist distinguishes between management and manipulation, and does not put words into the interviewee's mouth even when he or she knows just how to express the thought better. When an interview appears on the screen there is always the implicit claim that a direct, unmediated connection is being made between interviewee and viewer. If no images can be found with which to tell a part of the story, an interview scene is the nearest a documentarist can get to presenting the viewer with direct evidence.

Titles and junctions

Formal sequences are those with a functional purpose to play in the overall film. They relate to the context within which the film is seen. They include opening title sequences, end credit sequences, and sometimes also symbolic junctions between the sections.

Most television documentaries have an opening title, a signpost that marks for the audience the start of the journey with the story-teller on which they are about to embark.

The title can be utterly simple—a line of white text on a black background—or highly elaborate—a minute of more of self-contained image-spinning. Its ostensible purpose is of course to display to the audience the title of the film. But actually the title sequence has a much more important function than that. The opening title of a television documentary acts as a frame. The beginning of a film must set the story's world and time apart from the rest of life. It must separate off the individual film from the continuous flow of material appearing before it on the screen. The title answers the question: 'has it started yet?' It is a sign which says: 'the world of the film begins here.' Even productions designed for office or home video viewing usually need a title sequence to mark off the empty tape, hiss and shash from the prepared recording—even when that purpose is logically negated, as happens not infrequently, by delaying the title for some time after the start of the film.

When generic to a broadcast series or strand, the title puts the material in a wrapper designed to suggest a standard product, created to a uniform house style, giving an indication of the nature of the film to follow. Long running strands on British television like the BBC's *Horizon* or LWT's *South Bank Show* have won a reputation for consistently high quality and style. In such cases the opening title sequence is a guarantee to the viewer. There is a difficulty, however. Documentaries in these strands also have their own individual title, which must be included somewhere. Common practice is to make the programme title a single superimposed caption at some distance from the series title. The disadvantage of such double titles is that they may confuse the audience about the actual starting point of the film, which may seem to have a double beginning.

A title sequence should prepare the viewer for the story-telling and introduce the mood, subject or theme. Many examples show the power of appropriate title sequences. In *We Can Keep You Forever*,[1] a film about American GIs missing in action in Vietnam, the opening titles were the first thing the viewer experienced, and by themselves were able to generate such dramatic tension, using such powerful images and dramatic music, that the audience was already captive by the time the actual narrative began.

In *The Last Exodus*, the account of twentieth century Jewish history in Eastern Europe was framed with the 1991 story of the emigration from Moscow, the titles growing naturally out of the opening sequence and forming a bridge between the detailed present and the grand sweep of history. In *Imagina '89*,[2] a film about the latest developments in computer animation, the opening was an opportunity to excite the viewer by showing off some of the most spectacular achievements of the new generation of computer animators, with the titles themselves being the culminating example of the range of their work.

Formal junctions between sections of a documentary are sometimes marked with special transitions. These are often in the form of short title-like sequences, often making substantial use of graphics, and often with a textual caption bearing a section heading. These perform the same function for the film as starting a new page with a chapter heading does for a book. Such a division,

[1] BBC 1986
[2] BBC 1989

however, temporarily abolishes the viewer's suspension of disbelief. The effect, just as in a book, is briefly to make the viewer emerge from immersion in the screen world and become aware of the technicalities, and therefore the physicality, and ultimately the unreality, of the medium.

The documentary maker must, therefore, always bear in mind that linking sections of the film by means of graphic transitions breaks the flow. Each section has to work much harder than usual to pick up the story where it was left before the break. For this reason, dividing the film material up in such an overt way is unusual, though not unheard of, in narrative documentaries. Where it is a useful technique is in films which are predominantly explanatory in content, and where the explicit organization of the material is an aid to the viewer's grasping the entirety of the picture.

The use of written captions as headings in the middle of a documentary are a matter of fashion. Silent movies used title cards to indicate that which could not be explained visually. For a long time, perhaps in reaction to the association with the silent cinema, textual captions were thought of as too old-fashioned to be used. More recently they have become acceptable once again, as they come to remind viewers, not of the antique silent film, but of the up-to-date computer screen. In fact much of the graphic treatment given to screen images now owes nearly as much to styles borrowed from information technology—the Multi-media Look—as it does to the traditional sources: magazine and illustrated book layout.

Imagina '89, an hour-long production, was divided into five cumulative sections, each with its own short subtitle. In that particular work, the images which composed the main body of the documentary were in the main sufficiently spectacular to make extreme simplicity in the section titles a welcome contrast. The junctions made use of still captions, white lettering on black background, dissolving into vision and then, after a second or two, fading out again.

End credits

At the other end of the documentary, the End Credit sequence is the symmetrical complement of the opening titles. It acts as the other side of the frame, the marker that stands between the completed film and whatever follows on the screen. The information end credits convey is a matter of convention. But their function, to bring the documentary to a smooth end, is achieved without reference to their actual textual content.

At their simplest, end credits are no more than a list of functions and names scrolling up the screen against a plain background. Though it is entirely appropriate that those primarily—and legally—responsible for the work: the director, writer, producer, photographer, sound recordist, should make their identity publicly known, tradition—and often contractual obligation—in the film industry, unlike in almost any other creative medium, demands that everyone who played almost any part whatsoever in creating the work should have their name included in the credits. Inclusion is taken very seriously by television people, although clearly the credits are only of real interest to those working in television rather than to the audience, to whom many of the job descriptions are mysterious and unintelligible. It is an odd situation when what adds up to hours of time every day are devoted to broadcasting material which is largely meaningless to the viewers.

There is little resistance to the tradition because the closing credits perform an important function within the structure of the film. Just as the opening title smooths the viewer's passage from his or her real world into the world of the film, so the closing credits ease the viewer gently back out from the film into the real world. In older cinema fiction, the resolution of the final climax used to bring the story rather quickly to a close, plunging the cinema audience very suddenly back into their real lives, and sometimes leaving them rather disoriented. Most people have had the experience of staggering out of the darkness, unable immediately to detach themselves from the powerful emotions released by the film they were watching. The aim of the director was expressly to leave the audience partly stuck in the fictional world, so that the emotions and implications of the story continued to resonate for some time in the audience's mind. This was possible in the cinema, where there are gaps between the presentation and where the audience has to be allowed time to leave the auditorium.

Television is different. The flow of stories never ceases. It is not really possible for the television documentary maker to leave the viewers to their thoughts. Something else immediately takes over the screen, probably starting off another story about something completely different, right away. Allowing time for a list of names and trades to run through, sometimes for as long as a minute or two, gives the viewers a chance to ruminate over and, the documentarist hopes, to assimilate what they have seen.

If the credits are not presented as bald text, but as words superimposed over moving pictures, such images will not be visually demanding. It is almost impossible to read a long stretch of on-screen text at the same time as following a complicated action in the underlying pictures. Advantage is often taken of the fact that these particular words are not of compelling interest to most viewers, by letting the last shot of the film run on under the credits. Thus the time is used for a number purposes: to conclude the action, to summarize the film's thread in a visual manner and to allow the viewer time to re-integrate him- or herself back into the real world, at the same time as to provide the credit information for those who wish or need to see it.

The actual credit list is not always presented on a long scroll. It is equally possible to divide up the names and put them on the screen in the form of separate static captions. Such a form of presentation makes it possible to combine the credit list with the continuing action of the closing moments of the film.

If continuously scrolling text is to be used, a particular psychological factor must be taken into account. Just as happens with subtitles, changes of shot under continuous text have a disconcerting effect on the reader. The eye assumes that not only the image, but also the text, has changed. The viewer's eye returns to the beginning of the words and begins to read again, only then to discover that he or she has read the text already. To avoid this phenomenon, shots to be used under scrolling credits are either chosen to be long enough to continue throughout the entire sequence, or, if changes of shot are to be incorporated, the credits are allowed to stop before the change, and only continue again afterwards. Whichever is chosen, the final image will be one which lingers long enough to bring the film to a controlled end.

Formal scenes like titles and credits are at the boundary between content and form—the matter they serve to communicate to the viewer is arguably less important than the function they perform while doing so. For most other sequences, content and form carry equal weight. Telling an effective documentary story demands not only that the content is effectively managed but that the resources used to do so—the pictures and sounds—are properly deployed according to their own internal film logic. Underlying all are the processes by which those pictures and sounds are collected and recorded.

Section B
The Tools

It is not necessary for a documentary maker fully to understand the physical processes by which the raw material—the images and sounds—are captured and converted into permanent records, ready for editing into the final film. It is enough for a director to know what he or she wants, rather than the precise details of how to achieve it. The cine-photographer and the sound recordist will have the technical expertise to realize the director's vision. But when planning and designing scenes for a film, some appreciation of the technicalities can be useful in helping to make plain what is, and what is not, possible. The director should have enough knowledge to ensure that the vision is one which is capable of realization. Every film-maker should know at least something in principle of how the lens and the microphone do their work.

Chapter 6

The Lens

The use of the lens in film-making is sometimes described as 'painting with light'. The metaphor suggests that using a camera lens is like using a brush: that the result is under the total control of the user, the artist. That is not really the case. A lens acts on the light rays which pass through it according to the laws of physics. The photographer, still or cine, and the film-maker who directs the photographer's efforts, is actually working with those laws and their consequences.

It is probably most useful to think of the camera lens as a viewer's eye, borrowed for the occasion, and directed towards whatever the film-maker wants the viewer to see. Like a human eye, a camera lens is a converter of three dimensions to two, collecting light rays which stream from a three-dimensional scene and projecting them through a variable aperture—the iris—onto a flat surface: either onto a strip of film or onto the photosensitive screen of a video camera. The idea is to create, on that flat surface, an image which is, as far as possible, exactly what a viewer's eye would see if the eye were in the same position as the lens.

Thus both the eye and the camera lens are concerned with projection onto a plane, the conversion of three dimensions into two. In this respect, both painting and film-making are concerned with a similar task and film-makers have something to learn from the history of painting. For in a sense, the art of the photographer is the fulfilment of the long search by painters for a technical solution to the problem of representing three dimension on a flat surface: a way of recording where the straight light rays emanating from a scene intersect with a flat sheet.

The artists of the European Renaissance worked hard on this problem, particularly in relation to the design of *trompe-l'oeil* scenery for the new dramatic art of opera. Leonardo da Vinci and Albrecht Dürer devised a number of methods and kinds of apparatus for ensuring that the two-dimensional image corresponded exactly to the painter's-eye-view. Leonardo suggested:

'Have a large sheet of glass about half the size of a sheet of good quality paper, and affix it firmly in front of you so that it is between you and the thing you want to portray; then stand back so that you are at a distance two thirds of an arm's length from the glass, and use an instrument that will hold your head still so that you cannot move it. Then either cover or close one eye and with the brush or pencil trace on the glass what you see...'

Another way of obtaining a similarly accurate result was the *camera obscura*—a 'dark room'. This was already well known during the Middle Ages. Light rays pass from an exterior scene into a blacked-out room through a pinhole which focuses them onto a whitewashed wall at the back. Such 'rooms' were built in many sizes. Some painters used the camera obscura and its close relative the portable *camera lucida*—the light room—to help compose landscape scenes. Today's children still play with small pinhole cameras made of cardboard, with a translucent paper screen at the rear.

The great advantage of the pinhole camera is that it has no focus. That is to say: all objects, at whatever distance, are equally sharp. Each point of light in the picture cast on the back wall is a tiny image of the pinhole. The smaller the pinhole the smaller the dots of light making up the image and therefore the sharper the focus. When the pinhole is infinitely small, the overall focus becomes infinitely sharp. Unfortunately, an infinitely small pinhole lets through infinitely little light, so the picture is also infinitely dark. A pinhole camera must always find a compromise between sharp focus and a visible image.

The introduction of a lens solves this conundrum, though at the cost of introducing new limitations of its own. Unlike a pinhole, which brings all objects into focus on its screen, a lens at a given distance from a screen can bring into focus only objects at one particular distance in front of it. That distance is a function of the distance between the lens and the screen, the focal length of the lens. If an object is not at the appropriate distance its image will be out of focus. Anyone who has used a still camera will know that a decision has to be made about which objects in the scene are to be in focus and which not.

A camera obscura equipped with a glass lens was first demonstrated by Professor Daniel Barbaro in Padua in 1568: 'Close all the shutters and doors until no light enters the room except through the lens, and opposite hold a sheet of paper, which you move forward and backward until the scene appears in sharp detail. There on the paper you will see the whole view as it really is.'[1] But it was probably not until the seventeenth century in Holland that lenses were first regularly used in place of pinholes to project images for artists to paint from. The time was one of intense exploration of the science of optics. It was also—and perhaps not by coincidence—one of the high points in the history of European painting. Some scholars believe that The Netherlands

[1] The Faber Book of Science 1995

painters Jan Vermeer and Peter de Hoogh may have used a camera
obscura fitted with a lens to produce a number of their domestic
interior scenes. For in some of Vermeer's pictures objects or
characters in the foreground are painted slightly out of focus,
seeming to throw the middle-ground and background into the
distance. It is the first time such an effect is evident in the history
of painting.

Whether or not the great Dutch master really did use a camera
obscura, there are other reasons for photographers and documentarists to count him among the originators of their craft. For he
certainly was among the first painters to confront the problem
facing all television film-makers: how to suggest the illusion of
everyday reality and develop realistic spatial depth within a small
flat image intended to be viewed in normal light among everyday surroundings. Vermeer's use of a lens may well have been
the inspiration behind his manipulation of perspective and the
use of different planes of focus in his compositions. But it was his
ability to raise the naturalistic, the ordinary and the everyday to
the highest plane of art which makes study of his work a valuable
exercise for photographic image-makers today.

Early lenses were made of simple single pieces of glass. But
such lenses suffer from aberrations and distortions, particularly
at the edges of the picture. White light tends to be split into its
constituent colours, straight lines may come out as curves. To
overcome this difficulty, today's lenses are made of multiple
sections—they are compound lenses. Such lenses can almost get
rid of aberrations, though not without introducing other problems.

Light suffers losses, by reflection, diffraction and scattering,
when it passes from one medium into another. In a compound
lens, light has to cross between a number of pieces of glass
cemented together, losing something in the process at each
crossing. The result is a spreading of what should be a point of
light into a small disc, the 'circle of confusion'—much the same as
what happens in a pinhole camera when the hole is not small
enough. This causes the picture to become slightly fuzzy or blurred.
Additionally, as some light is lost altogether in crossing between
so many pieces of glass, the brightness of the image is reduced.

Earlier film cameras used a number of lenses, often mounted
on a revolving turret for convenience, rather than the single zoom
lens which modern cameras favour. Today zoom lenses are almost
universal. But, as the zoom facility is only made possible by
stacking yet more pieces of glass together, there are still cine
photographers working today who prefer to use—even insist on
using—fixed lenses, even though modern optics suffer far less from
the defects of compound lens design than did those of the past.

Focal length

The two defining characteristics of a lens are its focal length and its aperture.

The focal length of a lens specifies the distance between the lens and the screen on which it focuses but it is not necessarily a direct measure of that distance. A very short focal length may not allow enough room for the camera shutter between the lens and the film. A long focal length lens may be too unwieldy and need placing rather less than the focal length in front of the electronic screen. Modern lenses deploy various optical techniques to fold the light rays and overcome these difficulties. The best one can say is that a lens with a given focal length produces an image on the screen which is the same size as the image which would be produced by a pinhole at the focal length distance from the screen. In other words, a 100mm lens produces an image the same size as would a pinhole 100mm away from the screen.

A change in the focal length appears to accomplish no more than a change in the magnification of the image but this result is much more important than it may at first seem. It makes focal length one of a lens's key characteristics, responsible for controlling the perspective of the image. Though we speak of focal length, the distance between lens and screen is not what we are really interested in; much more relevant to us is the fact that the angle of view which a lens provides is directly related to its focal length.

The standard lens of a 35mm still camera usually has a focal length of some 50mm. This is intended to provide an angle of view equivalent to that of the naked eye. Film and video cameras are slightly different but their standard lenses are designed in the same way. Yet the view seen by the naked eye is not always what is required. Often a wider or a narrower view is called for. This is achieved by changing the focal length of the lens.

Given screens of the same size onto which to project, it is clear that the longer the focal length of the lens, the narrower the angle of its view (Fig. 6.1).

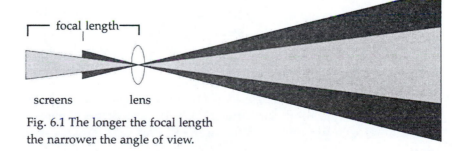

Fig. 6.1 The longer the focal length the narrower the angle of view.

Thus a longer focal length lens will appear to project a larger, closer image. A short focal length lens will project a wider view (Fig. 6.2).

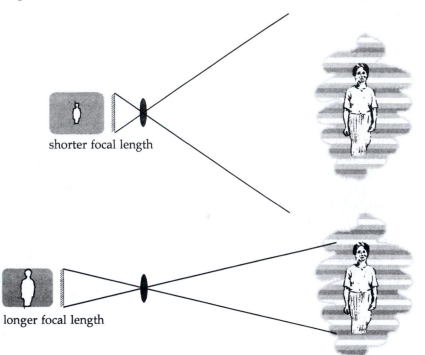

shorter focal length

longer focal length

Fig. 6.2 A shorter focal length lens will appear to project a wider image; a longer focal length lens will project a narrower view.

The focal length of the lens not only affects the apparent size of an object, it also determines the apparent spacing between different objects arrayed at different distances in front of a camera.

Consider a figure standing some distance in front of a building. If one keeps the size of the figure on the screen constant by moving the camera bodily backwards and forwards, the narrower the angle of view the smaller the amount of background that will be included in the image. The result is that a narrow angle lens will seem to compress distances and a wide angle lens will exaggerate them (Fig. 6.3).

This phenomenon is responsible for many familiar effects of perspective distortion. A narrow angle lens will make far-off mountains seem higher, distant buildings more imposing, a tyrant's statue in the background more threatening. Shoot with a narrow angle lens along a street and pedestrians or cars or telegraph poles seem more crowded together. Shoot down the length of a train as the carriage doors open and they will seem to disgorge a tight press of humanity.

By contrast, a wide angle lens makes any space seem larger and deeper. Small rooms are stretched, submarines made to seem less claustrophobic, city boulevards are magnified, freeways seem extended to infinity. Studio drama is often shot through wide angle lenses to make cramped sets appear more spacious.

Any movement through space towards or away from the camera is affected too. Because of the foreshortening effect, shoot an athletics race through a narrow angle lens from some way off and because distance is compressed, the runners will appear to be expending huge amounts of energy yet covering hardly any ground at all. Conversely, shoot a slow chase with a wide angle lens and characters moving in line with the axis of the lens will seem effortlessly to move the distance in leaps and bounds.

Narrow angle lenses must be used with care. Because of their greater magnification, camera movements will seem to be exaggerated. Pans and tilts need to be slower than with a normal or wide angle lens to maintain the same speed of movement on screen. When shooting with a narrow angle lens, the camera needs to be set up on a stable tripod to avoid any unwanted movement. Operating hand-held is inadvisable.

Use of wide angle lenses often results in distortion of the image. This arises from a number of factors, some being lens defects, others being the consequence of the geometry of projection.

Perspective can become greatly exaggerated. The size of an object projected onto the screen is proportional to the distance

Fig. 6.3 A wide angle lens will seem to exaggerate distances and a narrow angle lens will compress them.

from the lens. An object half the distance away from the lens is projected at twice the size. In a close-up of a figure with an outstretched hand in which the body is twice as far away as the hand, the hand will appear to be magnified to truly monstrous proportions.

This applies to all lenses, though it is most noticeable in wide angle lenses because they tend to work closer to the subject than narrow angle lenses. It is not the result of a defect. It comes from the fact that the proper perspective can only be presented to the viewer's eye when that eye is placed at the geometrically correct distance—the focal length—from the television screen. More exactly, since the image is actually enlarged to fill the television screen, the correct viewing distance is equal to the focal length of the lens multiplied by the magnification used to recreate the image. For example, if a frame of 16mm film shot through a 10mm lens is magnified some 35 times to appear on a television screen, it should properly be viewed from a distance of 350mm (about one foot two inches) to make the perspective seem natural. In reality the viewing distance of a television screen is never anything like that close. As a result many images shot with wide angle, short focal length, lenses appear to be distorted. The distortions are less evident when using narrow angle lenses, as the distance from viewer to television screen is more commensurate with the focal length of the lens.

Other perspective effects may be equally disconcerting. Straight vertical and horizontal lines may become curved in wide angle views, especially towards the edges of the frame. This is often what the eye really sees, but while the brain automatically compensates for it in interpreting the image, the camera gives us the image raw and unadjusted.

There are also problems associated with the need to project the image onto a flat plane. Because the light rays are channelled through nearly a single point, their focus lies not on a flat plane, but on the inside of a sphere centred on the lens. The focal length is the radius of that sphere. The shorter the focal length (the wider

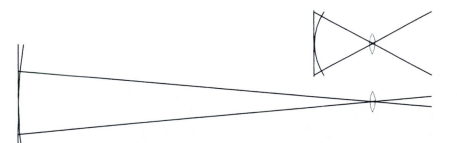

Fig. 6.4 Projection of a curved image onto a flat plane produces distortion away from the centre; the wider the lens angle, the more the distortion.

the lens angle), the smaller the sphere and the more pronounced its curvature. The longer the focal length (the narrower the lens angle), the longer the distance from lens to screen and therefore the larger the diameter of the sphere and the flatter its curvature (Fig. 6.4). A section of the surface of a very large sphere is not very different from a flat surface. But a section of a small sphere is.

All projection of a curved image onto a flat plane produces distortion away from the centre. The greater the curvature the greater the distortion. The result is that distortion around the edges of pictures becomes quite noticeable in images shot through a wide-angle lens.

This is a particular feature of very wide angle lenses, sometimes known as fish-eye lenses, which may in addition sacrifice some optical accuracy in the interests of cramming in as wide a viewing angle (sometimes as much as 180 degrees) as possible.

The distortions may not be very noticeable in shots that are relatively static. But objects moving through the frame will seem to alter their proportions as they do so. Panning or tilting the camera will make the objects in view change shape and size as if they were oozing. Such an image is disturbing to the viewer, perhaps only acceptable in its extreme form if the aim is to suggest disorders of mind or of perception: psychoses, nightmares, drunken fantasies, panic attacks.

Aperture

If the first defining characteristic of a lens is its focal length, the second is its aperture. This determines the amount of light which passes through on its way to the screen. The larger the aperture, the more light. The more light, the brighter the image. Thus aperture is a key factor in regulating the exposure of the image and therefore the overall tone of the picture.

On a still camera there are two ways of adjusting exposure: aperture and shutter speed. The faster the shutter, the shorter the exposure and therefore the darker the picture. The two adjustments: aperture and shutter speed, are both used together to provide for the particular circumstances in which the photograph is taken. But on both film and electronic cameras, the recording medium—film or tape—moves forward inexorably by 24 (or 25 or 30 depending on the technology) frames per second. The shutter speed is effectively fixed, and cannot be used to adjust for different light conditions. So a great load falls on aperture control. It also means that the lighting conditions under which moving images are filmed are much more constrained than with still photography. Hence film cameramen and women must be prepared to provide artificial lighting in circumstances in which a still camera would be able to operate by available light.

Measurement of the aperture of the lens of a still camera is given in 'f' numbers. These depend not only on the diameter of the iris, but also on the focal length of the lens. The shorter the focal length of the lens—the wider the viewing angle—the greater the amount of light passing through the lens. The 'f' number is mathematically derived by dividing the focal length of the lens by the diameter of the actual aperture (in other words: is the ratio between them). As both are defined in millimetres, the result is a non-dimensional number. Thus 'f' numbers grow larger as the effective aperture gets smaller—f22 lets through less light than f8. The brightness of the resulting image is inversely proportional to the square of this number. So as to make brightness increase twofold with each stop, the convention has arisen to make each 'f' number approximately the square root of a multiple of 2. Thus the usual 'f' numbers are f1 (square root of 1), f1.4 (square root of 2), f2 (square root of 4), f2.8 (square root of 8), f4 (square root of 16), f5.6 (square root of 32), f8 (square root of 64), f11 (just under the square root of 128), f16 (square root of 256) and so on.

These are entirely theoretical figures, however, resulting from the mathematical relationship between the size of the light passage and the focal length. Film and video cameras usually characterize aperture by empirical 't' numbers, based on the 'f' stops but with the light transmission physically measured by the lens manufacturer.

Generally, the aperture of the lens is set by the photographer to capture the image with the best possible overall exposure. Here there is a considerable difference between film and video. The ability of film to record many levels of illumination is far greater than that of video. The latitude of film means that even though shadow detail may not be visible in a straight print, the information is actually still recorded on the film and can be brought out by special development. The same goes for detail in the highlights of a picture. Thus the difference between highest and lowest usable exposure is far greater on film than on video. It is possible, for example, to shoot a film interview against a bright sky with the interviewee's face in shade and still get acceptable exposure of both. On video, the face would be almost in darkness and the sky burnt out to white. The video camera operator must be much more careful than the film camera operator to place the exposure right in the centre of the range.

Depth of field

If the aperture of the lens affected only the exposure of the picture, it would be a relatively simple matter to set correctly. But aperture also has an impact on focus, in particular on the range of distances in front of the lens between which objects will be in focus. This is known as the depth of field and is an important aspect of picture composition.

A pinhole projects a uniformly sharp image. A lens with an ideal pinhole-sized aperture would also create a picture which is focused all over. A wide open lens, by contrast, creates an image in which only objects at one particular distance are in focus. Real lenses are not ideal pinholes but neither do they entirely lack the pinhole effect. A real practical lens will project a picture in which a whole range of distances will be in focus. The smaller the aperture, the greater that range—in other words, the depth of field—will be.

If the lens is focused to infinity, the closest point to the camera that will be acceptably in focus is called the hyperfocal distance. This distance is proportional to the focal length divided by the 'f' stop (giving the actual physical size of the aperture). Given the same 'f' stop, the longer the focal length the further away the hyperfocal distance, therefore the closer to infinity, and therefore the narrower the depth of field. At the same time, the larger the 'f' number, the smaller the aperture, therefore the closer the hyperfocal distance to the camera, and therefore the greater the depth of field. The limiting condition is, of course, with a pinhole of zero aperture, when everything in the image from the lens to infinity will be in focus—but given zero exposure.

The depth of field in a shot will therefore depend on both the focal length of the lens and its aperture. Working close in with a wide angle lens—one with a short focal length—gives a cine-photographer great freedom, as the depth of field is large and the camera can follow most actions without much fear of losing focus. Working with a narrow angle, long focal length lens is much more difficult and demands far greater precision.

Since adjusting the aperture of the movie camera lens cannot be compensated by changing exposure, as with a still camera, it is important for a film-maker to recognize that working in different levels of illumination will have an impact on the depth of field. In dark environments, where it is necessary to work with the lens as wide open as possible, depth of field will be seriously reduced. Conversely, under very bright illumination, the lens will be stopped down and the depth of field correspondingly increased.

Chapter 7

The Microphone

The camera's lens and the recordist's microphone are not equivalent devices. A lens merely processes light rays so that they can then be captured on film or converted into electrical signals. Light rays enter from the front and leave from the rear. The microphone, on the other hand, is the device which actually performs the conversion. The task of the microphone is to receive vibrations from the surrounding air and change them into electrical impulses which can be recorded onto some medium, usually magnetic tape. Numerous different means have been tried over the years to achieve this, but for a long time, two devices have been in principal use: the dynamic microphone and the capacitative.

A dynamic microphone depends on the fact that when a wire moves through a magnetic field an electrical current is induced in it. If a magnetic field is moved past a static wire the same phenomenon occurs. The induced current is normally very small, but by increasing the length of the wire it can be made of measurable size. In a dynamic microphone, the wire is fixed to a diaphragm which moves in sympathy with the vibrations in the air. The wire is extended to a considerable length and wound into a coil, the whole coil vibrating within the field of a powerful magnet. The wire, though rather long and thin, has relatively little impedance—resistance to the flow of alternating current—and the result is a current flow of some magnitude, which does not need very high preamplification to bring it up to a level at which it can be successfully recorded. The simplicity and low cost of this arrangement makes it very attractive.

However, there are drawbacks to dynamic microphones. The coil assembly has a significant mass and a significant size and shape. These two characteristics mean that it has resonances of its own and vibrates more easily at some frequencies than at others, rather than moving totally and exactly in sympathy with the vibrations in the air. In particular the highest and lowest frequencies are less exactly reproduced. Moving coil microphones thus give a noticeable 'colour' to the sound they record, emphasising the mid-range, and giving less response at the extremes of the frequency scale.

Capacitative microphones depend on a different physical

property. When two conductive plates are brought close to each other and an electrical potential applied across the two, an electrical field is brought into being in between. Movement of the plates in relation to each other, as when responding to vibrations in the air, induces a change of voltage between them. The voltage change is extremely small but can be amplified to a usable level. The plates of the capacitor have very little mass and can be made to respond almost equally to all the sound frequencies which impinge upon them.

The result is a microphone which has an extended and rather flat frequency response with little unwanted colouration. Of course capacitative microphones have their disadvantages too. One is that they need a relatively high voltage source to make them work; this is usually derived from the mixer. Cheap 'electret' microphones, which are based on the capacitative principle, are often battery powered, but their sound quality is generally below professional standard. Another difficulty is that their internal impedance—resistance to alternating current flow—is so high, and the signal produced is so small, that capacitor microphones are very susceptible to electrical noise.

Whichever kind of microphone is used, the sound recordist takes care to capture only the sounds which are wanted, and to exclude those which are irrelevant, or disturbing, to the shot. To make this possible, microphones have directionality, that is, they are designed to treat sound differently depending on the direction from which it comes. Most microphones have either an 'omni-directional' or a 'cardioid' response—though since sound is a three-dimensional phenomenon, the same microphone may have both, depending on the plane in which it is operated. Thus a cardioid (heart-shaped) microphone mounted horizontally has a heart-shaped sensitivity to sound arriving in its own plane (Fig. 7.1). The same microphone looked at from the front is omnidirectional (Fig. 7.2).

For full directionality, the microphone capsule itself is set into a carefully audio-engineered housing which uses phase differences in the sound waves to cancel out, as far as possible, all sound from unwanted directions. Such 'gun' microphones, usually themselves housed in fluffy fur-covered, sausage-shaped windshields, have become a trademark of the sound recordist on location. However, many more kinds of microphones are regularly used. In particular, personal microphones, attached to the clothing of the speaker, and either connected to the mixer by a long cable or by a radio link, are among the most frequently seen. Such microphones require considerable skill in their use if rustles from the clothing and other unwanted sounds are to be avoided.

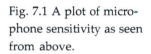

Fig. 7.1 A plot of microphone sensitivity as seen from above.

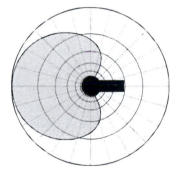

Fig. 7.2 Plot of microphone sensitivity as seen from the front.

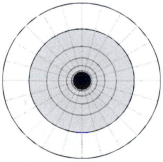

In the last few years, sound recording has become an even more demanding operation because of the introduction of stereophonic sound. Stereo sound is captured by using two microphones. At its simplest, the 'A and B' system, the stereo effect is obtained by recording separate left and right hand channels from separate left and right microphones, corresponding to the left and right ears of an auditor present at the scene. This demands great skill and sensitivity from the sound recordist as the final sound-world of the shot is decided at this time. The width of the stereo 'spread', once recorded on tape, cannot thereafter be altered; only the strength of the effect can be changed.

To offer greater flexibility a different technique, the 'M and S' system, has been developed. This also uses two microphones but in a different way. One microphone records a standard monaural signal. The other in effect detects and records the differences between the stereophonic sound of the scene and the monaural signal. Using specialized equipment, a stereo signal can be reconstituted from these two channels, while allowing for the stereo effect to be substantially changed. Thus final and irrevocable decisions about the sound quality can be deferred until later.

Section C
Building the Form

A television documentary is constructed not only of pictures and sound, but also time. Time is the universal though unrecognized factor that underlies all the work. As real life itself does, so television productions unroll continuously and unrelentingly from beginning to end. They don't speed up, slow down, reverse or stop. Without the regular and continuous unrolling of time they don't exist. Stop a film or a video and time is killed; sound and movement vanish; the film dies. Start time moving again and the production springs into action.

Time on television is not continuous as it is in life. Television time moves forward in discrete steps. On film, wherever we are in the world, time steps forward in paces of one twenty-fourth of a second. Television is different. In Britain and Europe, each step is one twenty-fifth of a second after the last; on American television it is one thirtieth. (In both cases a frame consists of two fields, each providing half of the lines which make up the television picture: field one draws the odd-numbered, field two the even-numbered lines.) The distinction is the result of different electricity mains frequencies. Thus do the chance decisions of engineering history influence quite unrelated fields.

When time is stopped, sound vanishes utterly but vision merely freezes. Without time, the very idea of sound—the movement of particles of air over time—loses its meaning. Sound is an analogue quality; it can be divided and subdivided down to the infinitely small—almost, though never quite, to zero. But vision is digital, atomic. Without time, vision, like physical matter, reveals itself as constructed of a series of discrete units. Beyond these, one cannot go. The indivisible atoms of television are the frames. An illusion usually called persistence of vision is what makes the viewer perceive movement when presented with a series of still frames.

To say that a thirty-minute film is a string of 43,200 individual frames, though true, tells us little. In the physical world, atoms are grouped in an ascending hierarchy to construct reality. Every sculptor knows that there are many graduations in between a piece of stone and the atoms of which it is ultimately composed. The precise nature of each level determines the character of the whole. The stone is made up of grains, the grains are constructed from crystals, the crystals are built of molecules and molecules themselves of atoms. Similarly a book is made up of chapters, the chapters of paragraphs, each paragraph of sentences, each sentence of words.

Film and video productions are constructed in a similar way. A film is made by joining together a series of sections, the sections are constructed from sequences, the sequences are built up from shots, and the unit of the shot is the frame. The meaning of a text cannot be deduced from knowing which words it contains, though in the end it is made up of nothing else. A documentary cannot be described solely in terms of the frames of which it is composed, though in the end here too there is nothing else. As with the atoms in stone or words in a book, a documentary depends on the arrangement, the order, the selection and the composition of the frames which make it up.

There is an exact correspondence between the number of frames and the length of the work. One can say a that thirty-minute film consists of 43,200 individual frames, a thirty-minute British video of 45,000. But one cannot say how many shots or how many sequences—there is no conversion table one can apply. A shot may have a hundred frames or a thousand. A sequence may have ten shots or fifty.

Nevertheless there is a relationship. The length of shots, of sequences, of sections, are still, though in a rough and inexact way, reflections of the length of the complete production. The number of frames in a shot, of shots in a sequence, of sequences in the entire work, will be of a similar order. Rhythm and pace demand that a short work contains shorter shots and shorter sequences than an extended production. A thirty-second commercial will have far shorter shots than a one-hour documentary. An extended film composed entirely of three-second shots would be unwatchable. A five-minute production made up only of ten thirty-second shots would be unconscionably slow. Thus film and video, like many other human creations that strive for an organic naturalness, are characterized by some of the self-similar qualities of fractals.

Self-similarity is that property of an object which makes areas of that object, when magnified to any scale, look similar both to the whole and to each other. A commonly given example is that of a coastline. At any magnification, from a representation in a printed atlas down to close observation by the naked eye, the edge of a sea shore looks similarly ragged. So much so that it is impossible to determine the scale of the image from its appearance alone. Similarly, when looking down at the ground from an aircraft, unless one can see objects like trees or buildings whose size is known, it is almost impossible to tell the height at which one is flying. Fractals are mathematical constructions which—amongst other qualities—display self-similarity. It is their self-similarity than brings fractals closer to nature than the rigid geometry of the drawing board. Fractals can be used to create convincing images of clouds, mountains, shorelines, forests, flowers. The self-similarity of film and video timings bring these works closer to the qualities of the real world too.

Though there is no limit to the possible magnification of a mathematical fractal, a real natural feature like a shoreline cannot be magnified indefinitely. Ultimately one arrives at the atoms of which the grains of sand are composed. By definition an atom can be divided no further. And so it is with a film.

Chapter 8

The Frame

The atomic unit of the whole film is the frame. The unit for the recording mechanism, cine or video, is the shot. The film or video camera is a time dependent machine. Between starting and stopping the camera, an arbitrary number of frames will be captured. The difference between the frames which make up the shot are the result of change over time—that is, movement; movement either of the camera or of the scene being photographed. Discount movement and the characteristics of all the frames in the shot are found to be collectively shared. Thus though one cannot compose the image of each single frame individually, by temporarily ignoring movement, the aesthetic qualities of the frames can be determined and designed.

A frame is a still image. Among its qualities are size, viewing angle, distance, perspective, composition, colour, tone, atmosphere. Its major characteristic, however, is its flatness. A camera is a converter of three dimensions into two. While a natural phenomenon of the human brain provides an illusion of movement where none really exists, no such assistance is on hand to help create the illusion of depth. The cine photographer must work hard to provide that visual sleight of hand.

Composition of the frame uses the same devices as are used in painting and still photography: compositional structure, key (high or low), contrast, focus. Many directors and cine photographers model their images on those by famous painters of the past, particularly those artists like Vermeer whose cool domestic interiors are among the finest examples of artistic realism. Textbooks of photography often contain rules of thumb for screen composition, invoking such considerations as balance, proportion and screen 'weight'. But because the frame is only a single one out of a continuous series, its compositional qualities can be rather different from those of a painting or a still photograph. Since the shot contains movement, the framing at the beginning may be quite different from that at the end. And the factor of movement leads to a quite different means of concentrating attention. Thus, where a painter would have to so construct the image as to lead the observer's eye to the principal feature of the picture, the cinephotographer may depend on movement in the frame to fulfil the same purpose.

Above all, a frame is a view; a viewer's-eye view. To design a frame is to place the viewer's eye in front of the scene. The aim is to create the illusion that the viewers are seeing what they would see if they were they actually there at the scene. This is what can be called the 'illusion of presence'. On this illusion is based the willing suspension of disbelief, which is central to the audience's involvement with all television, both fact and fiction.

While the illusion of presence applies both to the cinema and to television, the difference between the two media is considerable. In the cinema the illusion is assisted by the fact that there the images are life sized. Cinema images occupy the viewer's entire field of view. Around the screen is darkness. The size-estimation skills of the eye are applied directly to the screen image. Suppose a member of a cinema audience is seated at a distance of, say, 50 feet (15 metres) from the screen. A 6-foot (2 metre) image of a person on the screen is understood by the viewer's eye and brain as human-sized. Now the perspective effects of the real world apply. A 3-foot (1 metre) image is seen as twice as far off: 100 feet (30 metres). From the same 50-feet distance, a face, presented five times life size on the screen is perceived as only a fifth as far away: 10 feet (3 metres).

On television, the illusion of presence is far weaker than in the cinema. A television screen occupies nothing like the viewer's total visual field. The image is small, surrounded by other everyday objects which are usually bathed in the room's ambient lighting. In consequence, the sizes of images on a television screen are understood not so much as literal and realistic but as symbolic. The screen itself only symbolizes, rather than actualizes, the eye's visual field. The television screen is perceived, as the cliché has it, as a window on the world. Many older people still refer to watching television as 'looking in'.

To define precisely the eye's visual field is difficult. In tests, a normal pair of eyes can perceive an amazingly wide field, a horizontal angle of view of almost 180°. The owner of the eyes is, however, not normally aware of this large field, as the brain focuses on only part of it—that part on which the person is concentrating. It is as if the brain possesses a 'zoom' facility, able to zoom in on whatever takes the viewer's attention. In addition, a sighted person's eyes are never still, but constantly scan the viewing field. The smaller the area concentrated on, the smaller the total visual field scanned. The result is that a person is aware of a changing visual field which corresponds to what the brain interprets rather than what the eyes physically see. Combining the brain's zoom facility with the scanned field of attention produces the effective field of view.

The eye estimates the size and distance of an object on a television screen by judging how much of the screen's symbolic visual field it occupies. A head-and-shoulders image of a person on a television screen is interpreted to be at that distance at which the head and shoulders of a person would occupy the effective visual field of the eye in the real world—perhaps 3 feet (900cm).

Camera placement

The placement of the camera—more specifically the camera lens which represents the viewer's eye—can be at any point in a continuous spectrum of three-dimensional space. Applying the conventional co-ordinate system used in drawing graphs, one can call the side-to-side dimension the 'x' axis, the up-and-down dimension the 'y' axis, and the front to back dimension the 'z' axis. If we keep the distance between the camera and the photographed object—the 'z' distance—constant, the 'x' and 'y' axes are seen to be circles, with the 'z' distance the radius and the object at the centre (Fig. 8.1). Actually, to be pedantic, the 'y' axis is really only a quarter of a circle. We never shoot from under the ground—never? Well, hardly ever (Fig. 8.2)—and the back half of the 'y' semicircle is equivalent to the front, but with the camera moved to the other side of the 'x' axis. The framing of a shot in a documentary film depends on where the camera is placed on each of these axes.

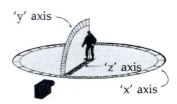

Fig. 8.1 The co-ordinate system.

Fig. 8.2 We never shoot from under the ground—never? Well, hardly ever.

The camera position on the 'x' circle is largely responsible for the composition of the image. If the subject to be photographed were alone in space, then choosing a point along this dimension would affect only the direction from which the subject is seen: from the front, the side or the rear. Normally, one would shoot a subject or an action so that it is directed towards rather than away from the camera. The exact position is usually chosen so as to reveal as much of it as possible. Often this means selecting a three-quarter view: towards the lens as well as slightly sideways, opening up the action by spreading it horizontally, thus allowing more of it to be seen and the effects of perspective to be revealed. The choice of which sideways direction, left or right, largely depends, as will be seen later, on the preceding and following shots.

The subjects of real frames are not usually isolated; a frame of a film almost always contains a multiplicity of objects. In a scripted film, the director has the opportunity to place the objects and characters where they will make the best picture. In most documentary filming, that job must be done by choosing the camera position instead. The positioning on the 'x' circle affects screen relationships in a number of ways. It can determine which

Fig. 8.3 Travelling along the
'x' circle around two figures
alters their distance and
screen position.

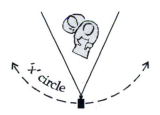

of the objects are 'upstage' (further from the camera) and which
'downstage' (nearer to the camera), it can ensure that none of the
objects which are important for the viewer to see are masked—
obscured from the camera—by others in front of them, and it can
effectively control the width of the action, ensuring that it is
contained within the frame. By imagining two figures standing
slightly apart, one can easily see how travelling along the 'x' circle
alters their distance and positioning on the screen (Fig. 8.3).

Perhaps most importantly of all, correct placement along the
'x' circle affects which object appears on the left of screen and which
on the right. If one draws a line between the subjects of a shot and
extends the ends to cross the 'x' circle, it can be seen that any shot
from one side or other of that line will place the objects consistently
left and right:

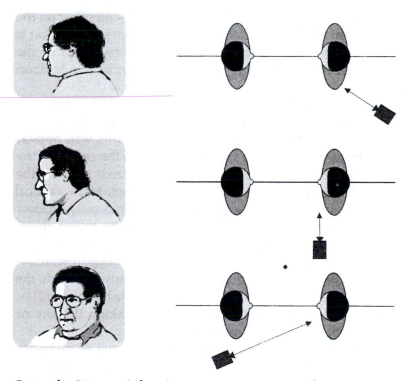

Cross the line, and the objects are reversed on the screen:

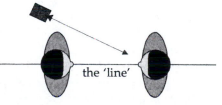

As will again be seen later, this 'line' is an important factor to bear in mind as it affects the way the shots can be assembled. Objects on the left of frame should normally stay on that side in successive shots, objects to their right should also stick to their own side of the screen. People facing to the right of frame should continue to do so, as should those facing left. Any action should therefore be photographed from either one side of the 'line' or the other, never both. 'Crossing the line' is regarded as one of a director's greatest potential solecisms.

Camera placement on the up-and-down axis, the 'y' circle, is much more restricted. The camera is hardly ever raised much above human head height, nor is it often placed below floor level. The difference in the appearance of a moderately distant lone subject, when filmed with a lens one foot above the ground and one seven feet above the ground, is barely noticeable. Yet that does not mean that raising or lowering the camera has no effect on the image, just that the pictorial impact is rather more subtle. What is changed by adjusting camera height is the perspective of the vertical features in the frame and the position of the horizon on the screen.

The normal way to photograph a subject is with the camera at the same height as the centre of interest with the lens aimed horizontally. In this position, all vertical features will appear vertical and parallel, and the horizon will be in the centre of the image. Raising the camera and tilting it downwards towards the subject produces what is called a high-angle shot. Here, vertical lines will appear to diverge towards the top of frame and get closer towards the bottom (Fig. 8.4). The horizon will be raised above

Fig. 8.4 Raising the camera and tilting it downwards towards the subject produces a High-Angle shot.

the centre of the screen, thus backing much of the image with the ground. Conversely, dropping the camera and shooting upwards— a low-angle shot—will make vertical lines narrow towards the top and spread out towards the bottom, while the horizon will be displaced to a lower position in the image, making the sky or ceiling the background to most of the frame.

These effects, though not gross, nonetheless have an influence on the way the audience views the scene. Powerful characters— or those to whom the photographer wishes to ascribe power—are often shot from a low angle, backed by the sky, making them seem to dominate the view (Fig. 8.5). By lowering the lens and pointing it upwards one can look at the world through the eyes of a child. In a film about children, all of the shots taken among the children would normally be shot from the children's own height. In contrast, the adult material would all be shot from a normal adult's height. The result would to give an impression of normality when shooting subjects within the adult's or the child's world, but a

Fig. 8.5 Powerful characters are often shot from a low angle, making them seem to dominate the view.

contrasting appearance, marking the difference in their views when observing each other's domain.

By raising the camera and angling it downwards, the audience sees the world from the viewpoint of a tall person or even a giant. A commonly used device is the high-angle shot at the end of a film, where the camera cranes up and looks down to provide the framing that some directors call 'the eye of God'. The effect is supposedly to distance the audience and make the concerns of the previous sequences in the film seem insignificant in relation to the overall picture of the world. Often the only real effect is to inform the audience that the director was well enough resourced to be able to afford to use a camera-crane.

It should be remembered that these effects are the result of angling the lens to the horizontal. Keeping the lens horizontal and simply moving the camera bodily up and down to match the height of a subject leaves the horizon in place and the image undistorted (Fig. 8.6).

Fig. 8.6 Keeping the lens horizontal leaves the horizon in place.

Shot size

Choosing a shooting position along the third, the 'z' axis, is largely responsible for the size of the subject's screen image. This is, as will be seen, not the same as choosing the magnification of the lens. Though there can be an infinity of different size of frame, by convention—and also by function—the frames of a film or video are usually categorized by the distance of the notional viewer's eye. The following names are standard, though their precise meaning, the precise size to which they refer, varies from director to director, photographer to photographer. They are, from furthest away to closest in: the long shot , the wide shot, the full shot, the mid-shot, the close-up, the medium close-up, the big close-up. These names do not define a precise size, that is, a precise placement of the viewer's eye. They are not absolute, but relative descriptions, depending on the nature of the scene and of the action taking place within it.

To choose between these frames, to determine the size of the television screen image of an object or scene, is to choose the distance at which the viewer's eye is placed. The illusion of presence depends on a convincing placement of the viewer's eye which in turn depends on satisfying inbuilt, as well as culturally determined, needs as to the distance between the viewer and the viewed object. Members of every culture learn early in life to defend an area of personal space around them. The size of that space depends on, among other things, the degree of formality in the situation: the more formal the situation, the further away the other person needs to keep. To allow the person actually to invade one's personal space is to allow an act of considerable intimacy. The placement of the viewer's eye in a scene follows similar rules. Camera placement involves the choice of an appropriate position between objectivity and intimacy.

The wide shot

The standard view instinctively adopted by an observer of an entire scene corresponds to what in the television vocabulary is called the wide shot. This shot gives that view of the entire scene. The eye is placed far enough away to be on the boundary of the scene but close enough to perceive the necessary details (Fig. 8.7). The wide shot is neither intimate nor distancing. It is the position taken up by a shy teenager arriving at a party: on the edge of, though not out of, the room. It corresponds to the view of the stage by the audience in a theatre. As in the theatre, it allows the viewers to feel themselves present while imagining that the real participants are unaware of the spectators' presence.

Fig. 8.7 Far enough to be on the boundary, close enough to see the details.

It corresponds to the theatre but is not the same. The real view of a real theatrical stage has width, height and depth. It is three-dimensional. A television frame has only width and height. It is flat. In the absence of an available third dimension, other ways must be found to indicate the depth of the view. The composition of the frame is the only tool available to that end.

Movement can help, as will be seen later. But mostly depth must be indicated by a series of visual clues and tricks such as overlap, parallax and perspective. Directors call it 'composing in depth'. These are the same devices as were developed over the centuries by painters and draughtsmen and draughtswomen. The image is first imagined as if built up of overlapping planes, like the cardboard dioramas in museum displays. Such an image can be thought of as consisting of three planes: foreground, middle-ground and background.

As on the theatrical stage, action takes place across the middle-ground. The foreground is the front of scene, the proscenium. The background is the set.

The foreground frames the action. It is an essential element of the artistic composition of the image. But it also has an even more important function. The foreground is perceived to be just behind the screen; it serves to push the action back and thus help create an illusion of depth. The human eye knows what size familiar objects should be. The difference between the actual size of an object on screen and the known real size of that object, is perceived as the effect of perspective. The contrast between the size of objects in the foreground and those in the middle ground cues the eye to perceive the middle ground as some distance away. The greater the difference between the screen size of foreground and middle ground objects, the further away the middle ground is recognized to be. The leaf of a tree shown at the same screen size as a human figure is recognized as close to the viewer with the human figure much further away.

Movement in a frame will be considered elsewhere, but it is worth noting here that foreground movement is often a feature of the wide shot. Movement of whatever frames the foreground of a shot adds realism. However, such movement must be handled with care. Foreground movement is magnified. Changes which would not be seen in the middle ground or background are clearly visible. Because the foreground is closest to the viewer it easily distracts attention. Movement in the foreground, unless continuous and random, like water rippling or leaves trembling in the air, takes the spotlight from where it should be: on the action. But such movement, if small and complementary rather than conflicting, can add greatly to the atmosphere of the image. Photographers frequently ensure that in a wide shot of an open air scene, for example, some foliage is included, drooping into the foreground top of the image. This is commonly called *dingle*. It is not unknown for an assistant to be deputed to shake it about a bit, to make sure that it is seen to move in an appropriate way.

The background of a frame is the set and setting for the middle ground action. It has functional and symbolic effects. Functionally, it pushes the middle ground action forward towards the viewer. Between the foreground proscenium and the background set, the action is forced into the middle ground. The illusion of presence, which depends on the illusion of depth, depends in turn on the action being in front of the background and behind the foreground.

Unlike a cardboard museum display, an image is not, of course, composed of simple flat planes. Though foreground, middle ground and background are distinguished from each other, in many images they are part of a single feature running from foreground to background. The illusion of depth in a frame is enhanced by allowing long features to run both in depth as well as across the image. A fence or wall, typically, would be so captured as not to run across the frame but at an angle, with part forming the foreground, part the middle ground, and the rest running away into the distance of the background (Fig. 8.8). Shooting at an angle makes the effects of perspective most evident.

Atmospheric perspective also contributes to the sense of distance. If very far away, the background to a scene may be fainter

Fig. 8.8 A fence, part foreground, part middle-ground, part background.

in tone that the middle ground. As in a watercolour painting, the further the background, the paler its tones and colours are likely to be. This is the natural consequence of the absorption of light by dust or mist in the atmosphere and is not an artefact under the control of the film maker.

The background of a shot does more, however, than just contribute to the three-dimensional quality of an image. The set of a scene tells the viewer where the action is taking place. The choice of background therefore has important symbolic and atmospheric consequences. It characterizes the location not only geographically but also adds emotional value to the scene. Choosing, or even dressing, the background is an essential part of placing the action in its physical, emotional and aesthetic context. Its contribution therefore to the content, not just the location, of the scene should not be underestimated. Film-makers usually take a great deal of trouble to ensure that the background to a wide shot is chosen to contribute as much to the meaning of the scene as possible.

The long shot

The long shot is usually captured from further away than the wide shot. It is usually flatter. The view is that of an observer totally disconnected from the action. The actual distance depends on the nature of the action and the scenic environment.

Where the wide shot reveals the action within its environment, the long shot focuses attention on the overall environment itself, of which the action is merely one element. Thus landscapes, both rural and urban, are what the long shot is usually all about, placing the action within a context of space and atmosphere.

Because of its nature, the long shot is not so much composed of a foreground, a middle-ground and a background, but is mostly all background. Foreground detail, which plays such an important function in the wide shot, may also be introduced into the long shot, but serves merely to emphasize the distance of the rest of the image. It is the middle ground that is most notable by its absence.

Where the wide shot is introductory to a scene or sequence, giving the viewer on overall impression of the scene, the long shot is often used as a device for temporarily withdrawing from the action and looking at it dispassionately from a distant perspective. The long shot dwarfs the subject.

Distance has its disadvantages on the television screen. Where in the cinema, the small size of the significant feature in the frame makes its own point, on television such a screen size makes the feature vanishingly small. In the domestic environment where most television is viewed, such a feature may not be noticed at all. The line structure of the television screen makes very small features on the screen physically unclear. An object needs at least a few screen lines to be recognizably drawn. Of the 625 lines making up a television frame (525 for NTSC as in the USA) only 576 (480) actually appear on the screen. Any feature less than 1/576 (1/480) of the height of the screen cannot appear, if at all, as more than a single dot. Thus there is a lower limit to the size a feature can be, if the viewer is to both observe and clearly interpret it. So the long shot is more useful to the cinematic film-maker than to the television documentarist. That is not to say that it should be entirely avoided. Only that great care needs to be taken with its use.

Because of its dispassionate nature and its disconnection with the action, and also because movement in the scene is minimized by the distance of the viewer's eye, the long shot lends itself most of all to the artifices of beautiful composition. Here the craft of the landscape painter is most profitably brought to bear on the image. Where in other shots too much attention to picture-making might distract attention from the substance of the image and the concentration on the action, the film-maker has an obligation to make the long shot as aesthetically pleasing as possible. And the problems associated with the small size of the main feature within the overall arrangement make care in frame composition particularly necessary. A tiny figure in a landscape cannot depend on movement to draw the viewer's attention. The structural composition of the image is the only way to concentrate attention on that particular part of the frame.

Group shots

In the wide shot and the long shot we are looking at the entire scene as a whole. As we come closer, we begin to pick out individual groups of objects or characters. It is impossible to say at what point a wide shot becomes a group; there is no sharp dividing line between them. But generally group shots contain no more than three or four, at the very most five, characters or objects. Any larger, and the group becomes too big to maintain its unitary nature.

Why would one wish to select out a group from the generality of a scene? Usually because one wishes to concentrate on the interactions between its members. To do this effectively, the camera must be placed in exactly the right position. In a scripted film, the director is responsible for arranging the characters in the *mis-en-scène* in the most dramatic and attractive way. In a documentary it is sometimes possible for the film-maker to interfere in an event enough to ask its participants to take up particular positions, but usually the composition of the image is controlled by careful positioning of the camera.

Groups of people interacting with each other mostly arrange themselves automatically and unconsciously in a rough circle. With the camera positioned outside the ring, some of the participants will necessarily have their backs to the viewer. More problematically, those in the front will mask—obscure from the camera—those at the back. Whatever actions or interactions take place within the circle will be hidden from the lens. The effect on the viewer is to be excluded from what is going on. In this situation the photographer, rather than attempting to peek between the foreground figures, will usually try to insinuate him- or herself into the circle, becoming part of it, and thus able to gain a viewpoint similar to the others in the group. As a result the sense of the group as a whole may be lost as the camera will only be able to see a restricted section—which section depending on the direction in which the lens is pointed.

Under such circumstances the previously mentioned concept of the 'line' becomes all important if the viewer is not to lose all geographical sense of the set-up: who, in other words, is standing where. With the camera positioned in the centre of the circle it is easy to see how different interactions between different members can place the 'line' now on this side of the camera, now on that. In consequence a particular speaker may first appear on the left of screen looking towards the right, later he or she may be found on the right, looking left. As a result, the audience may be left totally confused. It is possible, by very careful selection, to help the viewers make sense of such a sequence of images, but it is quite difficult. Most directors at the start of their careers try at least once to shoot a multiway discussion 'in the round'. The experiment is usually not repeated.

Even in a group, most interactions are one-to-one. In fact, nearly all human interactions are between no more than two individuals. When addressing an audience, a speaker's remarks will almost always be targeted to a single listener, or to a series of single listeners. Thus by far the commonest group shot is one containing only two participants: a speaker and a listener. It is called a two-shot, often abbreviated as 2-S (Fig. 8.10).

Two-shots can be of a range of sizes: from those which include both characters almost full length to those in which one of the characters appears as no more than a foreground frame for the other—the so-called 'over-the-shoulder' view. The two parameters

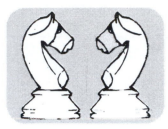
Fig. 8.9 Looking flat on.

Fig. 8.10 Two Shot.

Fig. 8.11 A photocall.

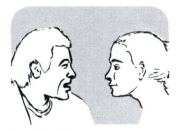
Fig. 8.12 Profiles.

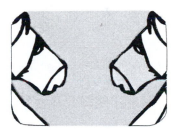

Fig. 8.13 The empty Space.

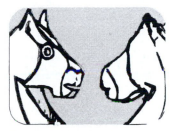

Fig. 8.14 At an angle.

Fig. 8.15 Over shoulder.

Fig. 8.16 Single subject.

Fig. 8.17 The interviewee.

which the photographer can vary are: the camera's position along the 'z' axis, the distance, that is, from the camera to its subjects. This, given constant lens magnification, determines their size on screen. The other variable is the camera position along the 'x' circle, which controls the angle between the lens and the 'line' joining the two figures. It is this angle which establishes the composition of the frame.

Where two people stand talking to each other, the simplest way to view them is flat on (Fig. 8.9). There are a number of disadvantages to this approach. Unless the characters are looking towards—'favouring'—the camera, as part of a photocall perhaps (Fig. 8.11), both will be seen in profile, a viewpoint which, though sometimes striking and making a strong interaction between the two participants almost visible, totally cuts out the onlooker and can therefore be rather alienating (Fig. 8.12). Such a view also ignores the preference for 'composing in depth', the aim of giving an illusion of three dimensions on the two-dimensional television screen.

In addition, the flat-on two-shot can only work where the figures are reasonably distant and their relatively small size allows them both to fit easily onto the screen at the same time. Where a closer two-shot is called for, filming the characters flat on gives rise to a split image, with the faces pushed to the edge of frame and an unsightly empty space left in the middle (Fig. 8.13).

In most cases, a two-shot will be so arranged that one of the characters is closer to the camera than the other, in other words so that the axis between them will be at an angle to the lens (Fig. 8.14). This brings in the necessary perspective effects to give depth to the image. The angle is controlled by moving the camera around on the 'x' circle, which at the same time determines how far apart the two figures appear: the narrower the angle, the tighter together. Where the figures are to appear large on screen, they will need to be brought very close together, at an angle to the lens approaching zero, that is to say, the 'line' between the two protagonists will be almost parallel to the axis of the lens. The foreground figure will be reduced to a sliver bordering the frame (the over-shoulder shot (Fig. 8.15) and will eventually be excluded altogether, leaving us with an image of just one of the subjects at a narrow angle to the lens (Fig. 8.16). This is the standard television image of an interviewee; it implies that the second party to the interaction is present but just out of frame (Fig. 8.17).

If both characters are looking at each other and at an angle to the camera, clearly only one of the pair will be favouring—facing towards—the lens. This will be the 'upstage'—away from the audience—character. Controlling what is 'upstage' and what 'downstage' are important compositional aids to directing the audience's attention to the action. Generally, the effect of perspective will be to point the viewer upstage rather than down, particularly when the upstage character or action is placed centrally on the screen. If, for example, one of the figures in the shot is performing an action with the hands, most photographers will try to position themselves so that the action is central and performed by the upstage hand.

The full and mid-shots

The long shot gives the most objective view of the subject, the wide shot less so. For greater intimacy, we define the images in terms of their subjects. A shot of two people is called a two-shot, a shot of one person is usually called a single. Categorized by its size on the screen, the full shot refers to a head-to-foot human image.

The full shot, common on the cinema screen, is among the least used in television documentary work. In part this is because of the difficulty of establishing an attractive composition for the image—the unsatisfactory relationship between the upright human figure and the recumbent (greater width than height) screen. In addition the detail in which a human figure's face can be seen in full shot is insufficient to read its expression clearly.

The mid-shot, however, is much more useful. It contains within the frame a human figure from waist to top of head (Fig. 8.18). It corresponds to a placing of the viewer's eye half way between objective and intimate. The mid-shot is the view of a person we get when initially introduced and shaking hands. It is the chosen view of the weather forecaster. It equates to the distance taken up by the audience when a formal lecturer says: gather round and look at what I am doing. The audience gathers round, but not so closely as to feel that each individual member is being individually spoken to. A television mid-shot is close enough for us to read the screen personage's expression and at the same time see the actions of the hands.

The mid-shot may be able to bring to the composition the same elements—foreground, middle ground and background—as make up the wide shot. Moreover the foreground may often be part of the action. In a demonstration, for instance, though the demonstrator is in mid-shot, the action the demonstrator performs will be seen as foreground action. This unity makes the mid-shot size particularly useful.

The mid-shot, being intermediate between the wide shot and the sizes closer in, is also available for linking the two together. In

Fig. 8.18 Mid-shot.

a scene with many participants, it is not always easy when going from a wide shot to a medium close-up to identify which character is the subject of the medium close-up. The mid-shot functions as an intermediary size; with it we can identify the subject of the following closer images.

The medium close-up

The medium close-up, often abbreviated to MCU, is the typical television framing of a human subject when speaking. It is the standard intimate view of a person on the screen (Fig. 8.19). If an average were constructed of all the frames shown on a television channel over the period of a day, it would probably approximate to a medium close-up of a single speaker.

Fig. 8.19 Medium close-up.

Film photographers differ in the tightness with which they frame a medium close-up. They also take care to keep important parts of the image away from the very edge of the screen. Since television sets vary considerably in their adjustment, screen images are composed to allow for sets which are 'underscanned', that is, those in which the screen cuts off a margin all round the picture. The image is composed within a 'safe area', often marked on the camera's viewfinder (Fig. 8.20).

In general one can say that an MCU is that shot which contains within the frame a person's image from shoulders to top of head. It corresponds to our normal view of a conversational partner. When we speak individually or privately to another person, the image of which we are conscious approximates to the television medium close-up. It is a view of some intimacy. Anything said to the camera by someone in medium close-up will be taken as addressed to the viewer—and to the viewer only. It is the standard image of the news reader, of the television presenter, of any other television personage who has a licence to address us, the audience, directly. That is to say, who may look straight into the lens rather than off to the side of it, a licence which is strictly reserved.

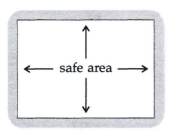

Fig. 8.20 The safe area.

In a framing as tight as the medium close-up, there are fewer planes available for composition of the image. In general there is the subject of the shot him or herself and the background. With the focus on the foreground head and shoulders, the background will often be allowed to go soft; that is, slightly out of focus. This will help in defining the depth of the shot. There is not enough space left on the screen to define the background with enough detail for it to add materially to the content of the image. The background will often add little more than a decorative element.

As a result, many film-makers try to avoid showing the background to a medium close-up in any detail. A plane coloured by a single tone is often chosen, sometimes with a decorative splash or streak of light. In an exterior, the background is often chosen to be far away enough from the subject to fall totally out of focus.

Modern techniques may divorce the background from reality altogether. The Blue Screen technique allows any part of the image detected as blue in colour (or green or red, but blue is commonly used because it is not normally found in human skin tone) to be replaced by a picture from another source. Thus any kind of background can be inserted behind a speaker's head, even moving images. Though the latter can add greatly to the interest and attraction of the frame, movement behind the head will always be a distraction from the foreground—which is usually the medium close-up subject's speech. Whether this is an advantage or a disadvantage depends on the documentarist's attitude to the material. Many of today's film-makers use such a composite image to add their own comments to what is being said. It must be recognized, however, that this will thrust into the audience's consciousness an immediate awareness that there is a film-maker at work, rather than accepting the flow of frames and images with the suspension of disbelief that is a more traditional film-maker's aim.

Close-ups

Close-ups fill the screen with the image of the subject. A big close-up concentrates on only a part of it. As with the medium close-up, photographers interpret the size of the shot in different ways. One photographer's close-up might be another's big close-up.
The differences between close-up, big close-up or even very big close-up (Fig. 8.21)—usually abbreviated to CU, BCU and VBCU—are related, not so much to screen size, but to the actual size of the subject of the frame. A close-up of a fingernail, for instance, will necessarily be taken from a closer viewing position than that of the finger to which it is attached, and both will be shot from closer than the CU of a whole hand.

The use of the close-up distinguishes the cinema film from the television variety. The CU is one of the key images of the television documentary because unlike in the cinema, where the viewer can choose which part of the screen to look at, the small size of the television screen makes it impossible for the viewer's eyes to concentrate on only the relevant part of the image. The television film-maker must do the selection on behalf of the viewer. This responsibility is an important one. It means that the director or cine-photographer must determine in advance what the response of the viewer to the image is likely to be. The flow of

Close-up.   Big close-up.   Very big close-up.
Fig. 8.21

frames should ideally be those that the viewers would have selected—albeit unconsciously—if they had really been present at the scene. Because the director makes the choice on behalf of the viewer, it gives him or her the opportunity to draw attention to details of the scene which have particular pertinence to the subject of the shot. The art of choosing close-ups is the art of selecting the significant detail which gives meaning to the scene.

The placement of the viewer's eye in close-up or big close-up position has implications for the way the viewer appreciates the image, particularly when the subject of the frame is a human face. Where, with an MCU, the viewer's eye is placed at a conversational distance from the subject, in a CU or even more in a BCU, the viewer's eye is placed much closer—so close, in fact, as to give the viewer the feeling, consciously or unconsciously, that he or she is invading the subject's personal space. In addition, the concentration on a single close image is symbolically suggestive that the normal scanning of the scene performed by an observer's eyes has been halted. The close-up of a face is the equivalent of staring hard at somebody. The viewer may become aware of feeling this whether or not the director wishes this to be the impression given.

The end result of these effects on the viewer of the close-up of a face may be subtly to alter the relationship between the viewer on the subject of the frame. The wide shot makes the viewer an observer of a scene which promises to, but does not yet, involve him or her personally. The mid-shot puts the viewer in the auditorium at a lecture or presentation. Because it is so close to the view of a person with whom we are conversing, the MCU can convince us that we are participating in a conversation. We can be made to suspend our disbelief that the person on the screen is aware of our presence. Hence the familiar pretence of television presenters: 'See you at the same time next week,' they say, when what they really means is *you* will see *them*. But the close-up and big close-up place the viewer in far too intimate a relationship for the viewer to accept that the person on the screen could possibly be aware of his or her presence. The viewer has been given a cloak of invisibility. Thus the close-up and big close-up make the viewer an observer again, rather than a participant.

The biggest close-ups of all begin to approach the view of the subject as one would see it through a microscope. There is no question of the subject of the image being aware of the viewer's presence, any more than an amœba on a slide understands that it is being looked at by a researcher. A big close-up of a familiar object such as a face can alienate the viewer, making the subject of the frame seem strange; just as a spoken word can, by constant repetition, become drained of its meaning so that one becomes aware, as if for the first time, of its sound.

Such an unusual view of a subject, particularly a human face, gives it unusual significance. A viewer will expect to see something of particular importance in the frame—and will usually find it, even when the director or photographer did not mean it that way.

The talking head

Fig. 8.22 Talking head.

If the most typical framing in the television documentary is the medium close-up, it is in the form of the talking head that it is most often found (Fig. 8.22). 'Talking head' is, of course, a pejorative expression. Such an image is considered too static and too unilluminating. It is thought to emphasize the literary, the words, in a medium that is above all visual. But while the talking head is criticized as a motif, yet it is the principal means by which the television documentary carries spoken exposition, explanation, narrative and expressed emotion. Human communication depends on far more than just words. The expressions that pass across a speaker's face while telling a story that has personal significance adds immeasurably to the text. Will Eisner, the great comic-book artist, emphasized the expressive potential of the human face: 'The face provides meaning to the spoken word. From the reading of a face, peope make daily judgements, entrust their money, political future and their emotional relationships.'[1] No film-maker should dismiss the power of the talking head to touch the audience.

The talking head may be speaking directly to the camera or to a seen or unseen interviewer. Though the phrase refers only to the head, what it really means is no more than a single person on the screen speaking. And this can actually be shown in every size of shot, from wide to close-up. Each of these framings will have its own effect on the viewer's response to the speaker.

It should not be thought inevitable that the closer the shot, the greater the communication. People also use their hands and their bodies to make an important contribution to the meaning of what

[1] *Comics and Sequential Art* 1985

they say. The more we concentrate on the face alone, the more we depend on purely spoken rather than total language; for some speakers, the closer we approach, the less information we receive.

A talking head in medium close-up is shown at the conventional conversational distance; intimacy is retained. If the speaker is addressing the camera, the viewer feels that he or she is being personally addressed. If the speaker is talking to someone off screen, the viewer is made to feel party to a private conversation. In mid-shot, the psychological distance between the viewer and the person on screen increases in proportion to the physical distance. As the frame widens, the speaker's words are addressed more to the generality and take on more of the attributes of a public performance. In full wide shot, the speaker's face may become so small on screen that the synchronization between the sound and the speaker's lip movements may be undetectable by the viewer. In this case, the speaker's words become—effectively—a voice-over. Such width of frame is purposeless when the speaker is addressing camera. When the speaker is addressing an off-screen presence, the conflict between the depersonalization of the speaker by going wide, the characterization made possible by showing more of the speaker's environment, as well as the greater visual design possibilities of a frame not solely taken up with displaying the speaker, is a conflict that may be hard to resolve.

The composition of the medium close-up talking-head frame betrays a revealing factor. By convention, the on-screen speaker is allowed 'talking room' also sometimes called 'looking room'. That means that the positioning of the head on the screen is not central, but displaced so that there is more space in front of than behind the head. It is as if the edge of the frame represents a solid obstruction, which must be kept at a distance so as not to discomfort the speaker. Most film-makers are aware of this convention as an empirical finding: the framing of the head looks more satisfactory that way.

The actual reasons for this judgement remain obscure. It may be the need to place the subject's eyes near the centre of the frame. It may be that the face has a greater screen 'weight' than the other side of the head, thus requiring a more central position on the screen. Or it might be that the on-screen character's speech or look is thought of as having a physical reality which, though invisible, must be allowed space on the screen—leaving room for a speech-balloon, as it were. It also seems likely that keeping the edge of the frame some distance from the face shows the viewer that the speaker's conversational partner is more than that minimum distance away, thus confirming that the exchange between them is not personal but public. It is certainly the case that placing the edge of the frame too close to the speaker's face gives the viewer a strange feeling of claustrophobia—not unlike watching a cat directly facing, and staring at, a wall.

Whether a speaker on the television screen addresses the camera or looks off-camera has traditionally been a matter of convention. The television presenter is usually the only character to appear on the screen who is in some sense licensed to address the viewer directly. This permission is somewhat paradoxical as it contradicts common sense: the sure and certain knowledge that whatever is happening in the scene has no real connection with the viewer observing the events on the television set.

The presenter role has a long and august tradition. Shakespeare uses a presenter in *Henry V*: the character called Prologue, who declaims: 'Oh for a muse of fire...' and is the only member of the cast permitted to speak directly to the theatre audience for fear of threatening the believability of the play. Ultimately the convention stems from the theatre's most ancient roots—the Greek religious drama. Is it too far fetched to see the television presenter as still in some ways analogous to the religious shaman or priest, the sole permitted intermediary, the bridge-builder between the congregation and the invisible Gods?

This question of eye-line—the direction to which the on-screen speaker is looking—touches on the instinctive human response to eye-contact. People are incredibly sensitive to eye-contact. A pedestrian in the street can tell from a considerable distance away, whether an approaching person is looking at him or her. In a television discussion if a participant even momentarily looks away from the presenter and directly at the camera, the effect on the viewer can be quite shocking and disorienting. For the accepted convention has been broken. It is as if the viewer's presence, conventionally that of an unseen bystander, is suddenly acknowledged by the participant. But since the viewer knows full well that he or she is not in reality present, the experience can undermine the suspension of disbelief and make plain the artificiality of the situation. Perhaps it is only convention which permits us to accept such a falsification from a licensed presenter, where it would not be acceptable from a 'real' participant.

Though it might seem that for an on-screen speaker to address the camera directly may provide a greater intimacy, that is not usually the case. Human communication depends for its total effect on an huge richness of non-verbal communication devices constantly being played out in the course of a conversation. When a speaker addresses the camera, there is no feedback, no response, from the glass lens. The result is to make the communication very much a one-way affair. Speech to camera therefore always reveals a certain artificiality. It has the feel of a lecture, even when a highly practised presenter tries hard to make the text seem improvised and personal. Add to that the peculiarly English interdict on using hand gestures to aid expression, and the presenter is driven by default to using a strangely mannered way of emphasizing individual words instead—often quite irrespective of their significance or importance in the sentence.

On the other hand, where a speaker is addressing a real person off camera, the flavour of the exchange is much more realistic. In fact the speaker can often come to seem quite oblivious to the camera's presence. In this case, the question arises: where to put the person to whom the on-screen speaker is speaking for this will determine the direction in which the speaker looks. The human eye, as previously noted, is highly sensitive to the direction of the look and can discriminate between exquisitely small differences in angle. Though the speaker may be addressing someone sitting or standing as close to the camera as can be, the viewer will be aware immediately, that the camera itself is not being spoken to.

The interviewer, by which is meant the person to whom the on-screen speaker is talking, may be placed in a wide range of positions. Usually this will be to one side or other of the camera, though some directors favour a position in line with and underneath the lens. Clearly, above the lens is impossible for practical reasons (unless the interviewer contrives to be suspended in the air.)

In general, the closer to the lens that the interviewer places him or herself, the more intimate the impression given. As we have seen earlier, the single image of an interviewee, speaking to someone just off camera, can be seen as the end result of a process of magnifying a two-shot, bringing the line between the pair closer and closer to the axis of the camera. Such a shot implies that the viewer is right next to the interviewer. Thus with the interviewer placed right next to the lens, the viewer is given the feeling that, though not being addressed directly, he or she is being included in the conversation.

Equally, the further from the lens that the interviewer sits or stands, the more the viewer is made a mere spectator or unconnected observer. The limit is when the speaker is seen in profile: the viewer is made to feel almost totally unconnected with the events on screen.

Placing the interviewer under the camera does bring the speaker's eye-line onto the vertical axis of the lens. Because of the eye's sensitivity to the direction of a speaker's look, the viewer is still aware that he or she is not being directly addressed. However, the fact that the speaker is constantly looking below the lens can give the interviewee's eyes a hooded look. The viewer feels that the interviewee is constantly looking down, making him or her seem somewhat shamefaced or even evasive.

In a film where the presenter or interviewer appears on screen, the back of the interviewer's head and top of the shoulder can be brought into the image in the framing known as 'over the shoulder'. This is the limiting magnification of a two-Shot—any further in and the interviewer would be lost from sight altogether. An image like this fixes the speaker's eye-line in a geographical relationship with the interviewer. It also makes explicit to the audience that the speaker is not in fact speaking to them, but emphasizes the reality of the exchange between interviewer and interviewee. The viewer again becomes a detached spectator, albeit included to an extent by close proximity to the exchange, but what is lost in intimacy may be made up for by making explicit the reality of the speaker's conversational partner.

Chapter 9

The Shot

If the frames are the atoms of which documentaries, like all films or video productions, are ultimately composed, then the shots are the molecules, irreducible component parts which nonetheless retain some of the characteristic of the whole.

Just as a text is usually made up of many sentences, though in theory it could all be one giant sentence—Friedrich Dürrenmat once published a novel that was all one sentence—so is the documentary composed of many shots, though, in theory, one giant shot could make up the entire work.

In practice, as we have noted, the length of a shot generally reflects the length of the whole film. Average shot length in a thirty-second commercial will be shorter than in a one-hour film. The pacing of a production depends largely on the length of the shots which make it up. The speed of the flow of time is the glue that holds the film together.

The shot is the result of adding the element of time to the frame; what is captured between the moment of switching on the camera and switching it off again. Time registers its presence by evidence of change. Each frame of a shot is changed from the one before. That change is perceived as movement. It is the importance of time that makes change and movement crucial to the film.

Without change or movement there is only the frame—an unliving image. Repeating the same frame without change results in a freeze. Film time stands still. There is only one place for the still frame in a film: when there is a need to freeze the action and bring time to a stop. Change and movement, bring life to the film. The nature of that movement determines the nature of the shot. Understanding how movement works in the shot is essential for understanding how the film works.

The self-similar nature of film leads to the tendency for each section to have a structure that mirrors the whole, each sequence to mirror the section, each shot to mirror the sequence. The structure in question is the narrative—the story. The overall film has a story, each section is built around a story, each sequence has a story and each shot tells a story.

The narrative of the shot

The story which a shot tells will usually be a simple one: a woman gets up off her chair and walks to the door; a man lifts a spoonful of soup to his mouth and drinks, a child wakes up in its cot and yawns, a soldier scans the horizon for enemies. In other words, the story of a shot will usually be that of an action. Even within this starkest simplicity, the structure of the shot's story will demand what all stories must have: a beginning, a middle and an end— even in a single shot.

What constitutes the start and the end of a shot's story? In general, the commencement and the completion of the action. The shot starts before the action begins and ends when the action is over. Shooting the shot demands that the moments of pause, of stillness, before and after the action are included. During the editing process, the pauses before and after the action will be adjusted to the pacing of the sequence into which the shot is being inserted.

It may seem that a shot which is above all static—a mother gazing at her sleeping child, for instance—has no beginning or end markers. And when shooting the image, this may indeed seem to be the case. But when the shots are being joined together into sequences, it is a rare editor who will not search the shot keenly for the slightest of movements—a twitch of an eyelid, a tremble of the lip—to mark the start and the finish of the shot. Reaction shots of the interviewer during an interview are often teasingly called 'noddies'. The movements of the interviewer's head are themselves narrative events—'the interviewer nodded' would be the description in a text.

The story may not, in the edited film, be told by the single shot alone. Shots which tell identical stories—different views of the same action—may be joined together. The sequence of shots may take the start of the action from one shot, the middle from another, the end from yet a third. At shooting time, it is not possible to predict exactly which portions of which shots may be selected. Hence shooting an action from different viewpoints requires the action to be repeated in its entirety each time. Even so, there may be difficulties in matching the action as between one shot and another. One of the principal complications is the action's speed.

Speed of movement

The shot's story unrolls over the time of the shot. The rate at which it does so is an important factor in its working. A shot will be placed among others in a sequence. The speed of the movements within it will have to relate to the speed of the movements in the shots on either side.

It may seem that this poses no particular problem, as similar movements will happen at similar speeds, but what is crucial is not so much the speed of the movement itself but its *apparent* speed on the screen. That apparent speed depends on the framing of the shot. The man drinking soup will move the spoon to his mouth at a speed that is natural to the action. In a mid-shot, his hand, taking care not to spill the soup, may traverse half the height of the screen in perhaps two seconds. In a close-up of his hand, the same speed will lead his hand to cross the frame in a small fraction of that time—the apparent speed of the action will be much greater. In a sequence composed of a mid-shot, followed by a close-up, followed by another mid-shot, the action will appear to speed up greatly while on the close-up and slow down again as the sequence returns to the mid-shot.

Thus in capturing movements of the shot's subject, consideration must be given to the way in which the shot will subsequently be joined to others in a sequence, and the apparent speed of movement adjusted accordingly, so as to seem equal on the screen. In any case, a close-up of the soup-drinker's hand traversing the screen in a fraction of a second is not a very useful or revealing shot. Movement in close-up will usually only look right when it is actually performed at a rather slower speed than is natural—one example of 'cheating' the action, manipulating reality to make it seem more real.

Direction of movement

Movement on the screen in the horizontal and vertical planes can vary between movements across or up and down it (the 'x' and the 'y' axes), and movements towards and away from the subject (the 'z' axis). The difference can strongly affect the impression given to the viewer as well as the viewer's understanding of the action shown.

Consistency of direction of movement is an important factor in helping the audience to comprehend the events being portrayed on the screen. Much will be determined when connecting the shots into a sequence, but since the sequence is made up of individual shots, the direction of movement in each shot must be the concern of the film-maker at the time of shooting.

It is obvious that the portrayal of a single action should maintain consistency of screen direction. In shots showing a woman getting up off her chair and walking to the door, the establishment of the geography of the room demands that if the woman is seated to screen-left of the door, her rise and walk must move her from left to right. If the action is covered by a number of shots, her screen direction must be the same in each. As mentioned earlier, this means that the camera position must be consistently on one side of her—to be exact, on one side of a line drawn between the woman and the door. This is known in director's jargon as not 'crossing the line'.

But what if the same location appears in a number of shots not connected together in a sequence? Standard film convention, as established in the cinema, suggests that the same screen direction is portrayed each time the scene is returned to. This is, of course, not a fixed rule, but many film-makers adhere to it as a way of helping the audience's mental understanding of the location.

On an even larger scale than the returned-to scene, a director may choose to give to an action or movement which plays an important conceptual role in a film, a consistency of screen direction which is adhered to over the entire course of the production. In a scene of armed conflict, for example, one side may always be shown as moving from left to right, while their opponents are always shown as moving from right to left. This helps not only with the mental image the audience maintains of the location of the conflict, but also helps with instant identification of which party to the conflict is being shown.

Other extraneous and purely cultural assumptions may affect decisions about screen direction. A shot of a transatlantic flight in an aircraft may make use of the audience's subconscious recollection of the map of the world looked at in the usual way: north at the top and south at the foot of the page. The airliner may thus be consistently shown travelling from right of screen to left if the journey is from Europe to America, and the other way round if the flight is from America to Europe.

All modern cultures share the same understanding of the map of the world. Thus screen direction to represent travel is likely to be universally appreciated. But another consideration that relates to quite different cultural assumptions affects movement on screen. The direction in which we read—left to right in European, Indian and south-east Asian languages, right to left in Semitic languages— makes us feel rather differently about actions which move from side to side on the screen. For readers of the Latin alphabet, the left to right direction is associated with the unrolling, the revealing, of information. For readers of Arabic or Hebrew, right to left is the more natural.

Movement on the screen has yet another important function which does not relate so much to its content but more to its practical effect on the screen image. Movement across or straight up and down the screen maintains the flatness of the screen's visual world. The movement of the subject brings it neither nearer to, nor further away from the camera. Movement directly towards or away from the camera has little immediate impact because it results in not very much change on the screen—the subject just slowly grows as it approaches or shrinks as it retreats. It may be hard to detect that an object like an automobile driving towards the camera is moving at all. Movement at an angle between the two—towards or away from the lens at the same time as to the side—combines the best of both planes and adds to the illusion of depth of the shot.

In a wide shot, where the illusion of depth is a primary consideration, movement at an angle is an important way of enhancing the illusion of presence. Such actions as people walking, birds flying, motor vehicles driving, will often make their best impact when travelling at an angle towards or away from the screen, thus making explicit the depth contained within the image. In a closer shot, which has by its nature little illusion of depth, movement towards and away from the camera may also be necessary to contain the movement within the frame. Side to side movements will necessarily be limited by the need to maintain them in vision. But even here, the action of a hand, for instance, when moving forward or backward in line with the lens, will help to sink the owner of the hand back into the imaginary space behind the screen, where a simple sideways motion would only emphasize the flatness of the image plane. Note, however, that at close-up size, it may be hard for the photographer to keep the hand in focus if its forward or backward movement is too great.

Subject and camera movement

The movement in a shot can be provided by the subject of the shot itself moving within a static frame, or the frame itself (or rather, the camera lens capturing the frames) can move. Often a shot will contain elements of both movement of the subject and movement of the camera.

Any movement on the screen must have a rationale, must be the effect of a cause. Where the subject of the shot moves, the purpose, the motivation of the movement is explicit in the movement itself. In other words, the action of a person or the movement of an object on the screen is part of the shot's storyline. The woman getting up from her chair and walking to the door is understood as performing a voluntary act. So is the man drinking soup. The rationale for their movement belongs to the world behind the screen and can be accepted as such.

But since the camera represents the viewer's eye-view of the scene, the effect of moving the camera is to represent a movement of the viewer within the scene. As the viewer is in reality merely watching a television screen, a way has to be found to give the viewer the impression that he or she is moving of his or her own volition. If it is the film-maker's purpose to draw attention to the fact that the viewer is watching a film rather than reality, camera movement can be used to contribute to that Brechtian 'alienation effect'. Otherwise the film-maker must find a way of persuading the viewer that the camera is moving in direct response to the viewer's own wishes.

Motivation

To motivate a camera movement is to predict the viewer's own automatic visual response to the images on the screen. That means that the camera must do what the viewer's eye would automatically do if the viewer were really present at the scene. Human eyes, and not just those of men on the make, are all roving eyes. Anyone looking at a scene will constantly be scanning different aspects of it, a process which, as mentioned before, builds up the eye's *effective* field of view. These eye-movements are largely unconscious and automatic. But there are other eye-movements— and sometimes body movements too—which, while instinctive, are consciously performed and can be, if necessary, suppressed.

If a person to whom we are speaking suddenly, in mid-conversation, glances to the left, we automatically respond by throwing a look in that direction too. If we are watching and listening to a conversation between two people standing in a doorway and one of the pair moves back so as to be hidden— masked, in film parlance—by the door frame, we again respond almost without thinking: we shift our position to bring the hidden speaker back into view again. If, while engaged in a conversation, we hear a strange noise to our side, we turn to see what is making the noise. In a television shot of these scenes, if the camera makes the moves that viewers would automatically make for themselves were they really present, in other words if the camera movement is properly motivated, the viewers may not, probably will not, notice that the camera has moved.

Motivation for camera movement is sought by the film-maker who does not wish to bring the artifices of camera work to the audience's attention. If the motivation is well done, the audience will not notice the camera movement, but will accept it, just as they accept a well-motivated change of shot. In many cases, the motivation will indeed be for a change of shot—after all, in the real world the eye does not pan across a scene, but skips from one point of interest to another. But audiences have become used to the moving camera as a substitute for the actions of the eye and even if conscious of a well motivated camera move, at least feel their need to see another view satisfied.

One of the commonest motivated camera movements is the track-in. It satisfies the viewer's instinctive desire to see something from closer up. A person on the screen speaking in mid-shot, if using a one-to-one conversational tone, will commonly stimulate in the viewer the desire to move in closer, the same movement that the viewer would make if engaged in conversation in the real world. The track-in satisfies the viewer's desire to make that move.

Zoom and track

Camera movements are of two kinds: tripod shots—movements of the lens alone, where the camera is pivoted on a fixed point, and travelling shots—bodily movement of the camera itself. Though the aim can be to change the framing of the shot in a somewhat similar way, the effect of each kind of movement is quite different.

Movement towards or away from the subject of the shot can be done by changing the magnifying properties of the lens—zooming—or by moving the camera physically closer or further away from the subject—tracking. The direction usually referred to as 'in' is towards the subject. Out is away from the subject.

The zoom lens is, historically speaking, a relatively recent innovation, and still suffers some optical disadvantages compared with fixed focal length lenses—more layers of glass to distort, diffuse and darken the image, the difficulty of keeping mechanical moving parts in pin-point registration. Nevertheless in television filming, zoom lenses are virtually the standard.

Effectively, a zoom lens varies the magnification of the image. Zooming in means increasing the magnification, zooming out implies decreasing it. Naturally, those portions of the image which border the edge of a less enlarged view are cropped—pushed out of the frame—when zooming in. Thus zooming in takes the central portion of the image and fills the frame with it. Conversely, zooming out—decreasing the magnification—brings new information into the frame around its sides. Nothing other than the framing is changed in the image itself. The zoom mimics the actions of the brain, when it selects a portion of our visual field to concentrate on. Though our visual field is potentially large—as was earlier suggested, extending horizontally to almost 180°—we are rarely aware of it. Most of the time, our brain concentrates on only a portion, larger or smaller, of that field. Everything outside that area of concentration is ignored—we are mostly unaware of it. To manipulate the zoom lens is to mimic the viewer's changing attention. When, in the real world, the viewer would auto-matically concentrate on a smaller part of the image, zooming in will satisfy that desire.

Only very rarely are there circumstances in which a person's area of concentration enlarges rather than shrinks. The use of the lens to zoom out is consequently very much more difficult to motivate. Only in circumstances in which the viewer yearns to see what is going on just outside the edges of the frame will a zoom-out not be noticed.

By contrast to the zoom, the track-in or -out does not merely change the magnification of the whole image at the same time, but actually changes the relationship between its elements. In shooting for the cinema, to ensure smoothness of movement, the tracking camera is usually mounted on a moveable dolly with rubber wheels which run along metal tracks fixed firmly in position on the ground. Sometimes shooting for television will use tracks and a dolly, but much more rarely.

Tracking in with the camera means moving the camera bodily towards the subject of the shot. As the camera moves closer, objects in the shot will be enlarged. But because they are all at different distances from the camera, the proportional enlargement of each will be different. In a shot containing a foreground object at a distance of ten feet (3 metres) and a range of mountains in the distance, a forward movement of the camera by five feet (1.5 metres) will halve the distance of the foreground object and enlarge it roughly to twice its previous screen size. The distant mountains, however, will hardly change. If they are two miles away (3.2 kilometres) the camera move will enlarge their image by roughly one two-thousandth.

These differences in change of apparent size are exactly what our vision system is used to when moving in the real world, and which it automatically computes when estimating distance so as to build up our normal three-dimensional view. Bodily movement of the camera therefore adds to the illusion of depth in the television image as well as potentially satisfying the viewer's desire to come closer or move further away. This is different from zooming movements of the lens, which simulate changes only in the viewer's area of attention.

Pan and crab

Horizontal movement of the shot can also be accomplished either by movement of the lens only, or by bodily movement of the camera.

Side to side movement of the lens, with the camera pivoted on a tripod, gives us the pan—the panoramic shot. Physically moving the whole camera from side to side, often done on tracks like the track-in and -out, is known as crabbing. The shot can be described as a crab left or a crab right.

The difference between the pan and the crab is much like the difference between the zoom and the track. Panning changes neither the perspective of the image nor the relationship between its elements, while crabbing moves each plane of the picture by a different amount, thus seeming to shear the planes against each other and re-enforcing, as does the track, the illusion of a three-dimensional space behind the screen.

Real eyes don't zoom. But the human head can surely pan. The panning shot claims to mimic a natural movement of the eyes and head. It should therefore be easier to motivate and to make seem instinctive than the zoom. But in truth the eyes do not pan in the real world. Rather they jump from one point of concentration to the next. Our attention does not smoothly move across a scene, at a regular speed, taking in everything on the way.

The only circumstance in which our eyes do this is when they are following a moving subject. If something we are watching moves at a steady speed across our field of view, our eyes will naturally follow it in a panning movement. This phenomenon is often used as a motivation for a pan—the camera follows a vehicle, a human figure, even an animal, as it crosses a wide vista. When successful, it leads the viewer to accept the panning shot as a natural visual response to a visual situation. Cine-photographers desperate to find motivation for a shot will sometimes follow anything that moves, even a seagull flying across the sky; though viewers may later puzzle over the significance of the bird.

If panning is not easy to make seem natural, crabbing the camera is even less like any action we perform with our eyes in the real world. There are a few circumstances in which we walk sideways: when trying to talk to someone who will not, or cannot, stop for us, for example. But walking sideways does not come easily to most of us; particularly when we cannot see where we are going and may easily therefore crash into an unexpected obstruction. A sideways-moving shot always carries with it some of that unease, even when movement of the shot is needed to follow a moving subject. For supporting the illusion of depth behind the screen the crabbing shot is unrivalled. But it is hard to make the audience unaware of its use as a device. Unless disturbing the viewer is the aim, crabbing shots are mostly found when representing the view from moving vehicles.

Crane and tilt

The third dimension of possible frame movement is up and down. When pivoted on a tripod, the action is known as tilting. Tilt up and tilt down are the two directions. Bodily movement of the camera requires a crane. The shot is known as a crane shot.

Tilting the head and eyes is a natural human movement. The nature of the kind of things we pass our gaze vertically over: masts, buildings, mountains, makes it a rather smoother action than we perform when we look around us on the horizontal plane. Consequently, tilting the camera lens is not so hard to make seem a natural movement.

Tilting the camera results in ending on a framing which is not horizontal—it is high-angle or low-angle. Or the camera may begin with the angled view and end up positioned horizontally. Either way, the camera movement is a link between a normal view of the subject and a rather different view. This can give the shot a strong sense of development and narrative. But the film-maker tilting the camera has to accept that the resulting angled perspective may seem distorted. When looking up the side of a building we are often conscious of the distorted view we receive, with the building's top receding into the distance in a way which rational geometry tells us is correct, but subjective assumptions can make seem unnatural—even in the real world. We can usually be persuaded to accept the strange perspective caused by tilting the camera in a similar spirit. As with other camera movements, motivation is all.

The crane shot is perhaps the most unnatural of all developing shots. There are very few circumstances in normal life when a person can expect to rise vertically into the air—or descend vertically either. Yet the crane shot is attractive to documentarists because of that very unusualness. A usable lift or elevator at a location, from which to shoot a (free) crane shot, is a delightful gift to a film director. Such a shot gives viewers a sight of the subject that may alter their perception and understanding of a situation. But, as previously suggested, it is over-used as an easy cliché when employed as a final ending shot for films—the 'eye of God' shot— offering little more than the spurious effect of seeming to put the small details of the preceding matter into an overall global perspective.

Crash zoom and whip pan

The premise of the above descriptions are based on the illusion of presence. The suggestion has been that if performed as a result of proper motivation, the movements of the camera will satisfy the viewer's instinctive response to a scene and remain either entirely unnoticed, or will at least be accepted as an appropriate movement in the circumstances.

But not all film-making seeks to make the viewers unaware that they are watching a film. Some directors find it dishonest to attempt to lull the viewers into a feeling that they are watching something real, and prefer to underline the artificial and one-sided nature of the medium. For such film-makers, the question of motivation for the purposes of sustaining the illusion of presence is not relevant. Of course even if trying to remind the viewers that they are watching a film, a film-maker does not necessarily want the flow of images to be constantly disturbing or surprising. A documentary in which every single shot is unexpected would be almost unwatchable.

And sometimes, even a film-maker striving to create a smooth and acceptable work will try to shock the audience out of its suspension of disbelief. Camera movements made at an unusual speed are well suited to such effects.

One of the commonest is the 'crash zoom': a zoom-in performed at so fast a speed that it draws attention to itself and makes the viewer immediately aware of the artificiality of the camera's movement. A crash zoom picking out a detail from a wider scene shouts loudly at the viewer: 'Just look at this!'

A 'whip pan', a panning shot performed at such a speed that it blurs the images between the pause at the beginning and the pause at the end, is less frequently used today, though in the past it has been a commonly used technique for moving from one scene to another. It is a purely artificial device, with no real analogy to the movements of a real human eye. Audiences understand it as a cinematic conceit. It has little place in documentary making today.

Combined movements

To keep the subject in vision when craning up or down, the camera has to be tilted at the same time. Most bodily camera moves are accompanied by simultaneous pivoting movements of the lens. To maintain an effective composition of the frame while moving the camera may need constant adjustment of the lens, both horizontally and vertically. It may also need some adjustment of the zoom setting. These lens moves are not usually noticeable within the overall camera movement.

There are times when two contrasting movements can produce bizarre effects: tracking out and zooming in on a figure at the same time, for instance, magnifies the background without changing the size of the figure itself. As the foreground figure gets smaller, the camera zooms in to compensate, thus enlarging everything else in the image. This is the equivalent of the real life impression one occasionally gets of the growing size of a mountain range when one is motoring away from it, the consequence of the greater apparent change in size of foreground than of background. Even the poet Wordsworth noticed this, while rowing across a lake, when:

'… the huge Cliff
Rose up between me and the stars, and still,
With measur'd motion like a living thing, strode after me.'

The hand-held shot

Thus far we have considered only images produced when shooting from a tripod or other camera mount. The result is 'classical', formal, stable, and—at its best—persuasive and convincing. The audience's suspension of disbelief is readily achieved. But there is another way of gathering the material in a much more informal manner, by operating the camera from the shoulder, without the constraints of a fixed mount. In a hand-held shot, all of the moves described previously may be combined, both at the same time and also by flowing seamlessly from one to another. A typical hand-held shot is one long movement from beginning to end. In fact purposeful movement is necessary in the hand-held shot as, unless the camera operator has an unusually rock-steady shoulder, any attempt to shoot a static frame with a hand-held camera is likely to result in a fidgety, unstable and distracting framing.

The result of hand-held filming looks quite different and has a rather different impact from that of formal shooting. The camera can move around, can duck and weave, can push its way between members of a crowd, can look over people's shoulders. Such constant movement cannot be motivated in the strict sense of the word. It relies for its success on sweeping the viewer up in the rush of impressions. A hand-held camera shot nearly always presents a point of view: that of the person behind the camera. A successful hand-held shot will lead the audience to identify with that person. It may be appropriate for representing the point of view of a character appearing on the screen. It may also be identified with a person never seen, but whose voice carries the narration.

For this reason, the hand-held camera is often used as standard in documentaries which offer personal reportage. In news filming, where hand-held operation may be the only possible option, and where audiences associate the informality with urgency, hand-held shots are interpreted as the reporter's eye-view. But a number of well-known film-makers also make use of this kind of shooting by preference, even though they do not themselves appear on the screen. (Nonetheless they often allow their subjects to address them behind the camera, and often including their own voices in the final edited work.) The result is to make the entire film very much the film-maker's personal vision. Intimacy and emotion are emphasized in contrast to objectivity. When used with skill and artistry, hand-held camera work can totally involve the viewer with the film-maker's viewpoint.

Shot sound

In the opinion of many film-makers, the sound accompanying the shot is among its most important and powerful elements. It contributes to the content of the shot as well as to its flavour and atmosphere. Just as the vision is part of an imaginary world behind the television screen, the shot's sound must conjure up a believable sound world. The sound world's significance lies in the fact that we respond to a shot's sound rather differently from the way we respond to the screen image.

Firstly, our consciousness of sound is not precisely located in space. The picture shown by a television screen will always, by definition, be fixed in the position of the screen—a small luminous area some distance away in the room. On the other hand sound is, as previously suggested, built up inside our heads. Though sounds may give the impression of having originated somewhere in the three-dimensional world, we become, so to speak, immersed in them, bathed in them; they become part of our environment.

Secondly, sounds seem to have a more direct access to our thoughts and associations. Just as smell can conjure up unexpectedly powerful emotions and memories, so our ears seem to be plugged in to a deeper stratum of our brain than our eyes. To generate true illusion of presence at a scene, the sound is among the shot's most crucial components.

Capturing the full richness and totality of sound at the same time as the visual shot is usually impossible. Thus film sound is almost always an artefact. Although, when well done, it is a convincing representation of what a person would have heard were he or she really present at the scene, in nearly all documentaries the sound of a shot is constructed after the event.

To be sure, in most cases, the foundation for the sound track of the shot will be the sound recorded at the scene. But much will be added to it at later stages of production to make it perform its full function.

Generally speaking, the viewers will expect the perspective of the sound to match the camera position. This is a demand of the illusion of presence. If the camera, and therefore the viewer, is close to something which is making sound, a viewer will expect to hear that sound from close to. If the camera, and the viewer, is some way off, the viewer will expect to hear the sound more distantly. A long shot will normally be accompanied by a very wide sound perspective, gathering in all the sounds from the entire scene—though some directors do delight in coupling wide vision with very close sound, as in the closely-miked hiss of skis played over a long shot of a solitary skier on a mountainside. A close shot will usually suggest much more selective sound, diminishing or even excluding all noises other than those coming from the subject of the close up. For in the real world we automatically exclude irrelevant sounds from our consciousness.

Thus at the time of shooting, film-makers will concern themselves with questions about what sounds are to be included and what excluded, as well as from what perspective to record the sound. The audience will expect to hear the sounds produced by objects which appear on the screen. They will expect to hear those sounds in a proportional relationship with each other. The further away the screen object, the further away the audience will expect it to sound. In a scene which includes a person speaking in foreground as well as a car driving in the background, the audience will expect the voice to be louder than the car.

The human ear, or rather the part of the brain that deals with hearing, applies extremely elaborate filtering processes to the raw sound before it arrives in our consciousness. Psychology textbooks often mention the 'cocktail party effect'. This is the ability of the human hearing system to select from among a chaotic babble of voices, just the one single voice to which the person is listening. Background noises are suppressed, extraneous sounds are ignored. The redundancy of information available to a person really present at a scene allows that person to fill in gaps in comprehension of speech from other senses; watching a person's lips move helps us actually to hear what that person is saying. The phenomenon is similar to that which happens when watching subtitles translating a language with which we are familiar but perhaps not entirely fluent. The subtitles actually help us to *hear* the foreign speech, not just to understand it. We are not necessarily aware of that transfer from sight to sound, it happens subconsciously.

The cocktail party effect, like other brain processes performed on sounds that we hear, depends on the fact that the vibrations which constitute the sounds come at us from all directions. Their different frequencies, phases, echoes, distortions all help the brain to distinguish between their different sources. But sound recorded as part of a shot at the shooting location, is compressed into a single—double if in stereo—channel on the recording device. All the sounds are inextricably mixed together. When it comes out of the loudspeaker at the other end of the chain, the brain can no longer separate its different sources. Thus while a conversation taking place in real life in front of a very high background of ambient noise can still be heard and understood by a person present at the scene, once recorded and replayed, the same conversation may be completely inaudible, or at least, unintelligible.

In consequence, what the film-maker will try to capture at the location will be a strongly selective version of the sound, concentrating on only those elements which need to be tightly synchronized to the image.

Modern microphone technology allows for great selectivity. Where there is a high level of surrounding noise, microphones with a very narrow angle of acceptance are used. But even if a directional microphone is so positioned as to reject as much as possible of the surrounding noises, the reflections of the ambient sound will inevitably find their way into the microphone's path. If care is taken, they will usually be sufficiently attenuated so as not to interfere with the foreground sound.

In later stages of the production, the sound scene will be built up by adding to the foreground sound both other sounds recorded at the location and further atmospheric sounds culled from elsewhere.

From the viewer's perspective, the sound of a shot can originate from an on-screen object or subject, from an object or subject which is off-screen but understood to be present at the scene, or, like accompanying music, it can be related to something in the film which is not at all part of the actual on-screen world of the shot. It is not always possible to distinguish between these three categories, which may subtly merge into each other. In addition, the sound of a shot can influence the viewer to reinterpret the visuals in a way which justifies the sound.

Thus, for example, a shot taken in a patch of English woodland might have bird song added to it at a later stage. The audience will accept the bird song as what they would expect to hear at that location. But were the sound of tropical insects substituted for the British birds, the audience would be likely to interpret the visuals in a different way—as a tropical forest perhaps, so as to justify to themselves the presence of insect noises. Unless the sound of the shot is quite clearly established as not coming from the visual scene, viewers will reinterpret what they see to rationalize the sounds they hear.

Few documentary makers would need or wish to change the audience's perception of the location of a shot from a British wood to a tropical forest. But one striking use of non-synchronous film sound is a television commonplace. Natural history documentaries are commonly shot without any sound at all. The sounds that the audience hears are all added later. Where the visual world of the film is at human scale, the added sounds are naturalistic, and viewers are mostly unaware that they were not recorded at the time of filming. But when such documentaries deal with the world of the small scale and the microscopic, the film-makers have to invent what they imagine a person would hear if scaled down to the same size as the subject of the documentary. Such productions also often make use of speeded up shots—plants growing visibly, for instance—and slowed down shots—humming birds hovering or cheetahs running are often seen examples. In such cases the documentarist must make an even more imaginative leap to suggest what the appropriate sounds might be. The resulting choices may well seem bizarre—dividing bacteria do not in fact rustle. But some sound is always necessary to give an impression of reality to what is actually an entirely artificial series of images.

Chapter 10

The Sequence

If the frame in a film is the equivalent of a word in a book, and the shot the equivalent of a sentence, then the sequence is a paragraph—a subdivision of the whole film, which maintains the same structure as the whole film but in miniature. It is composed of sentences—shots—strung together in such a way as to give the whole sequence a self-standing integrity. A sequence can be viewed by itself and, though it will not carry the whole message of the entire documentary, it will be a complete thought of itself.

Like a single paragraph in a passage of text, a sequence runs from one break to the next. Like a paragraph in a text, its function is to carry the content, the meaning, of the film from the previous sequence and hand it on to the next. Its function may be straight narrative, it may be description, it may be exposition. In *Modern English Usage*, Fowler describes the paragraph as a unit of thought, not of length. The writer, he tells us, is saying: 'Have you got that? If so I'll go on to the next point.' Much the same definition can be given to the sequence in a documentary.

What ties a sequence together is a series of unities. Not quite the dramatic unities that Aristotle prescribed, but an equivalent set that function to the same ends—to bind together the series of images, sounds and the events that they represent into a single whole. The unities which a sequence obeys are those of time, of action, and of character.

A sequence has a beginning, a middle and an end. Like a scene in a play—and even in documentary work, a sequence is often called a scene—a sequence follows a single set of characters performing a single action through a continuous stretch of time. The characters may be represented by a narrator and the action may even consist of the narrator putting forward an argument or an explanation accompanied by a series of mute images, yet it will still be perceived as a sequence as long as a single subject and a single visual treatment is maintained over a continuous passage of time.

A sequence's shape is given by its storyline. The sequence's story-line will begin with the start of its action, the starting point of its argument, and will end with its conclusion. If lifted out of context, it will be complete in itself. The audience should automatically recognize the beginning and the end of a sequence;

the viewers' conventional cultural assumptions and perhaps also their innate expectations will be satisfied. Yet at the same time, the beginning of a sequence will pick up the thread of the film from what came before it—unless, of course, it is the very first in the work—and the end of a sequence will hand it on to the next—unless, of course, it is the last sequence of all.

Picking up from what went before may be a matter of using a linking character, a linking location, a linking theme, a linking argument. The story is passed on from one sequence to the next like a relay baton. The handover depends on some of the subtler skills of story-telling: raising questions, suggesting consequences, hinting at complications, even faintly presaging doom. There will usually be some kind of connection, since the documentary form does not lend itself so easily to carrying ahead parallel storylines. Where a film's attention is shared between a number of protagonists, it will usually be found that they each represent a part of the real subject of the film—the collective.

A sequence is composed of a series of shots—vision and sound—linked together subject to the dynamics of the scene. It is a carrier of the 'illusion of presence'. The shots supply the viewers with what a real witness would see and hear if really present at the scene. Most film-makers try to make the viewers forget that they are not actually there. Thus the construction of a sequence depends on empathy with the audience, on satisfying the question: what would they want to look at and listen to if they were actually here?

A sequence can move the viewers around in the scene to look at and listen to all that is going on. A real observer both follows the action as well as looks constantly this way and that and listens here and there, to build up a complete picture of the pattern of events. The film sequence mimics this constant scanning of the scene by directing the viewer's attention to whichever aspect the director finds appropriate at that particular stage of the continuing action. The sequence can also switch subjective viewpoint and present the action as perceived by any of the characters within the scene.

The choice of shots

The shots which make up a sequence may usefully be classified by function into three varieties: establishing shots, narrative shots and what can be called 'look at this' shots.

Convention suggests that a sequence should begin with an establishing shot. It is the way we usually confront a new scene in real life. We stand at the edge and look in on things—to see where we are and what is what. It is our eyes' equivalent of the cinematic wide shot. And so too will a sequence often begin with an establishing wide shot, which sets out the geography of the location in which the action begins. The very first frames may not necessarily be wide, however. If the film-maker wishes to capture the attention of the audience for the new sequence, he or she may choose to start with some kind of striking and arresting close-up image. However, if the audience is to be kept *au fait* with what is going on, the close-up must eventually give way, or perhaps develop by tracking or even zooming—for this is one of the few cases where the viewer's wish to see more of the scene will justify a zoom out—into a wider shot.

Film is not restricted to a single location per sequence. So every time a new location is introduced, there will be a need to establish the new geography early on with a wide shot. Unless, of course, the film-maker deliberately wishes to hold back from the audience the knowledge of where they are. Then a wide shot towards the end will come as a surprising revelation. To offer no wide shot at all will keep the audience unaware of where the sequence is located and the relationships between all the things shown in its course. Viewers are likely to feel ill at ease, anxious even, as they wonder where the camera has taken them.

The wide shot which places the viewer on the edge of the scene is not sufficiently intimate or involving to carry the narrative of the sequence strongly. Nor, on the television screen, can the wide shot carry enough detail to satisfy the viewer's demand to see exactly what is going on. Narrative shots on television are from closer in, mid-shots and medium close-ups mostly, bringing the viewer right into the centre of the action and involving him or her in it directly. The narrative shots carry the sequence's story line, answering the question 'what next?' with 'this'.

On the other hand, if following the action only in closer shots, the viewer will remain unaware of what is going on elsewhere in the scene. To complete the picture, the third element of the sequence that the director will bring in are what can be called 'look at this' shots.

A real observer of a scene will be constantly looking around him- or herself, darting glances in every direction as the action unfolds. A film sequence provides the viewer with a similar experience by interspersing the narrative shots with others, mostly close-up shots of the significant details of the scene. What the film-maker is saying to the viewer is: 'look at this, and now look at this, and now look at this.' Since the film-maker is making the choice in advance on behalf of the viewer, it becomes the film-maker's responsibility to ensure that these close-ups are relevant and really add something to the viewer's understanding of the action.

The audience will in any case automatically interpret anything shown in close-up as being a significant detail. Audiences are fully accustomed to the use of tell-tale close-ups in cinema films. Anything included in close-up in a sequence must therefore be truly significant in one way or another, or the audience will be misled. Selecting and shooting the close-ups of what he or she sees as the significant details of a scene provides one of the documentarist's most powerful tools for expressing a personal vision and interpretation, and in consequence shaping the audience's response. As already suggested, many film-makers would say that the soul of a documentary scene is in its details.

Continuity

When joining many shots together to make up a sequence, the director must be strongly aware of the unity of time. A single sequence follows a single passage of time. Therefore each shot must continue the previous shot's place in time in an unbroken flow. Within the sequence, continuity of time, character and action must be maintained throughout.

It is clear that if the principal character in a documentary sequence is a woman first seen wearing a flowered skirt, she cannot in the next shot be dressed in a trouser suit. Equally clearly a man shown hailing a taxi at the end of one shot with his arm raised in the air, cannot be seen in the very next shot with his hands in his pockets. Because time throughout a sequence is perceived—and understood—by the audience to be continuous, continuity of action, of character, of costume, and of all other elements of the scene must be kept going for as long as the sequence lasts.

But as we have seen earlier, the time which the audience experiences as continuous is the *film time* of the sequence, not of the reality on which the sequence is based. A real event taking an hour to unfold, may be compressed into only five minutes of screen time. Though each individual shot in the sequence covers a real stretch of time, which cannot be speeded up or slowed down, film time may make continuous what are discontinuous periods of real life. Equally a number of consecutive shots may in reality represent a single event, either photographed with more than one camera at the same time, or with the action repeated as many times as necessary.

The compression of an event from an hour down to five minutes results from selection: choosing to shoot for the sequence only the highlights, only the most significant moments—the moments which carry the sequence's narrative, the sequence's story, in the most economical as well as the most persuasive way. Selecting which moments to shoot for the sequence is another of the documentary director's important creative acts.

The audience perceives the sequence's time as continuous. The sequence is actually made up of shots which may not be, and probably are not, continuous in reality. Thus it is often impossible to join together one shot of a character or action directly to the next. This effectively means hiding from the viewer the fact that the shots were taken at different times. It is in constructing the sequence out of its separate shots that this filmic sleight of hand is performed. By taking discontinuous shots of the action and interposing between them the close-ups of significant details—which are needed for their own purposes: to add meaning and comment to the scene—the film-maker can avoid confronting the viewer with the evidence of lapsed time.

Cut-aways and cut-ins

For instance, should the sequence be concentrating on an action performed by a principal character's hands, a girl rolling a cigarette perhaps, interspersing the action of the character's hands with shots of her face screwed up into a grimace of concentration allows the action to be represented by only its beginning and its end, without the tedium of having to follow the entire process. Such condensation of time is almost universal in documentary making, since actions which are short enough and interesting enough to be followed through in their entirety are rare. The interpolated shots may record reactions to the event, either by the participants themselves or others—concentrating on faces avoids revealing the time jumps in the event itself. Or they may introduce other relevant and significant details. In another example, the sequence may be telling the story of a boy's treatment at the dentist's. By interpolating shots of the dental nurse preparing the instruments and mixing up filling materials, the long, painful process of drilling the boy's tooth can be represented by only a few shots of its selected 'highlights'.

Such shots are known as cut-aways, because they cut away from the principal action. It is important to remember that even though cut-aways are there to serve a structural purpose in the sequence, the audience will assume that they are being shown these details because of their inherent significance. Thus cut-aways can never be simply shots of convenience but must always be chosen with great care.

A common situation in which cut-aways are needed is the

interview. If the film-maker does not wish to reveal evidence of editing by using jump-cuts or fast dissolves to join different sections of the interview together, cut-aways will be needed to disguise the discontinuities. Where the interviewee is performing an action at the same time as speaking, the cut-aways may cover details of the action. Where the film acknowledges the presence of an interviewer or presenter, the cut-aways may be shots of the interviewer's reactions—the so-called 'noddies'. In situations where neither of the above is possible, the film-maker may have difficulty in finding a suitable subject for a cut-away shot. One sometimes sees interviews, particularly in news or current-affairs programmes, where the director has in desperation chosen to use shots of the interviewee's hands, other anatomical parts, or even items of clothing as cut-aways. An episode of the political documentary strand *Panorama*[1] comes to mind in which the viewers were treated to a series of shots of the (female) interviewee's trouser flies—which were not even undone. A directorial lapse must have left these unintentionally framed shots as the only available cutaway material. Unless such images are in themselves truly revealing, they serve rather to mystify the viewers than to mask the editing. It is usually better to recast the sequence than to struggle on with such bizarre material.

Though sometimes confused with each other, cut-aways are different from the shots called cut-ins. Cut-aways cut away from the action. Cut-ins cut into the details. Naturally whether a particular shot qualifies as a cut-away or a cut-in may depend on what the principal action is perceived to be. A Mid Shot of the girl rolling the cigarette—which will include both her face and her hands—can be followed by a cut-in, a close-up of only her hands performing the procedure. If the real subject of the sequence is what the girl is saying while rolling up, the close-up functions as a cut-away. If we are concentrating on the rolling-up process itself, it qualifies as a cut-in.

While cut-aways allow time to be telescoped without difficulty, cut-ins may need greater care if they are effectively to collapse the action. In the case of the roll-up girl, the need for continuity demands that her hands be in the same position in both mid-shot and close-up. However her hands will be almost certain to adopt a similar position many times in the course of carrying out their task. By joining the mid-shot to a point much later in the cut-in, though one where her hands again match positions, the same compression of time can be achieved as with the cut-away. Naturally there is a risk that the viewer may notice the sudden change from a cigarette barely begun to one which is almost complete. Such a transition would usually depend for its success

[1] BBC 1985

on the movement of the hands distracting the viewer from immediately noticing the change.

Cut-ins are by definition photographed in closer framing than the preceding and following shots. Cut-aways can be of any size. But with both, the issue arises: from whose point of view are they to be presented? There are two possibilities. It may be taken for granted that all images are shot from the point of view of the audience watching the action. But film convention has made an alternative possible: such shots can also be from the point of view of a participant in the scene.

In the second example, the boy at the dentist's, deciding from whose point of view to shoot the assistant affects the direction from which the camera observes her. The cut-aways may be taken from the same position as the shots of the boy himself. Or the camera may be put in the dental chair, thus representing the point of view of the boy himself. In the latter case, the audience will be given a hint on how to interpret the cut-away by the action of the boy's eyes. If, in the previous shot, we see him anxiously looking around the surgery, a cut-away to his point of view will be expected. If he is sitting in the chair with his eyes closed, it will be clear to the viewers that he is not looking at anything and that any cut-away cannot represent what he is seeing.

Similar considerations affect the choice of point of view of a cut-in. Suppose the sequence to be of someone cooking. Suppose that the main shot, the master shot, is a mid-shot, and includes the table on which the character is preparing a dish. There are now two ways of shooting cut-ins, which will be close-ups, of the food on the table. They can be shot from the same general position as the master mid-shot—anticipating the viewer's desire to focus in on the detail of the action. Alternatively cut-ins could be photographed from the cook's position and therefore from the cook's point of view. It is the preceding shot which will determine the choice. Following a mid-shot showing the presenter and the demonstration, particularly if the presenter is looking to camera, a cut-in from the audience's point of view would be expected to follow. After a close-up of the presenter's face looking down at the demonstration, a cut-in from the presenter's point of view would be more natural. The first choice confirms the viewer's perception: that of an uninvolved observer. The second offers a way of getting inside the screen character's head.

Pace

It is possible to stretch a single developing or travelling shot into an entire sequence, it is often done in the cinema. But such a filmic tour de force is unusual in television, as the small size of the screen, and the distance from which it is usually viewed, make it hard to extract enough visual richness from a single shot to maintain interest over any length of time. The main exception is the single talking head, which may often occupy an entire sequence. Here maintaining the interest depends entirely on the appeal of the speaker. There are speakers who are capable of holding an audience's attention for as long as any film-maker might need.

Mostly, a sequence will be made up of a number of shots joined together. How long the sequence plays on the screen and how many shots it is composed of depend on a number of things: the place of the sequence in the film, the length of its other, neighbouring sequences, the overall pace of that part of the film, whether the sequence is at the beginning of the film or at the end, and probably many other factors too.

The film-maker ought to have in mind, at the time of shooting the sequence, what part it will play in the structure of the work and therefore what its mood should be: happy, sad, contemplative, exciting, tense, relaxed. The action to be filmed will have its own pace which the film-maker may also wish to, or be forced to, reflect.

Because of a sequence's unity of time, its pace will be carried from shot to shot by the pace, the speed of action, of each constituent shot. The shot's pace may come from the action of the subject of the shot, in other words the shot may be static but the characters within it may move, or else the shot may develop, track or pan or zoom with a pace of its own. As the shots are joined together, each shot's pace will seem to run seamlessly into that of the next. The film-maker will be conscious of those connections while shooting the scene.

Pace is also much affected by the content of the shot and by the viewer's understanding of its subject. No matter how fast the speed of action in a close-up, the viewer is aware of its small dimensions and automatically translates it into a world scale, dividing the apparent pace down many times in the process. In any case, as previously noted, for purely screen-size reasons, close-ups cannot contain fast movement. Thus the closer the shot the slower paced it tends to be.

Stills are not cinematic shots at all. Unless camera moves are imposed on a still subject, the use of a still will bring the sequence to a sudden halt, like a train unexpectedly hitting the buffers. When a still frame appears in a film it brings time to a stop and the flow of the sequence is paused. It is very hard for a sequence to pick up movement again from a still frame. Thus the use of stills is generally restricted to the ends of sequences.

Of course the pace may change over the length of the sequence.

Equally, one slow-paced shot will not inevitably be followed by another. The change of pace and the alternation of shots as well as the exact timing of their beginnings and ends will be dictated by the demands of the visual rhythm.

Rhythm

Rhythmic interest is found in an ordered deviation from a regular pulse. This applies to placing shots in a sequence just as much as to playing the guitar. Rigid adherence to the regular beat quickly becomes boring. Totally random deviations from the beat are incomprehensible. Rhythmic satisfaction comes from giving enough order to the deviations sometimes to satisfy and at other times to surprise the audience. But while a rock 'n' roller can hear the drum giving the regular pulse throughout the music, film and video have no such luxury. The sense of the regular pulse must be implied by the rhythmic flow of the shots themselves.

Sequences are often cut to music. Here the pace of the music will usually match the pace of the movements in the sequence. The cuts or other transitions in the sequence will be placed according to both the content of the shots but also to the beat of the music. Sound plays as important a part in establishing visual pace and rhythm as do the shots. Sound can motivate a cut or explain it. Music can demand a cut or deny it. But a sequence cut throughout on the same predictable beat of music without reflecting the content of the shots quickly becomes boring. When assembling the sequence, the editor will carefully take account of both sound and vision.

Sequence sound

Sound and vision are not equivalent senses. Sound vanishes utterly if the film is stopped, while the vision remains as a frozen frame. Sound is sensed serially, whereas all the elements of the visual signal are sensed in parallel, grasped at the same time. A given length of sound is far less information-dense than the same length of a series of images. A second's worth of sound, for instance, can convey relatively little, compared with a second's exposure to a picture. Much more visual information will be retained. Yet sound's ability to conjure up a whole world of associations and emotions, something that vision by itself cannot do, makes sound an essential partner in assembling sequences in television documentary work. Many viewers, not paying great notice to the TV in the corner of the living room, will have their attention immediately attracted by a change in the quality of sound. If you want to make sure that your entire audience is watching, a sudden and unexpected silence in the sound track will usually do the trick.

Just as visual continuity must be maintained throughout a sequence so must continuity of sound. In fact sound continuity is in some ways even more important than continuity of vision. When shots are joined together into a sequence, great efforts are made to smooth the transitions of sound.

Sounds in a sequence are of two kinds: those relating to the individual shots in the sequence—speech, effects arising from the action, noises off, sound atmospheres—and those belonging to the sequence as a whole—music, spoken commentary, sounds split off from their visual source. In the case of the last named, the sound may begin as the natural synchronous sound associated with an on-screen event, but then continue over other shots to which it is only related by implication. A sound may begin in one category and end in the other. Thus a talking head may go on speaking while the visuals move off, to show the viewer other things in some way related to the speaker's words. This technique, first used as a shocking surrealist device, has become an accepted convention in documentary film-making.

Of the sounds relating to the individual shots, there will be foreground sounds: speech, action effects—and background sounds: noises off, atmospheres. Where the shots in a sequence feature the same location, the audience will expect the sound background to remain unchanged throughout the series of shots. Atmosphere and noises off will be expected to keep continuity.

This often makes recording location sound quite difficult. A background noise such as a low flying aircraft may not interfere much with a screen character's intelligibility, but may make it very hard to include just a sentence or two of the character's dialogue, unless the chosen words begin before the aircraft noise is heard, and also continue beyond the plane's final fade-out. Otherwise, when joining the dialogue at the chosen point, the background sound would then suddenly cut in at full volume at the beginning of the shot and equally suddenly cut out at the end.

Hence most film-makers try to isolate the foreground sounds with highly directional microphones and record the background sounds separately. In assembling the sequence, the foreground sounds are first joined together along with the visual shots, and the background atmospheres and noises off are subsequently added across them all.

The unifying power of sound continuity enables sequences to be assembled from shots that may have been recorded at widely different times—and even in different places. It is not unknown for a film-maker to recognize the need for a cut-in close-up of some object late in the production process when all the rest of the sequence has already been shot. It may then be necessary to shoot the close-up at an entirely different location (of course excluding any background that might give away the secret). As long as background sound continuity is maintained through the new shot, the viewers will be entirely unaware of the dislocation of time and place. In one episode of *Life Power*,[1] a series of films about biotechnology, the director omitted to shoot a close-up of a bottle of tablets in one of the protagonist's hands. He continued to try to take that shot on every later filming occasion, finally succeeding in capturing the needed image some two months after and some thousands of miles away from the original scene. In the assembled sequence, the speaker's voice, of course, never faltered and the shot matched perfectly. Such are the dishonest ways of the working documentary director.

Sound also plays an important role in the way shots join together. When editing a sequence, most editors will overlap the outgoing sounds with the incoming ones, so that a very fast mix rather than an abrupt change of sound can be achieved. This provides a more aesthetically pleasing effect. But the timing of the sound change may not need exactly to match the change in vision. It takes the brain fractionally longer to analyse and comprehend sound than visual images. The eyes understand first, then the ears. Thus in switching from one shot to the next, the sound is often begun some fraction of a second before the new image appears, helping to motivate the change of picture. Editors call it 'telegraphing the cut', as if sending a message to the viewer that the cut is on its way.

Or the new sound can lead by a more noticeable time interval, priming the viewer to question the source of the sound, and to appreciate the dissolution of suspense when that source finally appears on the screen. Here the sounds of the subject of the shot is used in a way less like a purely naturalistic effect and more like a phrase of music.

Sequence music

Music has always been an important ingredient of the documentary film sequence, just as it is in fiction film technique. Nearly all films are, in a strict sense, melodrama. The music will usually be coterminous with the sequence, beginning with it and ending with it. In fact it is not unknown for some directors to lay the music down first and select the shots to accompany the music afterwards, rather than vice versa.

Music performs a similar task to the general sound atmosphere

[1] BBC 1983

of a sequence—but with even greater precision and greater impact on the viewer. Much sound is value-free, whereas music can have powerful emotional effects and is capable of helping to determine the response of the audience to what they are seeing.

The style of the accompanying music can be related to the participants in the scene itself or it can simulate the viewer's response. There are so many kinds of music with such a huge variety of associations that the choice is legion. The music can simply generate atmosphere or it can comment; it can be in ironic contrast to, or support the emotion of, the scene. The chosen music can be baroque, classical or contemporary; it can be popular or dance, folk or techno; or it could be that most familiar kind of late-romantic-style film music once characterized by the critic Germaine Greer in the unforgettable oxymoron 'Jewish Wagner'. Whichever is chosen, it will influence not only the response of the audience, but will reveal something of the attitude of the film-maker to the material.

Dramatic music, pastoral music, dance music, all change the way the viewers respond to the sequence. In *We Can Keep You Forever*, the documentary about American GIs missing but believed still to be alive in Vietnam, the music maintained such an unstoppable and high-powered drive from beginning to end, that it kept the mood only just on the sane side of hysteria—a perfect match for the paranoid fantasies of the men whose exploits the film was following.

Sometimes the music can be allowed to take over the narrative function of the film. In *The Last Exodus*, the documentary about the history of Eastern European Jewry and the emigration of Soviet Jews to Israel, the makers were unwilling to use real archive film of the holocaust to carry the necessary narrative. Instead, the film turned a painting, *The Dance of Death* by Nussbaum, himself an Auschwitz victim, and travelled across its details while the film's composer contributed a profound musical account of the *Shoah*.

Sequence music can belong to the first category of film sound: that arising from the events on the screen themselves, or it may be of the second: music not arising from the action but overlaid during the construction of the sequence.

Ethnographic documentaries often make use of the traditional music of the people who are the subject of the film. This seems a natural choice, particularly where the music is at one time the sound of an on-screen event and at another becomes the generic accompanying music for the whole sequence. However, there is a paradox hidden here. The response to the music of those whose everyday art it is—Amazonians for instance—will likely be quite different from the response of the documentary's audience. A comic song in Yanomami will not raise many smiles among English or French speakers. Location music will certainly not have the same exotic associations for its performers as for those eventually hearing it on film. Thus using music recorded at the location, while undeniably providing flavour and atmosphere, will not necessarily tell the viewer much about the feelings and responses of the participants in the scene. And the exoticism conjured up by the unfamiliar melodies may work against the sense of identification between viewer and subject for which the film-maker may be striving.

Some music is so well known and carries with it such powerful associations that it will always impose those associations onto the filmed material. No documentarist could use the Mendelssohn *Wedding March*, *Land of Hope and Glory* or *Entry of the Gladiators* in other than their stereotypical roles, without recognizing that the viewers will interpret the inclusion of such well-known tunes as a comment, or even joke, on the subject by the film-maker.

Sequence narration

Words of commentary accompanying a sequence are not in the same category as the other elements of the sound. Whereas screen dialogue, sound effects and music all form part of the sequence and help the viewer to interpret the images at an experiential level, a commentary imposes a purely intellectual layer onto the documentary. For this reason there are many documentarists who feel that if a film needs a commentary to explain it, then it has failed as a creative work. It is certainly true that some factual television productions are little more than lantern lectures or radio productions with pictures of dubious relevance added afterwards. Clearly for a documentary to work primarily as a film, the filmic elements must be the priority. Commentary or narration is added afterwards for the additional richness it can add to the viewing experience. Nonetheless, narration or commentary are an accepted part of the familiar television documentary sequence and will need as much care in construction as the other elements of the film.

Commentary accompanying a sequence can be of two kinds: that which is contributed by an anonymous narrator, a never-seen voice, and that which is a continuation of the speech of an on-screen character—who may in turn be either the subject of the film or its presenter.

The continuation of an on-screen voice over material shot at another time and another place seems paradoxical, but is the expansion of a perfectly naturalistic technique. A real participant in a scene, while engaged in listening to a speaker, will at times concentrate on the speaker, and at other times look around the scene—to survey the environment, to determine the reaction of other observers, to check on actions taking place elsewhere in the scene. Presented on film, such a situation is the direct parallel of a sequence in which shots of the speaker are intercut with other material from the same location.

When other visual material comes from elsewhere while the speech continues, the viewer is no longer in a situation ever actually experienced in real life. As suggested earlier, this is a technique first devised for its surrealist effect. What we have here is an overt fiction, and the viewer's understanding of what is happening on the screen is radically changed. But though it is a fiction it does have a real analogue. The extension of a character's voice over subsequent discontinuous shots parallels our experience of memory. We can bring back to mind, like a replay, the sound of someone's voice from the past, while at the same time being in a quite different location in the present.

The moment we switch from using a speaker's voice at the same time and at the same location as when the speech is being made, even if the speaker is not in vision, to using the voice as an accompaniment to other shots from another place, we are telling the viewer something about the time-slice which the whole sequence inhabits. The important question for the maker of a documentary sequence to establish for the audience is: which is the past and which the present? Is the speaker remembering and do the images represent the speaker's own memory. Or is the speaker the memory and the other shots the now? The distinction will determine the way in which the audience will instinctively judge the material presented to them. For we all assume, do we not, that memory is fallible, while the camera doesn't lie?

The images to which a character's voice-over is applied must be chosen with care; the viewer can easily be confused. Using a character's voice-over while showing that same character speaking on screen at another time, quite apart from the difficulty the viewer will have in distinguishing the voice-over from the actual sound of the shot, risks suggesting to the audience that the sound synchronism has failed. It can take some time for a viewer to work out that the voice in the voice-over is not to be taken as the synchronous sound of the image.

Once we have left the character's on-screen appearance behind, the voice may return as a voice-over at any time in other sequences—or at least for as long as the viewer can recognize the voice and remember who is supposed to be speaking. Every time the voice-over returns, the same original time perspective will be suggested. The film-maker will take care to ensure that the memory and the 'now' remain consistent; otherwise the audience may become disoriented.

All these considerations apply just as much to an on-screen presenter as to any other character in the film, perhaps even more so. For in a film which uses a presenter in vision, the presenter's voice will mostly be used for the overall commentary as well. But judging the time perspective represented by the presenter's appearances to camera may be more difficult. Many film-makers make a point of introducing the presenter at the beginning of the film in such a way as to suggest that this first appearance is to be understood as the present and the entire following documentary is a flashback in time. Indeed films of the reportage genre are sometimes set overtly in the past, the presenter saying explicitly or implicitly: 'I did this, I saw that, I witnessed the other.' Indeed the grammar of the spoken text usually makes use of the past tense, or at least the historic present.

The role played by an off-screen narrator, a commentary by a voice never identified as a character in the work, is rather different. Here the time slice of the words is that of a continuous present tense, no matter what tense the grammar of the text actually uses. The classic voice-over is understood by the viewer as an accompaniment to the journey of discovery that is the film. Thus the voice-over can express just as much surprise at the outcome of a series of events in the documentary as the audience feels. For in such a case the narrator is a surrogate for the viewer him or herself. The voice attaches itself to the images. It is the unseen presence behind the camera. Or rather, the character whose eye the camera is—the concrete embodiment of the illusion of presence that the viewer experiences. Often the narrator will be the voice of the film-maker him or herself; though that fact is not always revealed to the audience.

A consequence is that the selection of the voice for the narrator is crucial for the identification of the audience with the point of view of the film. Viewers are asked to identify themselves with the narrator. All the issues of sex, age, class and race are raised by this demand, particularly in the English language, but not uniquely—there are others, like Russian, in which culture, class, ethnicity and educational background are instantly made plain by the speaker's accent and dialect. For this reason some film-makers avoid the unidentified and unidentifiable narrator's voice, preferring to present the narrator as a character in the film, at least at the very beginning, and therefore to a large extent made actual and objective. From the moment that the narrator appears in vision, he or she no longer represents the viewer but merely him or herself, giving an account of the events which the documentary brings to the screen.

For many years *Horizon*, the long-running BBC strand of science documentaries, was narrated by the unmistakable voice of Paul Vaughan, called by one critic 'the first invisible star of television'. In an episode called *Rail Crash*[1] a man was discovered standing on an empty railway station platform. He turned towards the camera and spoke—with the voice of Paul Vaughan. It was an extraordinary moment, almost shocking. And it was recognized as such by Paul Vaughan himself, who felt it necessary to acknowledge the audience's inevitable surprise with the words 'Yes, this is Paul Vaughan.' Even screen-hardened television reviewers were moved by the moment; one newspaper expressed amazement that Paul Vaughan turned out to be 'beetle-browed and mildly trendy'.

Different varieties of documentary habitually make use of different styles of narration. Films dealing with current affairs, being second cousin to news reports, often adopt an urgent, slightly breathless style. Documentaries about children may match the subject with a gentler sound. Educational productions frequently use a voice with an authoritative timbre and style. Film-makers will take care, however, to ensure that their choice of voice and speaking style is not made by default and by cliché. All documentaries about women do not have to have a female narrator, all documentaries about the life of the poor do not have to be matched by a working class accent, all arts productions do not have to be narrated in the cut-glass tones of the academy.

A narrator who appears on screen must perforce adopt a relatively naturalistic style of presentation. Only relatively, however. Certain kinds of production have well-established conventions of presentation. News films, for instance, often make use of a kind of verbless language of headlines which viewers expect and understand. Once the narration is carried in voice-over, a certain formality is taken for granted by the viewer. The hesitations and deliberations of normal speech, even those artfully simulated by an on-screen presenter reading a prepared text, are not so appropriate when the speaker cannot be seen. By the same token, the film-maker is freed from writing in a totally naturalistic style. A commentary can be, and often is, composed in a far more mannered and stylized way than words intended to be spoken by a visible speaker. A British foreign correspondent has been known to cast his film commentaries in blank verse—though unnoticed by his bosses or the audience. In a previously mentioned episode of *Welcome to my World*, a shot tracking at great length past row upon row of grounded warplanes at an air force base, had the

[1] BBC 1974

presenter Robert Powell seamlessly switching in commentary from prose to rhyming verse. The stanzas were written to match the visual image and paced to accord with an accompanying drumbeat. Viewers remained only subconsciously aware that the conventions of the narration had changed:

'Where are the men of war today?
Not on the battlefield, where fate
Rules between armies of machines;
And silicon and armour-plate
Fight, without ever knowing fear—
Or hate.'

The effect was to supercharge the sequence with heightened emotion. The sequence—a single shot—was ended by cutting to a real conversation between Powell and an airman, which returned the film seamlessly to the world of prose.

The cut

Sequences consist of shots joined together. The joins, the junctions between shots, are the transitions. There are a number of different kinds, each affecting the surrounding material in a different way. By far the commonest in television documentary is the cut.

There is good reason for this. When introduced to a scene in reality, we do not stare fixedly in one direction, nor do we sweep our eyes across the scene in smooth panning movements. When watching an event, an action in reality, we constantly cast our gaze around—to observe reactions, to fill in the context, to be forewarned of other oncoming events. When we do this, our brain suppresses our consciousness of the movement of our eyes. At a cricket match one moment we are aware of looking at the batsman, the following moment we are glancing at the bowler, the next we are looking up at the sky to see if it is going to rain. The effect is as if we are switching abruptly from one view to the next. It is this sudden switching that the cut in a sequence of television images seeks to emulate. When well judged, the cut is no more noticeable than our switch of attention in a real scene. In fact, a skilful director and editor can ensure that a cut is not noticed at all.

Well judged means—as it did with camera movement in a shot—that the film does what a viewer's eyes would automatically wish to do. If the shots in the sequence are joined together in the way in which a real viewer would use his or her eyes in a real scene, the fact that a succession of different images follow each other on the screen will be largely unnoticed by the viewer. Whether this is the effect wished for by the film-maker depends on the film-maker's attitude to the material and desired audience reaction. However, even if the film-maker is striving to make the audience aware of the artificial nature of the work, for every cut in the film to be noticeable and shocking would be very wearying, and probably unacceptable, to the audience. A modicum of smooth and unnoticeable cutting is the norm in almost all documentary work.

Smooth cutting, like acceptable camera movement, depends on motivation. When a cut is well motivated it is less likely to be noticed by or disturb the viewer. Motivation of a cut depends, among other things, on what may be called 'pointing actions'. Thus, if a woman speaking on the screen suddenly points a finger to her left and says: 'look,' a cut to what she is looking at will almost certainly go completely unnoticed by the viewer, who will accept the change of image as if the viewer him- or herself had made the decision to look away from the speaker.

Most pointing actions are not so explicit. Any gesture, look or movement referring to an event or a sight off-screen by an on-screen character can act as a pointing action. For example, if in real life you are speaking to another person, who then glances to the left as if he or she can see something relevant to the conversation, you are likely automatically to glance to your right to see what he or she is looking at. In a film sequence, if a speaker on the screen merely glances to the left, a cut to another shot showing what the speaker is looking at will so mirror the viewer's own instinct that he or she is unlikely to be aware that the shot has changed.

Almost any movement can act as a pointing action. Just as in the real world any movement in a scene will attract our attention, so in a television wide shot, movement of any one of the objects in the shot will motivate a cut to a closer look. A wide shot of a scene in which a motor car begins to move will make a closer shot of the vehicle and its passengers automatically acceptable. A person fiddling with something in his or her hand, will justify a cut to a close-up of that object. Equally any movement in a closer shot which threatens to take the subject out of the frame will make the cut to a wider view instinctively acceptable. So, with a character sitting in a chair, the action of beginning to get up out of the chair will motivate a cut to the wider shot which will keep the character within the frame when standing up. In fact movement of any kind, even if not entirely motivating the cut, will usually sufficiently distract the viewer's attention from the fact that the shot has changed. It is as if following a movement with our eyes makes us unconscious of the switch of image.

When cutting to another shot on a movement, the question arises of how much of that movement to include in the outgoing shot and how much in the incoming. In general, cuts seem to work best if motivated by the start of the movement, but reserving the major part of the movement for the shot after the cut. Thus the total movement is split between the two. The two shots should match in the speed of their action. The viewer has great sensitivity to the flow of the movement between shots. Repeating part of the movement in both outgoing and incoming shots, even by only a few frames, makes a noticeable jump. Editors call it 'double action'. But a screen movement bridging two shots is not the same as a real movement. It is a representation.

Unexpectedly enough, shooting an action with multiple cameras and cutting live from one to another, as is done in studio video recordings—continuity cutting—can give the impression that part of the movement has been shown twice, even when logically it cannot have been. When putting together a sequence shot with multiple studio cameras, one often has to leave part of the movement out altogether to avoid this apparent double action. The pace of the sequence determines how much of the movement is represented. The faster the pace, the more of the action may be omitted. It is as if when switching attention in real life from one part of a scene to another, the time taken for our eyes to make the change is taken into account—as if we expect to miss part of the action while our eyes are readjusting.

Matching the shots

Actually, it takes a measurable time, even on film, for the viewer to take in the change from one image to another. The time it takes depends largely on the composition of the before and after frames. The main key to smooth transitions is that there should be as little movement of the eyes as possible when going from one shot to the next. Since the brain suppresses awareness of the movement of the eye from one view to another of a real scene, a cut which mimics that change of focus should also suppress awareness of movement of the eye. This means that the centre of interest in the image, the centre of the action usually, should be in the same place in the two frames, so as to minimize the movement the eye has to make. If the action in the outgoing shot takes place in the centre-left of the screen, the action in the incoming shot should also be placed in the centre-left. If the eye has to search the incoming shot to find where to look for the continuation of the action, part of the movement—as much as four or five frames—may well be missed. Where this is most important to allow for is not so much when cutting from a wide shot to a close-up, since in the close-up the action is likely to occupy most of the image, but when going in the reverse direction: from a closer shot to a much wider one. How often one finds oneself frantically scanning the screen to discover where the action is continuing.

Special considerations apply when the action of the sequence involves the characters on the screen interacting with each other. A screen conversation between two people will have one participant speaking left to right, the other, right to left. If shot in MCU, the 'speaking room' given to each character displaces their images slightly away from the centre of the screen. Thus the viewer's eye travels a short distance each time the shot is changed, not unlike a real observer watching a conversation. In wider shots, matching two-shots for instance—that is, shots in which both participants appear, the two matching shots each favouring one of the speakers—the displacement from the centre will be greater. Such a cut in any case implies a major change in the viewer's position, so should allow time for re-orientation.

The aim of putting shots together to cover a conversation or an event is as always to provide the illusion of presence. The shots in the sequence will mimic what a real spectator would do if present at the scene. From this follow a number of empirical restrictions on the way scenes are shot, which make sense if thought of in terms of the physical presence of a real witness. Where would a person place him- or herself if listening in to a conversation between two others? The closer beside the protagonists, the more involved would the witness feel. The conventional placement of the camera represents a position between, and almost in line with, both speakers. In practice, this is impossible to achieve, since the camera would block the view between the speakers. However, by placing the camera behind each speaker and zooming in (Fig 10.1),

equivalent onlooker's position

Fig 10.1 Matching medium close-ups simulate a postion in between the speakers.

an equivalent impression can be given. Cutting between the two views is the equivalent of a spectator turning his or her head from side to side, while following the exchange. (This is one of those cases in which it would be necessary to shoot the same conversation twice, once from each position, unless two cameras are used simultaneously.)

However, it is clear that wider shots that include the back of head and shoulders of either of the partners would imply a physical jump by the viewer through space from one position to the next. There has to be good reason for such a leap of viewpoint to be made. The viewer is better given the illusion of presence by going from such a wider shot to the medium close-up first, as if he or she had stepped forward into another position.

Conversations involving more than two screen characters can be arranged in similar ways, cutting between individuals and groups of people. The question to be answered in deciding on the shots is as always: where would the viewer be standing if he or she were really here, and how can one minimize—or at least rationalize—the viewer's implied movement from shot to shot. This is particularly the case when cutting from a wider to a closer view of the same subject. If the axis of the shot does not change— that is, if the change of size is achieved simply by using the zoom lens, the viewer can feel as if suddenly—and uncomfortably— jerked forward or backward, an effect often called 'tromboning'. It is almost always better to move the camera to a different position when compiling different sizes of shot of the same subject.

Overall movement must, of course, maintain screen direction across a cut. If a woman is walking left in one shot, she must still be walking left in the next. A man lifting his hand must continue to lift it, not be letting it fall. If it is necessary to change the screen direction in the course of a sequence, the switch is not made between shots, but a shot is introduced within which the change is made.

In the opening sequence of *Foundations*, from the *Living Islam* series, a religious procession is shown winding its way around the streets of Cairo. The marchers begin by going from screen left to right down smaller side streets, change over to from right to left for their entry into the old part of the city, and finally arrive at the main square going from left to right on the screen again. The first change of direction was achieved by a shot at a roundabout, following the marchers as they came forward and right, then panning with them as they turned screen left. The second turnaround was the result of the camera itself moving from one side of the marchers to the other, across the head of the procession.

The fade and the dissolve

'Fade up from black' says the traditional first line of a cinema film script. The image arises out of nowhere, preceded by nothing. It develops the incoming shot from an empty screen, a mirror of the opening lines of the book of Genesis in the Bible where 'In the Beginning' God creates heaven and earth and darkness is upon the face of the deep. The fade up from black is the archetypal transition technique for beginning a stretch of time or for opening an argument. The final fade down to black spells The End, even if the words 'The End' do not appear superimposed.

To fade out and then fade up again, pausing for a moment of black—of blank screen—in between, is by far the most divisive of separating techniques, marking not so much the end of a paragraph as the end of an entire chapter. It completely breaks the narrative chain of the film. It brings to a halt all story, all movement, all development. It says to the audience: 'That was then. What follows is now.'

The fade-out and fade-up are therefore most useful when structuring films into quite separate sections, when different and clearly distinct approaches, stories, arguments, accounts of some phenomenon are being marshalled. In *Imagina '89*, the hour-long documentary about the Monte Carlo Festival of Computer Graphics and Animation, the account of the event was divided into separate sections, concerning different aspects of the festival. The sections of the film were separated by a fade to black and fade up again. 'Chapter headings' in text were superimposed over the blank screen in between to indicate to the audience that the subject was changing.

But if one shortens the gap in the middle, bringing the fade-down ever closer to the fade-up until they overlap, a variety of mixes or dissolves is created. If the fade-out begins some time before the new shot mixes in, and if the outgoing image is not quite gone while the incoming one is still fading up, some linkage between the two is maintained. If the fade-out and the fade-up are simultaneous, what results is no longer a dividing device but another form of transition—the dissolve.

Dissolves are used in two ways in documentary work: where shots cannot practicably be joined together without a jump, or where a perceptible break in the flow of shots is actually needed. In a way, dissolves used for the first purpose—to avoid an unseemly cut—might be seen as an admission of failure. Yet they are sometimes unavoidable, and sometimes even to be sought after. To cut from a shot which is static to one which is already moving— a zoom, a pan—is unsatisfactory; apart from its inelegance, it jerks the viewer, like a standing pedestrian suddenly grabbed by a passing car. But a dissolve is, in itself, a kind of movement. So it can serve as a way to begin a passage composed of moving shots. It is also a way to connect moving shots to each other, adding the counterpoint of dissolves to the visual rhythm of the shots. It is often done to music. And it is often composed of moving shots, taken with a rostrum camera, of stills.

The dissolve is not just a useful technical device. For it does not simply join shots together, as does the cut. The effect on the viewer is quite different. The dissolve brings the element of time right into the image. It makes time visible. The cut emphasizes serial continuity, one shot after another. The dissolve's two independent images coexist on the screen during the same moments, as if in a kind of hallucination, or mental dislocation. The dissolve tells the audience something about time and place. The shots on either side of the dissolve represent either widely different times, or locations far from each other—or sometimes, confusingly, both. The director's task is to make it possible for the audience to distinguish the two.

Sometimes the answer is obvious. Dissolving from a scene in daylight to the same scene at night implies 'time passes'. Dissolving from a shot of a speaker to another, identically framed, shot of the same speaker—sometimes done to avoid a jump-cut in an interview while honestly informing the audience that material has been excised—tells the viewer that the two shots are not continuous in time. But dissolving from a scene at one clearly established location to another scene understood by the viewer to be elsewhere, may say—paradoxically—'meanwhile'; in other words, elsewhere but at the same time. The distinction between the two is independent of the characteristics of the dissolve. It is an intellectual distinction, engaging the viewer's under-standing of the meaning of the sequence. It is implied by what comes before and what after.

Dissolves are not merely junctions between shots but are effects in their own right. They have an impact, and an aesthetic value, of their own. They can be long, lasting over many seconds, or very brief indeed. The longer the dissolve, the more conscious will the audience be of the active presence of the film-maker. A documentary joined mainly by dissolves will largely forego the illusion of presence and make a much more objective impression on the viewer.

On film, the dissolve is a relatively simple device. The outgoing shot is faded out at the same time as the incoming shot is faded in. But though simple, the technicalities are somewhat demanding. For a smooth effect, the fade-out and the fade-in are not made linear. That would make the end too sudden. Instead, plotting exposure against time reveals an exponential curve: the ends of the slope become ever shallower. If not placed with considerable care, an exponential fade-out added to an exponential fade-in can result in a peak of brightness in the middle of the dissolve. The aim of a good dissolve is to maintain the same level of exposure throughout.

Video dissolves are available in much greater variety. Devices exist which can produce many different kinds of dissolves: beginning at the edges and progressing towards the centre of the frame, beginning in a selected position and moving out from there, sweeping down from the top or up from the bottom of frame, variations which bring the dissolve close to the wipe as an effect.

Whatever technique is appropriate to the medium, a smooth dissolve will need to place the centre of interest in the incoming shot in the same screen position as the focus of the viewer's attention in the outgoing shot. That is where the viewer's eye will begin to examine the new frames. The eye will be far more easily satisfied if the action or other focal point of the image is there ready and waiting for attention, in the very place where it is already looking.

More thematically elaborate dissolves are often employed, in which the new image arises out of a chosen place in the old. In the first moments of *The Last Exodus*, to suggest the dreams of the emigrants waiting all night for their flight out of the Soviet Union, the shot of an old man's face as he slept on a seat in Moscow's Sheremetyevo airport dissolved to an image of the rising sun, burning through from behind his closed eyelids, the sun itself then dissolving to a shot of the old city of Jerusalem, with the golden cupola of the Dome of the Rock replacing the sun's globe. The tone of the images changed with each dissolve: from the blue-black darkness and shadows of the Moscow airport night to the blood red of the rising sun to the bright daylight of Jerusalem the golden.

Image manipulation

The development of electronic video transitions has not only made many more kinds of dissolves possible, it has also rescued the wipe effect from the store cupboard of film history. In a wipe, a demarcation line, separating the incoming image from the outgoing image, moves across the frame. The movement can be horizontal, vertical, circular or yet more intricate.

The development of digital video has made entirely new styles of wipe transition possible. Since most documentary material shot on film is now transferred to video for editing, such techniques are available no matter what the original shooting medium. Converting the images into a series of numbers allows for elaborate manipulations picture-point by picture-point. Different shots can be contained in different portions of the screen and moved along arbitrary paths, to break up and reform at the programmer's will.

The wipe turns the screen image into an object in itself. Its origin may well have been in imitation of the turning of a page, the moment when our perception of a book shifts from immersion in the meaning of the text to the physicality of the paper. In fiction films, wipes often retain a literary flavour. In the television documentary, a greater stylistic inspiration comes from graphic design.

Because the image is treated as an object, it can become any shape. When used as a transition device, that shape is often derived from the content of one of the images by deriving from it a 'key', an area of the screen detected as containing a particular colour or level of luminance. Thus black and white archive film could be inserted into the windows of a modern colour image of a building, the transition made by zooming into the windows until the archive material fills the screen. Or the image-object's shape can be more fanciful. By 'mapping' the incoming image onto an object moving in the outgoing frame (or vice versa), the image can become almost any shape and undergo almost any degree of distortion. Some documentary makers delight in playing games with such images; though it must be said that on occasion, the games played tend to make a statement about the film-maker's pleasure in using a new toy, rather than make any real contribution to the subject of the film. Recently seen was a shot of a police car rolling itself up into the shape of a large bee, buzzing around the head of the prostitute revealed waiting underneath, finally diving down and disappearing into her cleavage. It was fun, but told us little more than that a new machine had recently been delivered to the editing room.

Part III

Producing a Television Documentary

Section A
Pre-production

Chapter 11

The Proposal

Almost every documentary begins with a proposal. Unless a film-maker is lucky enough to be able to work entirely from his or her own financial resources, some commissioning body or other will have to be persuaded to underwrite the project. The task of the proposal is to get somebody to say: 'yes I will fund this idea.' To get that to happen the film-maker must first identify potential commissioning organizations and then present the concept in as clear, as attractive and as persuasive a way as possible.

Where?

A documentary maker with an idea to propose must first to decide where to send it. An independent film-maker, or one at the start of his or her career usually has two options: to go directly to a broadcaster or distributor, or to approach an established production company. The benefit of the first course is that it cuts out the middleman—and the middleman's percentage of whatever profit there may be. Working in the second way, through an established production company, has two advantages. The first is that unless the film-maker has a company of his or her own with limited personal liability, if anything goes wrong, the film-maker is left financially responsible for the mess. The second advantage is that an established production company is likely to have good relations with a number of executive or commissioning producers among the broadcasters. One must remember that commissioning a film or video production involves the broadcaster in a financial risk. The money may be spent without the production living up to expectations. Many broadcasters try to minimize that risk by selecting producers and production companies with a known track record, with whom they have worked before and whose professionalism they trust. On the other hand, they are also always under pressure to develop new ideas and new talent.

If the film-maker decides to go it alone, he or she will need a knowledge of available television channels and funding bodies. as well as of who is responsible for commissioning their work. It is not very hard to get this information. Many film-makers will be aware of their locally accessible television or cable networks and production companies as well as other possible sources of finance. In some places handbooks published by a film-maker's group or association will contain the necessary information.

Where such a source of addresses does not exist, a documentarist's best way forward is to ask the advice of other colleagues and film-makers. Some film-makers are afraid to do so in case the person to whom they speak steals the idea. Bringing a subject to a production company's attention may possibly stimulate the company to develop the idea itself. There is no copyright in ideas—just in the way they are realized. In truth, although this does sometimes happen, it is really rather rare. Most documentary makers are honest and few creative people would wish to spend their time and energy on a second-hand theme. After all, a bare idea is usually so general that it is something nearly everyone will already have thought of it at some time or another. The risk of plagiarism is far outweighed by the advantages of sharing knowledge and information resources.

Different countries and states work in different ways. In some, like Britain, funding for the whole process from start to finish is usually provided by the broadcasting organizations. It is they who will pay not only for shooting and editing the production, but also for the development from a preliminary idea into a fully fledged working treatment. In other countries, the documentarist will have to find support from other sources, as the broadcasters will only come in to provide finance for the actual production when all the preparatory work and research has been done, and a complete 'dossier' has been compiled. In a few places, such support is provided by the state, elsewhere private financial institutions play the funding role.

Very often the amount of money from any single source will not be sufficient to cover all costs. Today, more and more film-makers are having to approach a number of different backers at the same time, putting together a package of complex financial deals. Many television documentaries are credited on the screen as 'co-productions', which once used to mean little more than co-finance arrangements, one leading partner taking editorial control of the work and the others simply coming in with a share of the money. These days co-production frequently implies an active involvement by all the named parties. The film-maker often has to perform a difficult balancing act to satisfy a number of collaborators, even in the form of collaboration known as 'presale', in which the right to show the film is purchased in advance at an advantageous price.

It can be especially hard if the co-production is an international one and the local culture of each different organization demands a different approach. British-American co-productions are one example of such a conflict. Though the culture of British television and that of the American Public Broadcasting Service are not so very dissimilar, other US channels, such as Discovery, A & E or Disney, have a very different outlook and favour very different styles. Collaboration between a producer in Britain and one in France or Germany involve a different kind of complication, even though the broadcasting culture may not be dissimilar. Co-productions involving countries which use different languages may even make it necessary to allow for the film to be shot in more than one language at the same time. If the film is in-vision presenter led, this may mean having more than one presenter standing by at each location; alternative interviews may need to be shot in more than one language, separate graphics—titles at least—may need to be prepared for each language. All this is within the realm of the possible, but it does increase costs which must be allowed for in the initial budget.

Where the film-maker is looking for partners to finance the production, it may be necessary to create different proposals for different funding bodies. Not, of course, to tell each a different story, but to make sure that the aspects of the story most relevant to each target organization are made quite clear. Some broadcasters are above all concerned with the factual content of the suggested film, often requiring detailed support and references from acknowledged experts in the production's field, others are far more concerned with the artistic treatment proposed and wish to see it described in detail.

Who?

Having identified a suitable organization, the next task is to discover to whom in particular to send it. Here it will be necessary to identify the specific department or strand of programming for which the concept would make suitable fare. The only way of really getting to know the subjects and styles favoured by the different strands of output coming from a broadcaster or production company is study: watching the output carefully, and noting the names of the executive or series producers responsible. For example, it does even the best of ideas no favours if it demands the use of a presenter when the strand under consideration invariably restricts itself to voice-over commentary.

The prospective film-maker should take account not only of customary style of a commissioning organization but also of the range of subjects covered over time—and not just in the strand in question. If a documentary about the same subject as the film-maker wishes to propose has recently been shown, even elsewhere, it is extremely unlikely that another bite at the same cherry will be commissioned. Unfortunately the quality of what has already been broadcast is not an issue here. It doesn't help to protest: 'Yes, I know that you recently showed a film about X but it wasn't very good, whereas mine will be.'

A film-maker with an idea to put forward will need to be familiar with other factors too: the kind of treatment the subjects are given in this strand of programming, the sort of budget allowed for—estimated if necessary from the perceived production values—and, last but not least, the length. It is not unknown for a naïve film-maker to send a proposal for a one-hour film to the editor of a strand of half-hour programmes.

Each commissioning producer or strand editor has his or her own likes and dislikes, favourite subjects, preferred formats. When writing the proposal it is obviously an advantage to know what they are. Mostly they are not mysterious or difficult to find out. A telephone call is often all that is needed to get a good idea of what the commissioning editor is looking for. Some broadcasters in the UK hold open days for their different sections, at which the person responsible for commissioning new programmes meets potential film-makers and makes clear the kind of production currently being favoured. These meetings are organized in the UK by PACT, the independent producers' association. Similar meetings have been held elsewhere in Europe under the auspices of the European Union's Media project. Going to open days and other such events is useful for the independent film-maker working alone, not only to find out more about what the market is looking for but also to meet other documentary makers and compare notes.

What?

The proposal will of course be written in such a way as to attract the commissioning editor who reads it. One must not forget that such individuals receive huge numbers of proposals every week. What does a commissioning editor want to know initially? In the experience of most documentary makers, the answer is three things above all:

    1 What is it about?
    2 Who is in it?
    3 What will it show on the screen?

and in some cases, important though not over-ridingly so, a fourth:
   4 How much will it cost?

In addition, some commissioning organizations may require further information in order to consider an idea for production. These details usually relate to their specific needs. Educational television broadcasters or producers, for example, are likely to want to be given a detailed account of the intended audience and the educational aims of the proposed film. Some broadcasters openly publish their proposal requirements, others depend on prospective film-makers speaking directly to the person responsible for commissioning work.

Note that the above list is hardly different from what would be in the billing—the published promotion for the programme in a newspaper or magazine tv listing. That is not surprising, given that the person commissioning the work will try to respond to the idea as an ordinary viewer, and is likely, therefore, to be attracted to precisely the same kind of production as are the general public. In addition the commissioning editor's first task will be to 'sell' the film to whoever makes up the channel's schedule. After that, the production will have to be promoted to the audience. A proposal which from the very beginning suggests to the broadcaster how it might best be pitched is likely to be received more warmly than one which depends on the commissioning producer's imagination to see its potential. (However, documentary makers should be wary of making claims that are not achievable. It is one thing to claim that, say, Sean Connery or Robert Redford will be the presenter, quite another to convince the broadcaster or production company that the big star has agreed to take part and will appear at a price that the budget can afford.)

The proposal should be a concise account of the project. At this stage a long essay is not the appropriate way to put the idea forward. Given the number of submissions arriving daily on their desks, commissioning editors are likely to read no further than the first few paragraphs unless their interest is immediately aroused. Some admit quite frankly that too long a proposal will simply not get serious consideration. Others openly request that no proposal should run to more than two pages long. Naturally such considerations depend on who the proposer is, and whether the commissioning editor knows his or her work. An Executive Producer at one large broadcasting organization admitted that she employs an assistant to send all proposals back automatically 'except for those that cannot simply be returned.' When asked what characterized a proposal that cannot simply be returned, she said 'one with ——'s name on the bottom,' referring to one of the best known and most distinguished producers in the industry.

The proposal's primary job is to generate interest and enthusiasm. The idea must be presented with sufficient clarity for anyone reading it to grasp the essentials right away. Covering up uncertainty in the approach with cloudy language will be unhelpful to the idea's prospects. Commissioning editors are quick to notice gaps in logic and fudges in concept. If the writer is not entirely clear over what the proposed documentary is really about, you can be sure that the person reading the proposal won't be either. Suggesting that the film might do this or possibly might do that is a sure way of courting rejection.

Who is in it does not just mean starry names. Of course, if the proposed documentary is to include well-known personalities with clear public appeal, this should be mentioned. But ordinary human interest is far more important to the success of a documentary than famous film-stars. If the film is built around a character, that character's personality should come over in the proposal as well as can be contrived. If the subject is a group of people, or if people are otherwise involved in the film, they should be described in such a way as to make them seem as immediately interesting to the reader as they are to the film-maker. Of course, many kinds of documentaries, wild-life films for example, are not about people at all. In such cases, the question who is in it is irrelevant. But it should be recognized that without strong characters on the screen, the proposer may often have a more difficult task persuading a commissioning producer to take the project further.

One most important point must always be borne in mind: if the proposed documentary depends on the willing participation of particular people, they must be asked for their agreement first. It happens all too often that an idea is accepted by a broadcaster and subsequently it turns out that the film-maker is unable to deliver the contributors promised by the proposal because they are unwilling to appear before the camera. Not only does this waste everybody's time but it puts a black mark against the name of the film-maker involved—a black mark which may take much time and effort to erase.

What will be shown on the screen is perhaps the most important part of the proposal. In advance of detailed research, it will not be possible to be specific about actual sequences and scenes. Nonetheless, an idea of how the subject is to be handled in terms of film values is absolutely essential to the success of a documentary idea. 'Remember, format is everything,' one executive producer advises.

The link between the idea behind the film and its realization on the screen is one of the main keys to the success or failure of both the proposal and the final documentary. Most subjects can be handled in a large number of different ways—through different participants' eyes, for example. A commissioning producer or editor will be looking both for achievability and originality in the proposed way of handling the subject.

Achievability is sometimes forgotten in the first flush of enthusiasm about a subject. Some film-makers put forward grandiose ideas which seem fine in theory but look obviously impossible—to the commissioning editor at least—in practice. Of course just because the style of handling a subject seems impossible to the commissioning editor, that doesn't necessarily make it so. It is the task of the documentarist writing the proposal to make sure that the editor understands that any difficulties in the proposed technique have been foreseen by the proposer—foreseen and solved. This applies not only to technical and logistical difficulties—'how exactly do you suggest getting permission to film in the White House lavatory for two continuous weeks?'—but also artistic ones—'how do you intend to make the viewer understand that the whole film is shot from the point of view of the pet dog?' The commissioning editor is not likely to believe that it can be done unless the proposal indicates how.

Originality is important in both the concept and its realization After all, many documentary ideas relate to a world which is already familiar to the television audience. The film-maker is saying to the viewer not just look at our world, but look at our world *my* way. The approach a documentary maker takes to the subject is his or her signature. The commissioning editor will be looking for a signature that is both attractive and original. However, novelty just for its own sake is not generally appreciated. The originality of the treatment must be appropriate to its subject if it is to appeal to the proposal's reader. It goes without saying that what seems original to one editor may not do so to another, just as what strikes one as appropriate may appear unacceptable to another. This is where the film-maker's knowledge and understanding of the likes and dislikes of the person to whom he or she is sending the proposal come into play.

The last inclusion in many proposals is some indication of the project's budget. At this early stage, it is not possible to determine exactly what all the costs of the production may be. Nonetheless, even at the start, it is important that the documentary maker shows a good grasp of the financial significance of what is in the proposal. Every strand of television programming will have a standard budget against which any idea may be judged. Though some commissioning editors are reluctant to tell prospective producers exactly what that target budget is, and will often say that it all depends on the kind of project that is being proposed, there are obviously extremes beyond which it is not possible to go. Too low a budget and the broadcaster may suspect the quality of the production, too high and the proposer may be excluding the project from serious consideration.

Whatever budget is suggested at this stage should be sufficiently close to the real thing that further discussion changes it by no more than a few per cent. It is not a good idea to start with an impossibly low cost, so as to attract a potential commissioning organization, and then at a later stage, to increase the estimate. Any commissioning editor will know very well what the costs of production of a particular project are likely to be. An unrealistic price smacks of unprofessionalism, if not downright dishonesty. In the worst case, a documentary maker can find him- or herself legally contracted and bound to deliver a film which is not achievable at the price agreed. Of course the budgetary target included in the proposal is only a first estimate. The full costing will be subject to later discussion in much greater detail and will be specified in the production contract if the project goes ahead.

What is best, at the start, is to divide the costs up and indicate how much is estimated to be spent on development, on pre-production, production and post-production. Before the idea has been fully worked out, it is quite hard to estimate these sums with any accuracy but with experience, a documentary maker will develop the ability to make a good judgement of how much will need to be spent on each part of the process. The beginner would be strongly recommended fully to imagine the final film, researched, shot and edited—how close the imagined production is to reality is not relevant at this point—and work out the costs accordingly.

SCRIMP

**A six part Documentary Series to investigate
and celebrate the ingenuity, craftiness and
tight-fisted stratagems of Britain's scrimpers.**
With
Ray Brooks & Rik Ball

Writer/Producer - Ian Davidson
Director/Producer - David Collison

Whether it's for survival or pleasure, economy or
profit, 'scrimping' offers many rewards. There's
ingenuity to be proud of, there are savings to be
boasted of, and there's moral superiority to be
savoured. In this series, which aims to amuse as
well as inform, 'scrimpers' from all over Britain
and from all walks of life reveal their inventive-
ness and thriftiness, their triumphs and disasters.

The programmes will be shot entirely on location,
in **North Devon**, **Tyneside**, the **West Midlands**, the
Brighton area and the **London suburbs**.

Programme 1 will draw on material from all five
locations but programmes 2 to 6 will each come from
a single, broad based location. The precise content
of progs. 2 to 6 will depend on research on the
ground, but it will always be subject to the ideas
set out in the Contents Overview (see following
pages). We have not ruled out the possibility of
shooting beyond the main locations when a good
story demands.

Ian Davidson
David Collison
January 1994

Front page of a successful
proposal from
3rd Eye Productions Ltd
to Channel 4 Television

Chapter 12

Costing a Production

All film-making involves a fight against the limits of money and of time—which usually amount to the same thing. At some point in the production process every film-maker— except perhaps for those lucky few who can indulge in documentary making from their own resources—will be faced with committing to paper, and perhaps to contract, a legally enforceable costing of the production. Getting this right is of course essential, not only to ensure that all costs are covered and that the film-maker gets some financial recompense for the time and effort expended, but also to arrange for there to be sufficient money left over at the end to invest in developing future projects.

Since the sums involved are often very large, sometimes exceeding one or two million dollars or even pounds for a series of films, there is a natural tendency among those not well versed in business culture to regard the fine details of costing as unimportant. The difference between £100 and £105 seems very little when viewed in the light of a £300,000 budget. But in film-making the old adage is never truer: take care of the pence and the pounds will take care of themselves. A meticulous attention to detail is the first requirement of proper budgeting, no matter how dull and boring it can be. Working out costs accurately may be rather less glamorous and a lot less fun than getting out on location with a camera, but accuracy in budgeting contributes as much, perhaps more, to the success or failure of the project as do the overtly artistic and creative processes.

A particular difficulty which comes up right at the start of drawing up the budget is that the needs of the entire production process must be predicted and defined in advance—usually before the full details of the film are known to anyone. The budget will define how much time research will take, how many days' filming will be booked, how much stock will be shot, how much the contributors will be paid, what the cost of bought-in stills or film will be, how long the editing will take, what special visual effects will be needed. Since such details simply cannot all be known in advance, the art of budgeting relies on accurate *estimation* of likely costs.

To be able to make an estimate with the necessary accuracy, a very full outline, and possibly treatment, of the entire production

must have been worked out first. As a description of the completed
film, it will imply all the elements which will be needed to bring
the project to the screen. It is true that experienced documentary
makers often work out budgets in advance of that kind of full
preparation. But they depend on knowing how much similar
projects have cost in the past. It is also true that producers and
directors working on the staff of broadcasting or production
organizations are often presented with a budget at the same time
as the title and subject of their next assignment. The consequence
of this, however, is that the film will be developed to match the
available finance, rather than to follow and perhaps to do full
justice to its subject.

Even estimating costs from a full outline depends on
experience—there are professional cost estimators who do nothing
else—and a film-maker starting out on his or her career will find
this rather difficult. Consulting other more experienced
documentarists is, as always, a great help. There are few film-
makers who would be unwilling to give advice and assistance to
younger or less experienced colleagues. But the best advice for a
film-maker preparing a budget is to be rigorously methodical.

As previously suggested, there is a great temptation to
underestimate production costs. To repeat: this is invariably a
mistake. Putting in too low a budget in order to ensure getting a
commission is a recipe for financial disaster. If the production goes
over budget, the film-maker may well be expected to suffer the
loss personally, at best cutting onto his or her own remuneration,
at worst actually having to pay money out of his or her own pocket.
The sums involved can become very large and involve a film-
maker in serious financial difficulty.

Though some broadcasters and production companies may be
prepared to vary the costs slightly in the light of unforeseen
circumstances, many will not recognize that circumstances can be
unforeseen—demanding that every eventuality has been allowed
for. Clearly there are some events which are so unexpected that
nobody could have predicted them: serious illness perhaps, or
midsummer snowstorms, but in general, the production process
should be so organized, and budgeted for, that most of the things
that all too often go wrong have been thought of.

There is a precedent for this. In four-camera or five-camera
television studio work, it was always demanded of the studio
director that script preparation must include full contingency
plans: if one, two or even three of the cameras cease to function—
not an uncommon event—the recording must still be able to
continue. A similar fall-back position should be in the back of any
film-maker's mind when working out how much a documentary

production is likely to cost. 'What happens if this goes wrong' is a question which should be applied to every category of expense.

The best way to tackle the compilation of a budget, and to make sure that nothing has been forgotten, is to work from a check list, going through each category of cost in turn and attempting to imagine the production process in as much detail as is possible at this stage. Most commissioning organizations for whom a film-maker may be producing a documentary will have their own budgeting forms, including every possible detail and often running to forty pages or more. Following such a form through from start to finish guarantees that each possible category of cost has been at least considered. If the film-maker does not have access to such a form, or if the project is still in the proposal stage and before any discussion of terms of contract has taken place, it is advisable to work from a personalized list. On the next page follows a—rather simplified—checklist of personnel, resource and other costs, which makes a suitable starting point for the calculations.

PRODUCTION STAFF
Executive Producer
Producer
Assistant Producer
Director
Researcher
Production Manager
Production Assistant
Secretary
Other Staff Fees

CONTRIBUTORS' FEES
Artists Fees
Walk-ons and Extras

PRODUCTION EXPENSES
Production Transport
Home Travel
Home Subsistence
Foreign Travel
Foreign Subsistence
Excess Baggage
Hospitality
Miscellaneous

PRODUCTION OFFICE
Office Rent
Stationery
Telephone
Postage
Legal Fees
Accountancy
Miscellaneous

PURCHASED MATERIALS
Purchased Footage
Purchased Stills
Consultants
Copyright
Repeat Fees

FACILITIES' COSTS
Rehearsal Room
Home Facility Fees
Overseas Facility Fees
Location Catering

PRODUCTION COSTING CHECKLIST

COSTUME AND MAKE-UP
Costume Designer
Costume Materials
Dresser
Make-up Designer
Make-up Materials

SCENERY
Design Materials
Scenic Designer
Scenic Materials
Scenic Workers
Scenic Transport
Scenic Storage
Atmospheric Effects

PROPS AND VISFX
Prop Buyer
Props Cost
VisFX Materials
VisFX Designer
Armourer

SHOOTING
Film/Video Photographer
Film/Video Assistant
Film/Video Equipment
Film/Video Stock
Grips
Grips Equipment
Special Facilities

SOUND
Sound Recordist
Sound Assistant
Sound Equipment
Sound Recording Stock

LIGHTING
Lighting Personnel
Lighting Equipment

EDITING
Cutting Room
Film Editor
Assistant Film Editor
Film Editing Materials
Negative Cutting
Off-line Equipment
Off-line Editor
Video Editing Suite
On-line Video Editor
Video Effects
Autoconforming
Commentary Recording
Sound Dubbing Mixer
Sound Dubbing Theatre

STOCK AND DUPLICATION
Film Processing
Film Printing
Film Opticals
Video Tape Stock
Film-to-tape Transfers
Tape-to-tape Transfers
Standards Conversion

GRAPHICS
Graphics Designer
Graphics Assistant
Graphics Materials
Rostrum Camera
Stills Photographer
Stills Assistant
Photo Studio
Photo Processing
Caption Operator
Computer Graphics

MUSIC
Composer
Musicians
Music Recording Studio

Some of the cost categories in the checklist—travel costs, for example, or bought-in still photographs—are absolute cash outgoings, independent of time and duration. But most—staff costs, filming days, editing—are costed by time: by the hour, the day or the week. So to calculate a budget from a checklist, the film-maker must first have drawn up an accurate time schedule for the entire production process. Naturally this can prove difficult at the earliest stages, before the full dimensions of the work have been recognized and filled in. At the proposal stage, it is very unlikely that the film-maker will have a complete idea of what the finished documentary will be like in detail.

Unfortunately this can lead to a purely monetary classification of films: the cheap, the medium and the expensive. A documentary maker with a particular subject may need to decide in advance which category of production cost to pitch for. Subsequently that category, rather than the needs of the subject, will tend to determine the way the documentary is made. If the documentarist suggests too high a cost, the production may not be commissioned, if too low a budget, the film-maker will be forced to operate within too tight a financial strait-jacket.

There is no way around this problem except experience: the gut feeling that such-and-such a film, about such-and-such a subject and treated in such-and-such a way, is likely to cost such-and-such an amount. But the clearer the idea in the mind of the film-maker, the clearer the schedule becomes and therefore the clearer the costs.

The schedule

The production process is usually thought of as divided into stages: development begins with the idea and ends with an outline or treatment, pre-production is the stage of planning and organization, production is the shooting and recording of the material, and post-production begins with the editing and ends with the delivery of the completed work. To be able to calculate the costs of each stage, its length must first be decided. Time in film making translates to money, so the first step in budgeting a production is to draw up a firm schedule.

Development

The development stage of a documentary film can take as long as a few years, some months or as little as a couple of weeks. Since development begins with the first formulation of the idea and can involve a great deal of reading around the subject, visiting locations and talking to experts, often while occupied with other work, it is sometimes hard to decide at what point serious development has actually begun. For the purpose of a schedule, and of costing, the commonly accepted starting point is when all other work is set aside and the film-maker's full attention is concentrated on the documentary in question. At that moment too, others may become involved in the work—a partner, an assistant or a researcher may be engaged.

How much of the preliminary work will be allowed for in the production's budget depends greatly on the commissioning organization and the size of the project. A producer developing a single half-hour film will obviously be allowed less time than if working on a six-part series of hour-long documentaries. For such a major piece of work, as much as six months preparation may occasionally be paid for. Usually, however, it is rather less. There have been examples of a broadcaster paying a producer for as much as a whole year's thinking and ruminating time. But this is very uncommon, and probably only happens when the producer is a member of the broadcaster's permanent staff. To specify the development period for the purpose of scheduling and budgeting, the film-maker will mostly need to negotiate the time allowed with whoever is putting up the money.

Not everyone involved in the development of the project will be working throughout the entire time. Specialist researchers may be taken on for short periods to provide the film-maker with briefings on subjects outside his or her expertise. It may be thought advisable to engage other production staff, a second or assistant producer perhaps, to undertake some of the other preliminary work so as to shorten the development period. The schedule will specify for how long these collaborators will be contracted.

Pre-production

Pre-production is where the practical work begins in earnest. It is the stage of researching, planning, selecting and visiting events, locations and contributors as well as deciding on and engaging the film crew who will shoot the material, and the editor who will work on it after that. Planning will involve further research to fill in all the gaps left in the film outline and to make concrete any parts of the treatment in which pious hopes substitute for practical proposals.

The time allowed in the budget for pre-production varies far less than that for development—usually between two to six weeks, depending on the complexity and length of the documentary, though some regular specialist television strands only give the producer a week to plan and organize the filming. The beginning of pre-production is where serious spending on overheads usually begins: an office is set up, its equipment bought or hired, and office staff—secretary, telephone receptionist—may be engaged. A production manager or co-ordinator, if one is to be taken on, will usually start work at this time, as will a producer's or production assistant—the job title varies. If there is to be a director as well as a producer, he or she will join the team at some point during the pre-production period, allowing enough time to become familiar with the subject, the treatment, and to help plan the shoot. It is not a good idea—though it happens quite often—for a director simply to be taken on at short notice just before the filming commences. Directing the shoot is a major creative contribution to the film and whoever performs this task should take a large part in the collective thinking of the team.

Towards the end of the pre-production period the producer and director, if there is to be one, will 'recce'—reconnoitre—the locations, preferably together with the film photographer and, if possible, the sound recordist, to decide on any unusual requirements of the shooting: location sets, visual effects, script prompting machines, special lighting, lenses or camera equipment, in fact any facilities needed beyond the bare minimum of a standard shooting crew with their gear. Stills may be taken at this time for reference.

To sum up: when scheduling pre-production time, the documentarist will decide how long it will take to plan and organize the casting, location finding, shooting and post-production, bearing in mind that the money-clock has now been switched on.

Production

This is the stage at which the material which will make up the film is shot. It comprises the filming and sound recording days. The number will depend on the number of locations, the complexity of the shooting and the time needed for travel.

The length of time the camera is running, that is the period between switching on to start the shot and cutting at the end, is far from the main consideration in calculating how much shooting time will be needed. Unless the locations are all in one place, travelling may take up large part of the shooting day and travelling time includes unloading and setting up the equipment at the start, and clearing up and loading the vehicle at the end. Allowing as much as an hour to clear up the previous location and as much as another hour to get ready at the next, suggests that to add two hours to the travelling time between locations may not be an over-estimate. Film crews are mostly contracted to work twelve-hour days, perhaps allowing for an hour's travel to the location from home, and an hour for the return journey. Film-makers must remember that a cine-photographer will have to spend quite a lot of time loading the equipment into the shooting vehicle before setting out, and unloading it at the end of the day's work.

The crew must also be given time to eat. For the sake of good relations between the film-maker and the crew, if at all possible an hour's meal break should be included in the middle of the day, rather than expecting everyone to work continuously while grazing on sandwiches or hamburgers as they do so. The British tradition is for everyone to repair to the nearest pub at lunch time. Each documentarist will have to decide for him- or herself whether the maintenance of good team relations is worth the potential slow-down after the consumption of a pint or two of beer.

Most film-makers pride themselves on leaving a location exactly is they found it. Filming can be an untidy business: the furniture in a room may need to be completely reorganized to allow the camera space to work, windows may need to be covered by black card or coloured transparent gel, cables may have to be routed through doorways and taped down, fuse boxes may require tapping or bypassing to avoid blowing domestic circuits. All of these changes demand the property owner's good will, which must be repaid by a meticulous concern to put everything back at the end as it was before the filming. Film crews all too often arrive at a location to find that previous shooting by others had been an unpleasant experience and had left chaos behind, making the householder extremely wary of allowing the crew freedom to alter the arrangement of anything. Time and effort must then be spent in trying to assure everyone concerned that this occasion will be different. Every film-maker owes it as a professional duty to others in the future to make sure that the next crew which comes along will be made welcome.

The time taken to set up each shot and—if an interior—to light it, will depend on its nature. Some shots can be organized relatively quickly while others take what seems an age to a director who has little to do but stand around biting his or her nails. For interior shots which must be lit, allowing an hour to set up and light is not necessarily too liberal. Clearly the speed at which each individual cine-photographer works must be taken into account—some are quite fast, others are famously slow. But even simply moving the camera to another angle in the very same location and setting up and re-lighting the shot can consume quite a few minutes. Allowing too little preparation time is a common failing which the film-maker drawing up the schedule will try to avoid.

A rule of thumb often used in television documentary work is that it is usual to collect enough material for between three and six minutes of cut film per working day. Since shooting ratios—the difference between the amount of film shot and the length used in the edited film—vary between a minimum of some 5:1 through a preferred 12:1 all the way to about 30:1 for some observational films (200:1 in some exceptional cases), this may seem to be an over-definite figure. Clearly the kind of shots being taken—action, description, interview, interior, exterior—all have a bearing on how much of the day's work is likely to appear in the completed film. So does the average length of shot in the film. The faster the average cutting speed, the more shots will be needed and therefore the more shooting time will be taken.

Shooting ratios tends to be inversely proportional to the difficulties of getting the shot. A sort of Parkinson's Law of Filming seems to operate here: the amount of footage exposed grows to occupy the time available in which to shoot it. Thus material which is difficult to capture will often achieve a low shooting ratio, while that which is easier to get will make the ratio expand. A short action sequence may take a long time to prepare but not occupy very much film or tape, while great lengths of interview are often recorded in order to make sure of the few moments which will be included in the completed documentary. As a result between three and six minutes of cut film per day turns out to be a reasonable estimate.

On these figures, a thirty-minute film will on average need a minimum of five days and a maximum of ten days shooting depending on the kind of material to be gathered. But every film is in reality different. Your mileage, as they say, may vary.

What is worth struggling for is to make the production period continuous. That is to say, the filming and recording days should, wherever possible, leave no gaps between them. Unless the film-maker is also the cine-photographer and is working from his or her home, dead time in between shooting days is a costly luxury. Obviously, if filming away from base, unused days in between shooting mean either unnecessary hotel bills or extra travel costs to and from the area of the locations. It may be also be difficult to find a film photographer who is willing to split a booking into separate days without charging for the non-working time. If the gap is too long, there are psychological consequences: partly because those working on the production may lose impetus and energy, but mostly because a kind of team spirit soon develops in the course of shooting, which can add much to the quality of the work, but which can equally quickly dissipate when not invoked daily.

Some non-shooting days cannot, of course, be avoided. Long-distance travel must be allowed for in the shooting schedule. It is unreasonable to expect people to spend more than a few hours in a car, train or aircraft and then immediately set to work without having had time to rest. Continuous working for more than a week is also not likely to produce the best results. In scheduling for television production it is usual to allow one day off for every six days worked. Though a seven-day stint is just about acceptable, few film photographers or sound recordists would be prepared to shoot for a fortnight without at least one rest day included.

Post-production

Once the shot material is in the can or on the cassette, post-production begins. This stage will take the film through the composing and editing process to the final mastering, copying and delivery of the work to the body which commissioned it. There is a great deal to do and much of it must happen at the same time. The film-maker becomes an orchestrator and conductor of complex resources. Time, yet again, is money, and a documentary maker will try to make sure that nobody on the payroll is sitting around doing nothing because the next operation cannot begin until some other has been completed first.

One aspect of post-production is concerned with the gathering of extra material:

- commissioning, execution and rostrum photography of graphics and still photographs;
- creation of film opticals and video effects;
- translation of any foreign language dialogue and preparation of subtitles;
- creation and preparation of identification captions;
- collection of missed and extra shots and sounds.

The other aspect is the assembling of the work. Some of these processes are common to both film and video, even though the technology used may be different:

- picture and sound editing;
- track-laying of sound;
- sound dubbing.

From then on the process divides for the two media.

For film:
- negative cutting, answer printing, grading, show printing.

For video:
- 'on-line' editing or conforming onto a master tape.

Both film and video may finally need to have video cassette viewing copies made.

Most film-makers will try to begin the gathering of graphics, stills, and other extra materials as soon as the need becomes apparent. Editing cannot of course be completed until all required elements are available to the editor, so having everything ready from the start avoids unnecessary delay. This is one of the reasons why to prepare a full treatment of the work before starting production is an advantage. However, shooting does not always go as planned and the need for the extra images or sounds is not always recognized until some way into the editing process—sometimes even only right at the end. Such delay carries a time and therefore a money penalty.

Broadcasting organizations allow on average a minimum of two weeks to edit a thirty-minute, and four weeks to edit a fifty-minute production. Productions of quality can take considerably longer. Editing time is not strictly proportional to running length, as some overheads and some processes always take about the same amount of time, while variables such as the shooting ratio also have an impact on the duration of the post-production stage.

If the shooting ratio is large—as previously mentioned, certain kinds of documentary can be shot at a ratio of anything up to, believe it or not, 200:1—the viewing of the rushes, always the first stage of editing, can become a very extended operation. Rushes (the raw shots straight from the camera) must properly be viewed in real time, so if the shooting ratio is 12:1 for a one-hour documentary, this stage cannot be completed in less than 12 hours. The rushes for a series of six fifty-minute films shot at 20:1 cannot be viewed in less than 100 hours. As there is a limit to the length of time a person can usefully concentrate on screen images, 100 hours of rushes cannot realistically be viewed in under two to three five-day weeks .

The physical process used to cut film was once very different from that used to edit videotape—video-editing used to be a comparatively crude technique, involving much copying from one tape to another. But the development of technology has brought the two close together. Film is now regularly transferred to tape for post-production on 'non-linear' or 'virtual' computer editing systems. 'Non-linear' because unlike in previous video editing techniques, material can be removed from, or added to, anywhere in the production. 'Virtual' because the computer strings together the shots at the designated cutting points only during replay, simulating an edited film without any actual edits being made. This allows the editor to work as if on film but with the speed and convenience advantages of the electronic medium. Progress with the technology is continuing. It will soon become the norm for the editing computer to be the platform for all picture and sound operations, beginning with the raw footage and ending with the delivery of the completed film as a digital signal to be recorded directly onto the final master tape. The same is true for the re-creation and mixing of the film's sound.

But this change of technology will not necessarily greatly affect the time a film-maker needs to set down for post-production—except for those documentaries produced on such a low budget as to make high quality assembly and editing an unaffordable luxury. (Electronic editing and mastering does avoid the wait for prints to come back from the laboratory. Film editors often had to view and check them when already engaged on the next project.) A documentary maker will still allow between four and eight weeks of post-production for a fifty-minute film.

The very final stage of post-production after delivering the work should allow time for clearing up the production office. Invoices need to be paid, 'thank you' letters to be written, documents to be packaged up and stored. If the documentary is for a broadcaster, contributors need to be informed of the scheduled transmission time, or if none has yet been agreed, they need to be told how to get the information later on. This is an integral and essential part of post-production and should be budgeted for. How long this stage takes clearly depends on the documentary's complexity, but for a fifty-minute film, a week is by no means too long.

Budgeting notes

What follow here are some notes and pointers to help in drawing up the budget. One proviso should be borne in mind from the beginning. Many broadcasting organizations maintain union agreements—covenants which regulate the pay and conditions under which staff involved in a production are expected to work. Such agreements may regulate the employment of actors and musicians, of cine-photographers, sound recordists, editors and other technicians. Different organizations, in different countries, set up widely differing agreements, which may well override whatever deal the documentary maker may try to draw up with his or her chosen collaborators. It is essential to discover whether any such agreements apply to the production in question, and if so, how its provisions affect the engagement of staff and craft workers, before the budget becomes part of the legally enforceable contract between the film-maker and the client.

Production staff

Some film-makers work primarily on their own or just with friends. Even so, everyone working on a documentary deserves to be paid at a rate appropriate for the job. These rates are usually well known to anybody working in the industry. To repeat: in many countries trade union agreements or agreements with a film-makers' association lay down what the pay for any category of production staff should be. In other places the pay will depend on an ad-hoc arrangement for one production only. In some films the executive producer—the person carrying overall responsibility for overseeing the work—is supplied and paid for by the commissioning organization. In other projects, the executive producer is part of the production team and must be costed accordingly.

Given that the rate for the job is known, whoever prepares the budget will have to decide how long the production process is going to be and for how long each member of the production team will be expected to work on it. The producer will of course be working right through from beginning to end. So will a production manager, if one is included. A director may be brought in later in the pre-production stage and may leave before the clearing up process at the end. A researcher may be engaged just for the development and pre-production period, may also be required to attend the shooting locations, or may possibly be needed for even longer, until after the commentary has been written.

Other staff may occasionally be engaged for shorter periods to perform specific tasks. If filming in foreign locations, there may be a need for an interpreter or a local fixer to work on a particular shoot. Sometimes and in some places security personnel must be recruited to look after unattended equipment. In some countries taking on a government minder at the production's expense is a non-negotiable condition of filming. Whenever working in a foreign country is envisaged, the advice of other film-makers who have recently worked there should be sought.

Contributors' fees

Most people in most places expect to be paid for taking part in a film. The sums are not necessarily very large but they must be allowed for. Even where participating in a film could be regarded as part of a person's job—spokespeople for organizations or government departments for example—financial recompense may be insisted on. Where the film-maker wishes to take advantage of a person's special knowledge or experience, that person may expect to be paid rather more than the film-maker believes to be reasonable. This often happens with university professors and lecturers whose normal salary does not match their idea of their own importance. When one academic expert was asked why he was demanding $1,000 for a half-hour interview, he pointed out that the fee was in payment not for half an hour of his time, but for twenty years of his experience. Even in some cases where the film-maker's purpose is to support or to publicize a cause, those involved have been known to demand fees on the grounds that 'you are getting paid for making the film, why shouldn't we get paid for being in it?'

Presenter's fees will normally be agreed in advance with the person being asked to appear in that role. Sometimes, however, the commissioning organization will have its own rates for presenters which must be adhered to. Some broadcasters, for instance, wish to make sure that the fees paid to particular personalities are part of a general payment policy, taking account of experience and level of exposure and ensuring that the artist maintains a steady progression of rising fees over time, rather than an unpredictable switchback of greater and lesser remuneration. The only way to discover if this is the case is to consult the broadcaster before discussing money with the artist.

Actors, professional walk-ons and extras are part of the world of fiction film-making and are not normally used in documentaries. However, the older rigid distinction between documentary and fiction conventions is dissolving. Many documentaries now being made include scenes featuring actors, often in costume and sometimes even speaking prepared lines. Actors in documentary work are usually engaged by the day and do not require rehearsal time. Union agreements may be in force which set a minimum fee for any actor appearing in a production funded by the documentary maker's client.

Walk-ons and extras in documentaries are different from actors, since they are not, in practice, required to be professional performers. Many contributors to a film may be classified as walk-ons. Circumstances often arise where a film-maker wishes a member of the public to appear in a shot for artistic reasons. An example might be where a street cleaner is required to carry on his work in the background of a scene. Such people often wish to be paid and if their contribution to the image is important it may be worth spending the money.

Production expenses

This is one of the categories most often underestimated. It is very easy for such costs to get quite out of hand. Production expenses relate specifically to travel, food and accommodation both at home and abroad. Home and abroad are divided so as to make currency conversion calculations easier.

Camera crews and production teams usually supply their own transport when on their own turf, the cost of which is included in the travel expenses they submit to the production. Production transport refers to those cases in which vehicles need to be hired so that the entire team can travel together—for instance when working in busy city streets with no parking facilities.

Excess baggage, often quite a large amount, refers to the cost of air transport of the filming equipment. This may be difficult to calculate accurately in advance, as the exact weight of the equipment needed cannot be known until the precise details of the filming have been worked out. Most airlines allow a certain weight of baggage per ticket. When travelling by air, it is usually most cost effective to pool all the baggage of both the crew and the production team and set the total weight against all the flight tickets together. In this way, each person's allowance contributes to the whole. This cannot be estimated in advance either, so it is best to calculate what the excess baggage cost might be if the crew were taking a standard weight of equipment and there were no baggage allowance at all. In this way, the budget is likely to be over rather than underestimated.

Hospitality is a cost usually associated with expense-account staff of a broadcasting organization or major production company. However, while including a large amount for hospitality in the budget may be a questionable practice, film-makers will quite often find themselves in the position of being expected to buy someone a drink or take them out for a meal. There is no reason why the film-maker should be out of pocket as a result.

In some places also, palms need frequently to be greased in order to assure co-operation from officials, bureaucrats, even from policemen. An allowance should be made for 'lubrication', if working in a country in which this practice is accepted as the norm. It may not be morally admirable, but it may be essential if the documentarist is to succeed in filming at all.

Production office costs

Here are collected the overhead costs relating to the setting up and maintenance of the production office. How elaborate the infrastructure needs to be varies between both documentarist and project. Some film-makers, particularly when making one documentary at a time, are happiest working solo, operating entirely from their homes. Others with larger projects prefer to have the support of a team and rent an office to go to in the mornings.

Telephone, postage and photocopying costs as well as stationery and other consumables always need to be included. Charges for heating and lighting are often extra to the office rent and should be allowed for. Legal and accountancy fees may need to be paid to professionals responsible for advising on contracts and for auditing the accounts. These are unglamorous aspects of film making, but documentarists, particularly those with little experience, are well advised to seek professional assistance when dealing with their clients, who will nearly always be so represented. Such costs are legitimately part of the production budget.

Purchased materials

A documentary film does not necessarily consist of footage shot in its entirety by the production team and containing no other elements. It is often necessary to buy in extra material, sometimes archive film, sometimes scenes from old movies, sometimes amateur videos. Even the recordings from surveillance cameras are occasionally put to use in documentary productions. Such material can vary in cost between next to nothing: duplication costs only, and hugely expensive: moments from Hollywood studio productions.

Historical documentaries often make use of old photographs or reproductions of works of art. The rights to show such images must almost always be purchased. Even when a famous painting, for example, is centuries out of copyright, a photographic reproduction of the work, made by the museum or gallery which owns it, will probably not be.

Anything written especially for the film comes under the heading of copyright costs. If the film-maker engages a writer to produce the commentary, this is the place to include it in the budget. Bought-in briefings on specialist subjects belong here too, as do translations, if any of the scenes are in a language foreign to film-maker or the intended audience.

Facilities' costs

Shooting film or video is often an intrusive activity, particularly when taking place in a private home. A film crew's work can also carry a financial cost for the property owner, resulting from the use of electricity for lighting and of the telephone or other facilities. Occasionally damage can also be caused, in spite of every effort to be careful. It is customary to pay a—usually—small fee in compensation for the cost and disruption. Damage must, of course, be fully compensated. Commercial premises will usually levy a charge for the privilege of filming. Even filming in the open air on private land or in a public park may carry a cost. In some countries and cities permits must be purchased if there is to be any filming in public at all.

Costume and make-up, scenery, props and VisFX

Pure observational documentaries have not traditionally needed to budget for any of these facilities, which are more commonly associated with theatrical presentations. But as factual television programmes, particularly on historical subjects, now increasingly include dramatized scenes, costume and make-up are beginning to find a regular place in the documentary budget. Budgeting for drama is, however, beyond the scope of these notes, and documentarists who find they need to work with actors will be wise to consult film-makers experienced in fiction.

Dramatized scenes are not the only circumstances in which expenditure on costume and make-up turns out to be necessary. Presenters, for example, may wish to buy clothes specially for the production. In contrast to the usual gender stereotype, women presenters often supply their screen clothes from their own wardrobes; it is frequently the males who demand an expensive visit to the outfitters. Women fronting documentary productions usually look after their own make-up, while a male presenter may need the attentions of a professional to powder a shiny nose or spray-set unruly hair. The way a presenter looks on screen is the responsibility of the film-maker. If a particular image is wanted, the production may have to pay for it.

While props and visual effects (VisFX) are principally needed only in educational productions or for technical demonstrations, location scenery sometimes features in documentaries today. Films which include much interview material may prefer to have all contributors shown inhabiting an identical-looking set. Rather than bringing many interviewees to a single place—which may not be possible or financially feasible—one option is to take a single set to many locations. The word 'set' of course, covers a wide variety of possible constructions, from the simplest kind of plain backing to elaborate trompe-l'oeil scenery. While simple drapes can easily be erected on location by the production team, more complex constructions may need expert setting and striking by professional scenic crews.

A more common eventuality is the use of the blue screen technique—also known as CSO (Colour Separation Overlay) or Chromakey—which makes it possible to insert any desired background into blue areas of the picture during post-production. Many documentaries now use this technique to provide interviewees with a setting appropriate to the subject of their contribution. Some film-makers own their personal rectangle of blue felt, which they take on location with them. Great care needs to be taken to set up the blue screen without wrinkles or shadows, which would interfere with the later electronic switching of the image. If seriously large areas of blue screen are needed, the documentarist should budget for scenery professionals to do the work.

Shooting, lighting and sound

The filming schedule will say how many filming days will be included in the budget. The nature of the shooting will determine the size and the composition of the filming team.

The absolute minimum size of a video shooting crew working to professional standards with synchronous sound is two: one person to operate the camera, the other to control the recording of the sound (recorded onto the same tape as the picture), as well as to assist the camera operator when necessary. Unless the location sound is intended to be no more than a guide to the editor, a documentary will not use the sound automatically recorded by a camera-mounted microphone. On the other hand, for simple set-ups, lighting can often be undertaken by the photographer without the need for extra lighting personnel. Almost all video cameramen and -women as well as sound recordists will have and use their own equipment—camera, a simple lighting kit, sound mixer—for which they will charge a daily rental fee.

The minimum crew size needed for working with film is three. 35mm film, a very expensive medium, is now very rarely used in documentary work—and only for the most prestigious productions—but even shooting on 16mm film is a more elaborate enterprise than working on video. Given the greater cost, 16mm film is generally reserved for projects which aim for a higher level of production quality than video shooting. The operator of the camera will need an assistant, an extra pair of hands to load the camera magazines with film stock, operate the clapper-board, look after lenses and filters and undertake various other tasks which working in the medium of 16mm film rather than video demands. 16mm film sound is mixed and recorded onto a separate tape-recorder synchronized with the camera. The photographer may well own the camera itself, and the sound recordist the tape recorder and microphones. They will charge a daily rental fee. Extra equipment demanded by the shoot—special lenses, for example, or unusual filters—will need to be planned for in advance and hired from a specialist source, usually at a daily rate.

Should the shoot need special filming facilities—tracks perhaps, or other unusual camera mounts—an extra crew member, called a grips, must be budgeted for, together with the necessary gear. And some shoots may demand even more elaborate and expensive organization: a camera crane may be required, or even a helicopter or light aircraft.

It is exceptional for the project's own photographer not to do all the shooting, though when shooting on film, a lighting cameraman or -woman may delegate to the assistant the actual operation of the camera. But certain kinds of filming may need extra camera staff. When the event to be filmed is large scale, complex and unrepeatable, it can sometimes be cost-effective, or even essential, to shoot with more than one camera at a time. While an assistant film photographer may be able to work a second camera for short periods, if such filming is to be extensive an additional operator will need to be taken on. The same applies when certain camera mounts are involved—the Steadycam, a stabilized hand-held camera mount, for example— which needs particular expertise to use. Slow-motion, high-speed, photomicrographic, infrared or other out of the ordinary techniques of shooting may need an experienced specialist to be added to the team.

Daily hiring rates vary widely among photographers and sound recordists, and all special or extra requirements will affect the filming costs. As with other staff, trade union agreements may be in force which limit the film-maker's flexibility in striking a deal. A minimum rate may be specified as well as a maximum number of working hours per day; work beyond the union agreed limits may be subject to overtime payments. Documentarists will need to consult the proposed cameraman or -woman before drawing up the shooting budget.

Editing

This short word covers all the processes which take the raw footage captured by the camera through to the completed work. Editing inevitably comprises a series of highly technical processes, which the documentarist must understand to some degree in order to be able to work out this section of the budget. Calculating editing costs is further complicated by the differences between working on 16mm film or on videotape.

If editing on 16mm (or 35mm) film, the producer will hire a film editor, usually an assistant film editor too, and a cutting room. Many editors own or rent their own cutting rooms and work with one preferred assistant. They mostly offer an inclusive price per week for the complete package. If editing on video, the editor will almost always work solo, since most of the film jobs of synchronizing, logging and filing are not required.

The editing budget should include time for editing preparation. The necessary processes for 16mm film are the synchronizing, rubber numbering (printing code numbers along the edge of both picture and sound rolls, to help maintain synchronization) and logging of picture and sound rushes. For video edited by the 'off-line' technique, no synchronising is needed, but the master tapes will first have to be sent for copying onto working cassettes with time-code visible on screen ('burnt-in time-code'—BITC) or encoded as a machine-readable signal at the top of each frame ('vertical-interval time-code'—VITC). Editing by the 'non-linear' or 'virtual' computerized method, spreads the preparation time throughout the editing period, as the video-tapes must be 'digitized' (transferred as a digital signal) onto the computer's hard disk as and when the material is needed. Though the capacity of computer hard disks is continually increasing, few set-ups can today hold more than about twenty minutes of material at any one time. Thus non-linear editing may involve loading completed sequences onto permanent storage of some kind—writable video-disks are often used for this purpose—as well as digitizing rushes into the computer. Some editors engage an assistant to carry out this work overnight as, with current technology, these processes can only be done in 'real time'; in other words, a one-hour tape will take one hour to digitize. Many non-linear editors also have working copies of the master tapes made before undertaking any other operations, to preserve the originals from possible wear and damage in the playback machine.

When editing on 16mm film is complete, the edited rushes (the 'cutting-copy') are sent off with the original negatives for negative-cutting. A specialist editor, again often working overnight, cuts shots from the rolls of negative and sticks them together exactly to match the cutting-copy, frame for frame. This edited negative is then sent to the laboratory to make the print. Edited film negatives are printed through a set of coloured filters, to allow shots made at different times and in different places to match in brightness, contrast, tone and hue. This process is called 'grading'. The first 'answer' print returned by the laboratory is viewed by the film-maker and editor; any colour defects are noted and communicated to the lab. The grading of the next print is adjusted accordingly. Depending on how long the laboratory takes, perfecting the final 'show' print can stretch over many days, sometimes weeks. Some payment to the editor for this work, though it does not represent a continuous engagement, should be allowed for in the budget.

When working with video, the purpose is to create an 'edit decision list' (EDL), a list of the time-code at the start and at the end of every shot. If the off-line method is used, the list can be prepared manually—going through the edited tape and noting down the numbers on the screen (BITC). This list constitutes the instructions to the 'on-line' editor, who copy-edits the camera master-tapes onto the final master, a process known as conforming. One can buy computer software with which to record the list onto a computer floppy disk, which is then used to control the process automatically—auto-conforming. Preparation of an EDL can be achieved without human intervention by means of a device which reads the time-codes from the coded information at the top of the screen (VITC) and outputs the list onto a disk as well as onto a printed hard copy. An EDL on a disk, holding the instructions for autoconforming, is also the final product of non-linear computer editing.

All conforming must be done in 'real time' plus the time it takes to change from one source tape to another. If the conforming is to be done by a human on-line editor, each edit point must first be found, then rehearsed, perhaps adjusted and rehearsed again, then the edit made and finally reviewed. Creating the final master by this means is a time-consuming process; eight hours for a simple half-hour documentary is not too much. Some documentary makers prefer to work this way because it gives them the opportunity to make fine adjustments up to the last minute. Autoconforming reduces the time needed by at least a half and usually more than that, though having manually to change the source tapes between shots inevitably delays matters. It can sometimes help to speed the process, if material from a large number of different source tapes is copied onto a few compilation tapes first.

Methods of dealing with the production's sound also range from the physical cutting of magnetic tape to the application of the latest digital electronics. Whichever path the film-maker chooses, the production's images will be accompanied by a sound track, created by a dubbing mixer in a dubbing studio or theatre, from anything up to twenty-four or more separate sound tracks running in parallel. The tracks will carry the synchronous sounds of the shots themselves, all extra sound effects needed—some of them may well need to be specially recorded—plus any music which accompanies the pictures. Preparation of these tracks is called 'track-laying' and sufficient time must be allowed for it to be perfected, either by the main editor, or by a separately contracted sound editor. Once the production has been track-laid, a dubbing chart—instructions to the dubbing mixer relating to the bringing in, fading out and mixing of the sounds—will be drawn up. By tradition, commentary is recorded last of all and only added to the sound mix on top of the music and effects track (M and E) at the very end.

The editing and mastering of a documentary is a highly technical procedure and is yearly becoming more so. As the processes get ever more technological their requirements change; it is hard for film-makers to keep up with the latest developments. All documentary film-makers, not just those with little experience, are well advised to consult an editor before committing an editing budget estimate to paper.

Stock and duplication

This category of costs includes many which are often forgotten or can mount up quickly beyond expectation. Where the difference between a modest profit, breaking even, or making a loss on a production is small, stock, duplication, transfers and other such processes can easily swing the balance from plus to minus. Unfortunately, though there is little difficulty in estimating the total amount of stock to be used in collecting the material for a documentary—either rolls of 16mm film or video tapes—the number and kinds of transfers which will be needed are often hard to predict in advance.

The amount of shooting stock can be calculated using the projected shooting ratio: a half-hour documentary shot on 16mm film at a ratio of 10:1 will use roughly thirty ten-minute rolls of film—the standard load of a 16mm camera magazine. Developing the shot material and making the first rush print are, like almost all film-related processes, charged at a cost per foot of film. A foot of 16mm film represents 1.6 seconds of time. (Unfortunately a 35mm foot is different, running at 0.64 seconds per foot because, of course, it carries fewer, larger frames per unit length. To complicate matters still further, some 16mm film machinery only measures in 35mm, rather than 16mm, film feet.) Thus a more exact calculation shows that a thirty-minute production shot at 10:1 will in fact take 11,250 feet of 16mm film, which is just over twenty-eight 400-foot rolls. Answer prints and show prints, opticals and other effects are all calculated per foot of film. So is making duplicate footage ('dupes'), such as are commonly made from the cutting copy ('slash dupes') after the editing is complete so that work on the sound may continue while the cutting copy itself is sent off for negative cutting.

Videotapes come in different lengths, though not all equipment is able to use all sizes. It is very much cheaper than 16mm film and, of course, needs no processing but allowance must be made for the production of viewing copies, usually on a domestic format of some kind, VHS for example. If incorporating tapes from other countries, a documentary maker should be aware that the way the colour signal is encoded on the tape varies from country to country. Three forms of encoding are currently in use: PAL as used in Britain, SECAM as used in France, and NTSC as used in the United States. Conversion from one standard to another can be expensive.

Graphics

Under graphics are classified those elements of a documentary that put images on the screen derived from sources other than location shooting with a film or video camera. Some kinds of graphics work, however, particularly those used for opening title sequences can involve the shooting of models, sets and sometimes even live location action by the graphics designer rather than by the film-maker responsible for the overall production. The graphics designer is often given the task of looking after all aspects of the production that relate to its graphical style.

Graphics work is often very expensive. Title sequences can occasionally cost almost as much as the rest of the film put together. The designer's fee is usually calculated by the day, sometimes by the hour. Additional costs run up by the graphics design process—illustration, model building, special film or video effects—are charged separately. Graphics artists are well used to working to a given amount of expenditure; the graphics budget is best discussed directly with the designer before settling on a figure.

If still photographs of a location are needed for inclusion in a documentary, the stills photographer will be booked by the day to accompany the shooting crew. Stills have to be recorded onto tape or film before they can be edited into the production. The procedure is undertaken with a rostrum camera, a camera fixed in a rig which can be controlled, zoomed, moved in and out or side to side, with great precision—these days mostly by computer. This is necessary as still photographs, either prints or transparencies, are physically small in size yet may be required to occupy the whole screen. It is not advisable to try to save money by shooting the stills with the main location camera, as manual operation does not provide the required control.

Screen captions made up of letters or figures—for use in credit title sequences or for the identification of speakers—were formerly created as optical effects on film but are now almost invariably generated by caption generating machines and superimposed on the screen image at the last stage of video-editing. A production all on film will usually be recorded onto videotape for this purpose. A specialist operator, who is familiar with the particular machine in use, will also have to be booked. Most editing suites have a caption generator permanently installed, but an additional charge is commonly levied for its use.

Computer graphics, where required, can be the most expensive of all production processes. Computer animation, particularly if photo-realism is called for, occupies expensive hardware for long periods of time. Such animations are designed as wire-frame images, showing only the outlines, and then filled in or 'rendered' as the final process. With current technology this monopolizes the computer hardware for many hours, sometimes even days. As with so many other categories in the budget, the only way to estimate the cost of computer graphics work with any degree of accuracy is to discuss the needs of the production with a computer graphics facility company before committing to a figure.

Music

Music for a documentary can come from commercially available recordings or it can be specially composed. Many familiar title themes have been taken from commercial recordings. All such recordings, whether specially issued for use in films ('mood' music) or released into the general entertainment market, will have to be paid for at some time—often by the broadcaster as part of an annual payment to an appropriate rights organization. This, of course, shifts the burden of the cost from the documentary budget to the commissioning organization.

Specially composed music has the advantage of originality and being created to fit exactly to the documentary's various timings and atmospheres. It is, however, relatively expensive.

If music is composed for live performance and recording, musicians will have to be engaged and a recording studio hired together with its staff. If only one or two musicians are involved, there are few complications. If more players are needed, the usual procedure is to engage a musical director (the conductor) who takes on a 'fixer', who in turn selects the individual musicians making up the band. Musicians' contracts for productions to be broadcast on television are in most countries subject to union agreements. The number of hours which constitute a session are generally rigidly adhered to. It is commonly forbidden for music from a single session to be used in more than one production; in the case of a series, each episode must have its own music recording session. Such agreements change all the time and a film-maker should make enquiries as to the present situation before committing him- or herself to the budget.

The music is recorded with the musicians—or at least the musical director—watching the pictures, so that exact timings can be maintained. Not surprisingly, a number of attempts may be needed to get this right. A common estimate for music of any complexity is that a two-minute title theme takes a single four-hour session to record. Incidental music, which may need slightly less precision, can be accomplished in rather less time. But if the music involves a number of musicians, is in any way difficult, or needs any kind of adjustment, five minutes of finished recording is all that can realistically be expected from a four-hour session.

An alternative approach is to commission the score from a composer of electronic music, who will create the entire sound (or sometimes just most of it) using an electronic synthesizer or sampler, and will record the mixed and layered result directly onto a digital audio tape. This can then be synchronized to the picture during the sound dubbing process. The advantages of absolute accuracy and relatively low cost may be offset by the synthetic sound quality of the result, though this may be entirely appropriate for some kinds of production. Care should be taken since in some countries union agreements require that a single electronic composer taking the place of five live musicians must be paid five times the single session performance fee.

Chapter 13

Outline, Treatment, Script

Film consists of sounds and pictures but can also be described in words. Most documentaries begin as verbal descriptions and most such descriptions are written down. Written accounts of a prospective film can range from cursory notes to a fully worked out treatment. The progress from one end of the range to the other parallels the film-maker's development of the production's shape, from the first glimmerings of the idea, to being ready for the camera. While the process can be contained entirely in the mind, and some documentarists prefer to keep it so, as with arithmetic, working out the details can be greatly helped by putting them down on paper.

An idea of the finished film is the starting point of all documentary making. The film-maker may begin by knowing none of the film's details, neither the characters, nor the locations, yet in some sense he or she will already have in mind an idea, a design, a shape, a form; psychologists might call it a Gestalt. The form is like the armature of a sculpture but it is, at the start, invisible. It cannot be seen or described in words. It is little more than a feeling. But a feeling with a shape, if there can be such a thing. And it only comes slowly into view as the sculptor adds clay to it, piece by piece.

For most film-makers, the production process consists of filling the details into just such an imaginary yet unimagined form. Only when the work is finally complete can the form be seen. Only then can the film-maker know how close he or she has come to achieving his or her aim. The process is difficult to describe, but somehow one knows whether the final film matches the initial unvisualized, idea. The pre-production process: the preliminary research, the writing of an outline, the further research, the writing of a treatment, the preparation for shooting, all are ways of ensuring that the footage captured by the camera is the material which will best bring the form into reality.

The initial, unvisualized form can be sparked off from many quarters. A television documentary may begin with a programme-maker's idea; an in-house communication may start with a check-list of information to be included; a commission for a corporate publicity video may start with a specification from the public relations department. If lucky, a documentary maker may be asked to put in a proposal to fit a television channel's given brief.

The documentarist's first response to the initial idea, wherever it comes from, will be to investigate, to immerse him- or herself in the subject. Books will be read, newspaper clippings checked, but most of all people will be sought out. The film-maker will wish to get a feel for the subject at all levels, particularly the detailed experience of those most familiar with it. Sometimes, when the subject lies in an area with which everyone is familiar, this will suffice. In other cases, the film-maker will go to experts for their opinions. In yet others, the results of public opinion surveys will be consulted. No one can tell how long the process of familiarization should be. It will take as long as necessary for the film-maker both to get a grasp of the area of concern and to form the beginnings of a feeling for what the film should be.

Of course a few days, weeks or even months immersed in the subject will not make the film-maker an expert. But that is not the point. The film-maker does not have to be an expert but a perceptive observer and a sympathetic listener, with a concern to notice the unspoken, detect the unperceived, and pick out the significant details which form the pattern of events and relationships that will be the substance of the film.

It is at that point, the point at which the film-maker forms a notion of the film that he or she will begin to set down an outline on paper. Even those documentarists who take the most stringently observational approach to their subjects start with an outline in their minds, even if it is never actually committed to paper—writing it down can seem limiting and prejudicial to those who prefer to think of documentary making as an objective empirical scientific enterprise. But most of us find that setting down our thoughts on paper rather than keeping them only in our heads helps us to look at them critically.

Outline

Creating an outline is the essential first step in pinning down the initial idea and giving it some concrete substance. In this sense, writing an outline is like an experiment, a series of tests, to find out where the boundaries of the unvisualized shape may be, or like a painter's first attempts at a sketch, an effort to pick out and make concrete an invisible drawing from the blank surface of a sheet of paper.

To begin with, the initial outline need be no more than a simple list of elements which may go to make up the finished film, put in order. At this stage, with none of the details yet known, a film-maker will be no more than probing the formless idea. Like the artist trying out a line on the paper to see whether it matches the imagined drawing, the notes which make up the first outline will only be tentative. Yet even now they will begin to tell the film-maker something about the finished work. Like a painter's sketches too, a film's outline is disposable: it gets constantly rewritten, sections are erased, are changed, are switched around.

Like the armature of a sculpture or the sketch for a painting, the outline makes a framework which gives the documentarist his or her first view of the overall structure of the final production. The importance of this cannot be over-estimated. For when documentaries fail, it is as often as not because of failings in the structure of the film, rather than in the execution of the filming and editing.

These first attempts will already be set down in filmic terms. They are not literary ideas. The outline is not the framework for a theoretical presentation. The style of outline used in some quarters, which begins with the intellectual content of the piece in words— set up the opening premise, develop the argument, reach the conclusion—can lead a film-maker to ignore the fact that the completed work is to be a film experience rather than a written text. To go down the wrong path at this stage can lead to a documentary which is little more than a lantern lecture. So the entries in the outline list will be shorthand for film sequences like perhaps: 'ski slopes with music—fast cutting;' or 'moody night scene in airport—prospective emigrants;' or 'band rehearsal in drummer's bedroom—beer cans and cigarette smoke.' Added to the shorthand description will be notes about what the purpose of the particular section is to be: 'to show subject's skiing skill;' or 'to meet subject of film for first time', or 'to witness the first stage of developing the band's musical arrangements.'

The notes in the outline will contain references to the subject to be treated, the locations envisaged, the characters to be filmed, the atmosphere to be sought. In short a breakdown, in order, of the sections of the film, with an indication of their content.

The notes in the outline will give the first indication of what the shape of the final film might be and how the theme, story, or argument of the film might be handled. Even though they are but a highly compressed, economical shorthand for ideas that are still vague in the mind of their creator, the outline will yet say something about the completed project. Even at this stage one can ask questions of it: Can the film achieve its aim? Does the form work? Is the content too much or too little to be contained within the envisaged length, is the theme too simple or too complicated. Is the line or thread of argument through the film clear enough? Do the stated elements add up to some kind of whole?

Does the completed film have a point to make and if so does it succeed in that aim?

The individual sequences will be studied too. The first question to be asked is: is the idea for this section of the film the obvious one or is it original. Many documentarists make a practice of discarding their first idea, and sometimes their second and third, on the grounds that those are the ideas everyone else will have had too.

Again, the film-maker will want to make sure that the sections of the film can do their job in a visual way, or else will recognize that they need support by interview or commentary. Some film-makers go so far as to demand that a film should be able to be understood without any sound at all. Only that way can it be said to depend on entirely filmic values. But that goes too far. Film has had synchronous sound for some seventy years now. It is as much part of the art of film as the images are. But synchronous sound is not the same as commentary. If film needs constantly to be explained by a voice-over, it is probably not doing its job.

A third question which the film-maker will ask of the sections of the outline is about their feasibility. At this stage the film-maker will not necessarily know any details of locations and personalities. But it will be possible to know whether a sequence falls within the bounds of achievability. If a particular point can only be made by some means which is not within reasonable grasp—an elaborate computer animation perhaps—then the film-maker may have to think again.

The importance of having these notes written down at this stage now becomes clear. For right at the start, when no expenses have been incurred and no commitments given, the film-maker can adjust, change, alter, elaborate, switch round, lengthen or shorten the items which will go to make up the completed work. In other words the shape of the idea can be massaged until it adopts a satisfactory form. Already now, the documentarist can see whether the film is balanced, whether and where there is too much exposition and too little enaction, whether the pace is likely to be maintained or if longueurs are already evident.

The question may well be asked: how can one write an outline before detailed research has shown what characters, locations and events are available for filming. The answer is to use the imagination. At this stage, where nothing is yet fixed and no decision is unchangeable, the film-maker has the opportunity to dream up any sequence he or she feels will do the job. The outline is at first only a statement of intention and nobody will hold the film-maker responsible if the very first intention cannot, in the event, be realized.

Of course a framework of knowledge is essential even to begin the outlining. But a film-maker does not need to start with more than an overall grasp of the subject he or she proposes to film. In fact many film-makers feel that too great a knowledge of the subject *too early on* in the process can be harmful. What is needed for outlining is an overview, not a fine-grained image. A documentary must necessarily simplify the complexity of the world in order to encapsulate it. In any case, the film-maker's work will be communicating with people many of whom may know little or nothing about the subject. It is useful at this stage to be in a similar position. That way the film-maker will not be taking prior knowledge by the audience for granted.

It is quite true that a documentary maker, representing him- or herself as a seeker after truth, would be reluctant to admit to having a mind already made up even before exploring the reality in any depth. But, to admit for a moment the scientific paradigm of the documentary maker's work, even in a scientific experiment the scientist must first propose a hypothesis to be tested. No physicist or chemist for example, begins a research project with a completely open mind and unformed opinion, not having any idea of what the results of the investigation might be. In fact most scientific papers begin with the hypothesis which is to be proved or disproved.

The key issue is how much the film-maker is prepared to change his or her mind in the process of researching and outlining. The process is an iterative one: outline, research, rewrite the outline, more research and so on. As the work progresses, the documentary's form is defined ever more clearly until the film-maker is satisfied that the form and shape of the project is as close as possible to both what he or she understands to be the truth as well as the original, unimagined, form in the film-maker's mind.

In the process of going round and round the outline-research cycle, the outline will grow in size as more and more details are fixed. Locations will be decided on, interviewees selected, stock footage and archive sequences traced, events to be shot will be pinpointed and entered into the production schedule. By the end of the process, the structure of the film and the items through which it is to be realized will be fully determined.

At this stage, the film-maker will be able see in his or her mind's eye a much more detailed picture of what the final work will be like. The outline has turned into a treatment.

Treatment

A treatment is a full description of the completed film, scene by scene, sequence by sequence, couched in the 'historic present' tense. Many documentary film-makers avoid writing a treatment, feeling that the image of the film in their head is sufficient to take them forward to the shooting stage, and fearing that to fix too much detail before the shooting begins might limit their response to the actual location. Others find that the discipline of describing the specifics of what the final production will look and sound like, is an important help in developing their theoretical ideas and making them practicable.

A treatment, if suitably written, allows a film-maker actually to run the movie before it has been made: to ask questions of it; to determine the balance of different elements; to see whether it is successful in its aims; even to determine whether it is interesting or enjoyable to watch. A treatment is, in effect, a virtual film— with both the advantages and disadvantages of any form of virtuality. It is protean, can change its shape, can be altered, switched round, manipulated, all with no cost and little difficulty. But at the same time, it is of course not real, and demands a leap of the imagination to experience not so much its content, but its associative, emotional, sub-intellectual impact.

A treatment fully written out will face the film-maker, even at an early stage, with the reality of any problems, conflicts or paradoxes hidden in the outline and covered over by slick and easy forms of words. Vague ideas, attractive in their feel, will seem very different when the film-maker is faced with the task of turning them into concrete realities. It is easy to specify for instance: a sequence showing John Smith wrestling with the controls of his aircraft. But what does that mean specifically? Writing the treatment will make it clear how the scene will begin and end, how long it should be, how its atmosphere will be captured, what kinds of sounds the viewer will hear, precisely what sorts of shots are required, and a host of other features which go to make up the completed sequence. It is of course true that clever editing can in the end make almost anything 'work'—though editors are well known for protesting about missing shots, wrong sizes, inappropriate framings. But there is no doubt that solving such problems at this stage, before any footage has been shot, can avoid the need for first aid and intensive editing care later on. Solving problems in advance is almost always better than leaving them to find their solution later on. Most film-makers know that sufficient thought and preparation put in at the start can repay its effort by saving a day's or even a week's work later on.

The treatment will not just be an account of what the shooting will need to include but will take the process forward to the editing, dubbing and beyond. As a virtual film, it will be a description of the finished work, ready for viewing after everything has been completed. It will therefore imply what needs to be done to achieve that completion, not only in shooting, but in all the stages of post-production.

That is not to say that writing a treatment is a literary exercise. Film-makers are not, and do not have to be, writers. The excellence of the style in which the virtual film is composed is not an issue—unless, as is sometimes the case, a condition of the film-maker's contract with the broadcaster or other commissioning body demands the delivery of a full treatment before shooting starts. Occasionally film-makers have engaged professional authors to write treatments. Jean-Paul Sartre is reputed to have once written a 600-page treatment—albeit for a fiction film—though there is no record of the film ever having been made. But in such cases it is more the writer's concept of the subject that is being sought rather than an impression of how the film will look and sound. A film-maker's treatment is primarily for the film-maker's own eyes, not another reader's. So how well or not it is expressed in words is irrelevant for the task in hand, which is to concentrate the film-maker's own mind on what needs to be done to realize his or her vision.

Later on, during production and post-production, the documentarist may find it useful to show the treatment to other collaborators: the cine-photographer and editor, perhaps. Certainly many cameramen and -women welcome the opportunity to get an idea of the complete film on which they are working. It makes it possible for them to make suggestions and add their own contribution—as happens all too infrequently in the television industry. Film and video editors, on the other hand, often prefer to work only with the material with which they have been presented. At that stage, they believe, the producer or director's original vision is no longer relevant to the task in hand, which is to make the best possible film out of the material actually shot. However, since there are at least as many ways to edit the same material as there are to play a duplicate hand at bridge, it surely cannot do any harm for everyone working on a documentary to know what the film-maker has throughout been striving for.

Script

A treatment is not a shooting script. A treatment is the description of a completed film, while a script is the detailed instruction manual for shooting it. Of all the documents written in preparation for a documentary film shoot, a script is the least often used. And if a form of script is compiled for a scene, it will be most likely not be a shot by shot chronological description but more of a shopping list, noting a selection of images which will probably be needed.

For a documentary maker to work exclusively from a shooting script, a condition sometimes imposed by contract, particularly in the corporate video field, is to put on a set of blinkers. It restricts the film-maker's ability to respond to the scene as it plays itself out in reality, it prevents the camera from seeking out previously unobserved details, it makes it impossible to adjust each shot in relation to what happened in the previous one. As long as the documentary maker has a clear image of the scene in mind, the shots which are required to create it will usually be determined in the course of an interactive process: the way each shot goes will lead the film-maker to respond with a decision about the next.

A shooting script also pre-empts the editing process and risks tying the editor's hands. Most film-makers will make allowance for the fact that deciding precisely which shots to use, for how long, and how they are to go together is best left until later. The construction of an individual sequence depends to a great extent on the sequences on either side; its exact delineation must wait until all the shooting, for all the sequences, has been completed. Unless the film-maker does all his or her own editing, a second person's eye on the material, as from an editor, almost invariably improves the end result. Even novelists benefit from the suggestions of a book editor; a film-maker is no different. To pre-empt such a process by rigidly defining the film in advance with a script can condemn the work to mediocrity.

Preparing a shooting list, if not a shooting script, is a useful exercise as long as it is not regarded as definitive and complete, and as long as the film-maker feels free to depart from it as necessary. A shooting list, rather than a script, is an advantage in circumstances where following a scene or an event will need the film-maker's full attention and concentration, with the risk that certain indispensable shots may be forgotten in the heat of the moment—a disaster which happens all too frequently. A list can also help to decide on the order in which to carry out the filming. Where time is short, or circumstances are difficult, shooting must often be planned with the precision of a military exercise.

The critical difference between a treatment and a shooting list is that the former is usually written—at least in its first version—even before any locations have been identified and visited, before contributors have been selected and spoken to, before any of the concrete details of the shooting are known. A shooting list depends entirely on the reality of the location, its appearance and topography as well as the individual characters to be shown inhabiting it. Consequently it will be the very last matter to be attended to before the shooting begins.

Writing a shooting list, or a shooting order, can be thought of as a kind of recorded rehearsal, as the film-maker proceeds through the process of shooting the sequence in his or her imagination, trying to foresee all the images that might be needed in the course of assembling the sequence, and trying to predict and therefore to forestall any untoward eventuality which might occur during the filming. But of course not every possible occurrence can ever be foreseen. The shooting list can never be more than a foundation, a rough preparation for the real thing.

Naturally, none of these limits apply to the shooting of dramatized sequences. Where filming to a written script is concerned, whether with dialogue or not, a full shooting script, prepared in advance and discussed with the artists wherever possible, is always beneficial if not essential.

Chapter 14

Research

Research is the foundation for all non-fiction film-making. The word sounds serious, scientific, impressive even, though possibly a little dull. It has strong academic associations. But research for a television documentary is no academic exercise; it is practical, sometimes exciting and often fun. For many film-makers the research is the most enjoyable stage of the documentary production exercise—the time for finding things out.

To do so, the researcher brings to bear on the problems an armoury of techniques many of which are more closely related to the world of the private detective than to that of the university library. In some ways research is easier than detective work. Informants are usually far more willing to give information to someone introduced to them as making a television programme, than to someone claiming to be an employee of the Philip Marlowe Detective Agency—the opportunity to be interviewed on TV is generally more appealing than the chance of appearing in the witness box at the Old Bailey.

Films may be researched by the film-maker him- or herself, or by a researcher engaged for that purpose by the production. In many cases both the documentary maker and one or more researchers work together, especially when making a film which is not based on pure observation. If a documentary is about an idea, a concept, an area of knowledge, the first essential for everyone working on it is to get a grasp of the subject.

Documentary research can therefore be divided into two kinds, usually carried out at different stages of the production process. Naturally there is some overlap. The first kind of research can be called theoretical, or content research, and must be done before anything else can happen. Content research may continue throughout the production process, but at some point, the emphasis will change to the second kind of research, which can be called practical, or production research. Content research informs the members of production team about the subject area in which they are working. Production research provides material for the shooting and the sound recording.

Content research

The first task of content research is to collect and collate sources of the information needed to make the film. The result may be a list of books, publications, magazine articles, newspaper cuttings which need to be read. Or it may be a list of experts, consultants, lecturers, witnesses, activists who should be spoken to. Research needs a good knowledge of available libraries, both of books and newspaper cuttings, museums and collections of written archives. Many companies, institutions and newspapers maintain collections of their own materials to which they are usually happy to allow a researcher access. A number of handbooks are available in different countries containing lists of such collections.

The second task is to absorb as much of an understanding of that information as is possible or necessary. Every documentary maker and researcher will have his or her own preferred way of gaining understanding of a subject. For some documentary makers, the pile of books, magazines and other documents may be the best possible informant of first resort. For others, personal contact and long conversations with people who understand the subject are the most comfortable ways of introducing themselves to the issues. Some researchers prefer to be already well briefed about an area before going off to talk to experts. Others are happier to receive information verbally than in writing.

The difficulty of the first approach is knowing when to stop delving ever deeper into the subject. Documentary makers have been known to become so involved as to abandon the production and end up with a PhD thesis, and consequent doctorate, instead. The other approach, learning about an area by directly consulting the experts working in it, has the advantage that a preliminary filtering takes place. Experts mostly restrict their explanations to what they think essential and relevant, as well as to what they believe the lay person can understand. Of course there is the danger that the film-maker will only receive a highly partial view. Many different sources of information will have to be consulted, just as many different books will have to be collected, to avoid bias and prejudice.

Whichever approach is taken, desk research or going out to speak to experts—and most content research is a combination of both—the task is initially to compile a survey of the subject of the film, to get an idea of what is known about it, what is its history, what has been written about it, what is the available evidence, who are the experts and where they are to be found. For some subjects, particularly those dealing with ordinary events and everyday life, a good level of general knowledge is all that is needed to form a working overview. For others, some science documentaries for example, or perhaps films dealing with such arcana as the world's financial markets, even a superficial understanding will only come after serious specialist study. Whichever class the subject in question may belong to, the film-maker will need to become familiar enough with its details as to able to hold a reasonably intelligent and informed conversation about it. This will greatly help later on when trying to secure the co-operation of contributors to the film. Many film-makers will themselves have had the experience of being consulted by non-experts; they will know their own reactions to daft questions and ignorant comments about their own business.

This first stage of exploration will take different amounts of time depending on the subject and the film-maker. The documentarist who works regularly in the same field has an advantage here. A producer of science films or a television financial journalist, when first presented with a new theme for a documentary, will probably already know quite a lot about the general subject area and may need to do little more than check up on the latest published papers or articles. Neophytes have to put in rather more work to bring themselves up to speed. Their recompense is the excitement of engaging for the first time in a new subject area and looking at the world from a fresh perspective. It is surprising how little time it takes for the members of almost every documentary making team to make themselves so familiar with their subject, that its best known concepts and most famous names quickly become the small change of conversation in the production office.

Production research

While content research is about discovering and understanding the story, and in the process creating the outline of the production, production research is about filling in the details and tracking down actual material for filming, leading to the full development of the treatment and perhaps a shooting script. The items usually to be sought are: people, events, locations, visual materials and sometimes props. Many of these categories go together, as in a documentary they will almost always be connected with each other. The choice of an event to film will necessarily specify the people who take part in it and the location where it takes place; the choice of a person to appear in the production will mostly define the locations where he or she is to be seen.

People

People to be found will include those who are to act as advisers, experts and consultants as well as those who will actually appear in the production. Finding people is a central task and a major skill of the television researcher—finding items in the other categories may well depend on first locating somebody who knows where that item is to be found. This is where detective work comes into play. It usually starts with the telephone. The first step begins with a name, perhaps mentioned in a newspaper article, perhaps known to someone in the production team, or perhaps located through an organization or institution. Journalists from local radio or television stations or local newspapers are often a good starting point too.

In many cases the first name is only the entrance to the maze. It is too much to expect to discover the central target in one go. The first contact will often only be the starting point of a lengthy process. From the first person spoken to, the researcher must usually follow a long and convoluted trail leading from person to person, contact to contact, until the goal of finding just the right contributor, the one with the right qualities, the right experience and the right knowledge, is reached.

Once the right person has been tracked down, contact will have to move from telephone talk to a meeting in the flesh. In spite of all our era's progress in communications technology, there is no substitute for face to face conversation when trying to determine the suitability or otherwise of a contributor to a documentary film. Where the film-maker is not personally carrying out the research but collaborating with a researcher, the researcher will often conduct the first meeting, leaving the film-maker to pick up the contact at a stage nearer the shooting time.

What does a documentary maker look for when selecting— 'casting'—contributors to the production? Clearly some matters are of basic importance. What are mostly sought are primary rather than secondary sources. That is, those with direct personal experience or knowledge of what they are required to speak about. Secondary sources are those who can report on not what they themselves, but only what others have done or experienced. This is the equivalent of hearsay evidence, which is no more valuable to a film than it is in a court of law. Naturally, there will be some cases in which a primary witness is impossible to find but film-makers usually make every effort to seek out a contributor with personal knowledge. The problem is greater when engaging experts to comment on or to provide a framework of understanding for a subject. For an expert's contribution to be truly useful and authoritative, the expert should have done the research or other scholarly study him or herself. The use of all-purpose television pundits to comment on matters far beyond their own expertise is, though not uncommon, not very helpful.

Honesty and truthfulness must of course be assured. No documentarist would wish a film's argument to be founded on dishonest testimony. Unfortunately there are some people for whom appearing in a film is such a lure that they are prepared to say almost anything just to get in front of a camera. There are also those with an axe to grind. When selecting contributors, the researcher will need to keep an open mind and a sensitive nose to detect the signs of the *parti pris* or the hidden agenda. Coming in on a subject without a long and deep understanding of its complexities—the inevitable situation of the television documentarist—makes it all too easy to be captured by those who nurse a wilfully distorted view. Television history has many examples of films which were fatally flawed because they expressed the documentarists' too gullible acceptance of the face value of what someone had told them.

Equally, the contributor must not only be honest and truthful but must also appear to be so. Sadly, some contributors, while in reality scrupulously and totally honest, can make a shifty and untrustworthy impression when speaking before the camera. Coaching them a little in self-presentation can help. In part, an aspect of the film-maker's skill is in putting subjects at ease when filming, so that they come over as relaxed, natural and straightforward. Of course it is not always possible to detect problems in advance. Many film-makers will have had the experience of cultivating contributors for a long period of time in the conviction that when filmed they will perform as splendidly as expected, only to find that when the camera crew arrives their *sang froid* has completely and catastrophically deserted them. Sadly, there are some people who become so nervous when being filmed that an air of relaxation is totally impossible for them. They speak, if they can get the words out at all, as if from a prepared text, become totally wooden and unnatural, or worst of all, respond to the interviewer's questions with frozen silence, like a rabbit mesmerized by a snake. Nobody is to blame for such an outcome and it is a matter of plain courtesy to avoid making the contributor feel that he or she has let the film-maker down. In the event, shooting may sometimes be completed using a so-called 'strawberry filter'—no film or tape in the camera—to avoid making the contributor feel a failure.

The final task of the researcher is to prepare the subject for the actual filming. It is important that contributors know what will be involved and what is expected of them. The contributor should be given a clear idea of the filming process, particularly how long it will take. The researcher should make it clear that agreement to be filmed has consequences which must be accepted in advance. Filming can be a disruptive process and it is as well that everyone involved understands and accepts this at the outset. It is important to try to avoid a situation in which limitations on what can be shot are suddenly placed on the team at the time of filming. Most documentarists find that if they are open and honest about what filming involves, the contributors will be prepared for most eventualities.

Contributors should also be given an honest account of the theme and other contents of the film. There is often a temptation to misguide a subject, in the fear that a truthful exposure of the purpose of the documentary may put them off agreeing to take part in it. This is not a fruitful way for a documentarist to behave. If the film demands honesty from an interviewee, it is only fair that those making the film should be equally forthright about their own intentions. There is a somewhat *macho* attitude not uncommonly found, particularly among those working in current affairs and politics, which suggests that all is fair in love, war and film-making; that the important thing is to get the material on film or tape and never mind what it takes to get it there. This may work on a single occasion. But once bitten, twice shy—such participants are unlikely ever to agree to take part in a film again. This may not matter to the documentarist at the time, but it hardly leaves a good taste in the mouth. Many film-makers would seriously deprecate such a short-sighted way of working.

On the other hand unrealistic promises should never be made. A film-maker should not promise to give the contributors the final say about their contributions. Those taking part in the film should know from the start who has editorial control over the production. When working on a film for a private client, it is not unreasonable that the client should have the final word over what is or is not included. In all other circumstances, a film-maker should make it clear from the outset that editorial decisions will be the responsibility of the film-maker or the commissioning organization. It is acceptable for the production to promise to make a preview of the completed film available to the contributors for their comments, as long as it is understood that the contributors will only be able to make suggestions and that the film-maker commits him- or herself to do no more than take the comments into consideration.

Locations

Location research for a documentary is rather different from the location finding which is a frequent aspect of drama pre-production. Documentary locations are largely predetermined by the intended content of the relevant sequence. If the content is the location itself, for example in a travel documentary, the location is a given fact and is determined from the outset. If the content is an event, the location is equally fixed; it is usually not possible to change the place where that event occurs. If the subject for filming is a person, the location will be wherever those activities occur which are part of the contributor's life.

So rather than searching out a location which has a particular look or suits a particular action, location research for a documentary works the other way round: it mostly involves finding out what the place is like, what its atmosphere may be, and what visual contribution it may be able to make to the production. It is also important to seek out any disadvantages it may present to the shooting process. Where in a drama, the conclusion may be that a different location should be found for the shoot, in a documentary this is generally not possible and the research will be limited to helping the filming team prepare for both the pluses and minuses of the given place.

Researching locations in the home country is fairly straight-forward. Location research for foreign filming will include extra tasks that may not directly relate to the documentary itself but rather to the logistics of filming it. There is an overlap here with the planning and perhaps the recce stage of the pre-production process since few documentary productions are well enough financially endowed to be able to afford multiple journeys to the filming destination. Some of the information needed may be possible to acquire by telephone research from the production base, but it may fall to the researcher during the trip to find interpreters and fixers, ascertain legal and bureaucratic requirements and possibly to make contact with local film photographers and sound recordists, if it is decided to take on such personnel locally rather than shipping out the entire crew from the home base. It may even be necessary to grease a few important palms to make the filming possible at all.

Events

Event research can be the most difficult of all, as the event concerned may be a once-only occasion for which full preparations have to be made without anyone from the production team ever witnessing the occasion themselves. There is little that can be done other than to get as much information as possible about what is supposed to happen, where and how. And to get that information from as many viewpoints as possible—they may differ remarkably.

Alas there is much that can—and often does—go wrong on the day. For the documentary series *Face Values*[1] the team filming the New Year's Eve ritual in the village of Comrie in Scotland were given an exhaustive description of the occasion. There would be a torchlight procession around the bounds of the parish—a ceremony which had taken place annually for some hundreds of years. The problem for filming was that so many people were to take part in the procession that once it had passed any particular shooting position, the camera team would find it impossible to move through the dense crowd and get back to the head of the march. Using information provided by a number of local informants, a complex shooting plan was drawn up using five camera positions in different parts of the village. Unfortunately allowances were not made for the earlier part of the ritual, which involved a long drinking session in the village tavern beforehand. When the moment came, the participants had imbibed so much whisky that they staggered off in a direction exactly opposite that for which the crew were prepared. The moral? Prepare for everything that could possibly go wrong—it probably will.

Other materials

Many documentaries contain materials which are not directly filmed for the production but borrowed from elsewhere. Sequences from news films and other documentaries—television or film—may be included, as may still photographs and printed or written documents which are to be shot under a rostrum camera.

Seeking out these items is usually the task of specialist researchers who gather, over the years, an extensive knowledge of where appropriate film and stills libraries can be found. As with archive research, there are catalogues and books available with lists of film and stills libraries as well as museums and other organizations which have collections of visual materials. Failing that, most broadcasting organizations maintain catalogues of sequences from their productions which they make available for the use of other film-makers. Feature film companies, too, have extensive 'back catalogues' which can be consulted.

Though some libraries issue catalogues in both printed and electronic form, film and stills research can in some circumstances be quite expensive as viewing copies may have to be made—at the production's expense. It is important to have a very clear idea

[1] BBC 1975

of what is needed before approaching a library, as while some charge only for any material finally included in the edited documentary, others charge for all material supplied. The researcher will also need to check on what rights to the material are available and the cost of clearing them.

The research report

Unless the film-maker is researching the documentary alone, most productions require researchers to write a report on what they have found. This may seem an unnecessarily formal way of going about things, but there are a number of advantages to having everything written down in black and white. To start with, it concentrates the mind to collate all the information gathered, to sort it out and to commit it to paper. In fact many documentarists who work only by themselves, nonetheless still compose an account of their researches for future reference, when the fresh memory of the visits they have made and the people they have met have long since faded from the mind. If the film is being made by a team, it is a great help to have all the information available in the same form to everyone working on the production. The exact format of the report is not important—some researchers write an extended personalized account of their experiences, others simply supply notes containing the essential information in an easily assimilable way.

ALCOY

We can't miss Alcoy. The symbolism of the Moros Y
Christianos is simply too rich. What's more it looks
like brilliant fun and we have an official invitation
from one of the leading characters.

This type of festival is quite widespread, but
nowhere else is it quite like at Alcoy, a rather lumpy
town of 70,000 people in the hills of Alicante province.
The Alcoy event purports to commemorate an actual
historical event - the defeat of the Moors in 1257, with
the aid of St George.

The number of people taking part in the actual
event is limited to 12,000, who are divided up into 14
groups of Moors and 14 of Christians. Each group has its
own traditions, costumes and plans, to upstage the
others.

I met and chatted with this year's Alfares (the
lieutenant) of the 'Cristianos', Francesco Javier
Vicedo, who assured us that we would be his honoured
guests and have complete access to his group's
activities. Appropriately enough for our film six, his
group is the 'Crusaders'.

Good close access to the fiesta denouement scenes
might be difficult, but with a brazen film crew and
perhaps some staging, we should be able to get really
good action sequences.

The rough schedule of the Fiestas is as follows:

24.4.91 On the first day there are various preparatory
rituals, music and celebration of St George's day. Vast
qantities of 'plis-plas', a vicious mix of coffee
liqueur and coca cola, are consumed.

25.4.91 The second day sees the emergence of the bands
and squadrons in their full regalia. Our man will appear
after a ceremonial breakfast with his bodyguard of
knights. Up to this moment, the costumes have been a
closely guarded secret. I have seen the design of our
Alfares's gear, and it is fantastic. It is also costing
more than £5000.

The squadrons then process through the streets,
often with camels, or even elephants, as well as vast
floats. More 'plis-plas' is drunk as feasting, dancing
and singing go on into the night.

pages from a research
report written by Jeffrey Lee
for *Living Islam*

26.4.91 On the final day, after a Moorish embassy to the castle (a temporary structure in the main square), the battle is joined in earnest. Those with hangovers are kept on their feet by the constant roar of exploding powder from hundreds of muskets as the morning battle leaves the moors in charge of the castle after hand-to-hand combat. Our Alfares will be taking part in all these activities, which should help us get better shots.

In the afternoon, it is the Christians who approach with an embassy, and then after another battle and staged sword fight, win the day. The fiesta climaxes with the appearance of 'Sant Jordet' a boy representing St George on a white pony.

Unlike other villages Alcoy does not humiliate the vanquished. The nearby village of Benares that has its fiestas around the same time as Alcoy, ends them with the 'Despojo', the ritual conversion of the Moors in the town cemetery. By all accounts the village takes this very seriously. People in Alcoy look down on this sort of activity. As Franceso puts it, 'Here, we're all Moors.' The Benares fiesta might be on 25.4.91. We need to check as Easter is interfering.

Other villages such as Biar and Villena, go even further than Benares, carrying around an effigy of 'La Mahoma'. This is a representation of Muhammad as a sort of dragon or dragon-man that is reviled by the mob. Generally the Moor is represented as a thing of evil.

The whole Moros Y Cristianos thing is so rich with imagery - Islam reviled, St George spearing Moors instead of dragons, Muslims being walloped, triumph of the West, that we shouldn't pass it up.

Other bits and bobs include a vast painting of the battle inside the church of Alcoy, various paintings and sculptures of St George, and the fiesta museum, replete with the costumes and relics of fiestas gone by.

We might even be able to get the comments of some Muslim onlookers. Arab traders come to sell goodies to the crowds and it's possible that we'll get something good from one of them - if we can find them in the throng.

Alternatively we might even find some Arab big-wigs coming to watch. They enjoy it, it seems, and one rich Kuwaiti even offered to buy the whole museum of the fiestas.

Section B
Production

Chapter 15

Production Planning

With all the research completed, the characters, events and stories chosen, the treatment of the film rewritten to take account of the results of the research, a plan for the shooting and sound recording needs to be drawn up. At this stage, unless the film-maker is operating alone, shooting and recording the material him- or herself, the documentary making process becomes a team effort. Apart from the film-maker, there will be the camera crew—film photographer, sound recordist, perhaps assistants and grips, and possibly others too. The documentarist, acting now as producer, becomes the manager of that team. To the previously exercised skills of imaginative artistic creativity, he or she will have to add the techniques of management. The larger the team, the greater the control needed. Management will involve managing people: the production team, the camera and sound recording crew, as well as the contributors and any others involved even peripherally in the production. It will also include managing resources: a given amount of money will have been allocated to shooting and the planning process will need to ensure that the best possible use is made of it.

Managing the team

The selection of the shooting team will be among the first tasks to be undertaken by the film-maker in the role of producer. In some cases of course, particularly if working as part of a production company with its own staffing policy, there may be little choice. In other cases, the whole world of freelance film craft workers is open to the film-maker. Matching the interests, experience and abilities of the crew members to the subject of the film is obviously a first priority. Film photographers often specialize. Particularly where the subject of the shooting demands a very particular way of working. Drama cameramen and camerawomen are accustomed to spending much of their time concentrating on the finest details of lighting, composition and choreographed movement; most documentary filming does not allow for such single minded pursuit of visual refinement. The skills of the wild life or natural history photographer, which may have been developed over many years—learning to sit in a tree or to hide in the underbrush for weeks on end, waiting for a particular creature to show up and do its stuff—these are not easily matched without the requisite experience. Equally, the way of working of the ethnographic photographer, who may be used to spending a great amount of time, and perhaps even living, with the film's subjects for long periods, is not at all appropriate for working on those documentaries which need a swift, accurate and highly targeted response. On the other hand, a camera operator who is used to shooting hand-held and getting directly involved in the hurly burly of political, social or military action may not be the right person to shoot a thoughtful and perhaps formal account of a concept or an idea. The adage that there are 'horses for courses' is never more true than when shooting film. Sound recordists are a little less specialized, though to shoot an elaborate rock or orchestral concert, it may be advisable to book a recordist with both the relevant technical expertise, as well as a particular interest in, and consequently a good ear for, the music in question.

Once having chosen the crew, good management involves striving to get the best out of everyone working on the project. In making a documentary the greatest expense is on human resources and it would be a waste not to realize the most possible benefit from the investment. To best achieve this, everyone involved in the production should be given a clear idea of the nature, aims and manner of the entire project. Film photographers and sound recordists are not simple artisans, hired to perform a single task with no involvement in the overall enterprise. They are practitioners of an applied art and respond best to being treated with appropriate respect. Their style of shooting will have a great influence on the feel of the complete work and they will need help to understand the artistic aims of the production as well as, of course, the individual practical details of what they are required to shoot. Though the film-maker may already have strong views about what he or she wants, making everyone else feel part of the enterprise by listening to comments and discussing options is often a valuable help in improving the end result. What this boils down to is to try to infect the entire team with the same eagerness and enthusiasm which has carried the film-maker through to this stage of the proceedings.

This does not mean that the documentarist needs to give up his or her personal vision. What a film-maker wants to achieve and the means by which it may be achieved are not the same thing. By strongly putting forward the first, but listening openly to suggestions and proposals for the second, new possibilities for improving the work often come to light, ideas which may well not have occurred to the documentarist him- or herself. In addition team members who are not so close to the project as the film-maker, may well foresee problems that have escaped notice until now.

A less pleasant management task that often arises when managing the team is the defusing of friction within the team. The production process is often an intense experience for all involved. As a consequence, tempers can quickly fray. Where crew members are not accustomed to working with each other regularly, animosity can develop between different craftspeople, all carrying out their own tasks as well as they can. Problems which naturally arise when a number of people are concentrating single-mindedly on only their own particular aspect of a collective enterprise, may come to be seen by one or other of those involved as, at the very least, a sign of insufficient consideration or, at worst, of intentional interference.

Where the team is mixed in gender or sexual orientation, the sexual dynamics of the situation can also lead to problems. Because working together on a film can be such a highly emotionally charged experience, team members, often living together for many days and often under difficult and stressful conditions, can soon develop a disproportionate intimacy. It is not unknown, nor even uncommon, for team members to develop sexual relationships with each other that can be very damaging to the common purpose. There are no simple ways of dealing with such situations. Tact but firmness is called for if the production is not to be allowed to go off the rails.

A similarly subtle approach is often needed when working with a presenter. The division of responsibility between director and presenter will need to be established from the beginning. There is often tension between the two. Presenters are frequently very self-confident, extrovert and demanding—not to say egotistic. Such characteristics are the tools of their trade; a shy and inward-looking presenter is no great benefit to a television producer. But there can be a cost. The documentary maker may feel that the presenter is being unreasonable and overbearing, a monster even. Most experienced film-makers have a long list of presenter horror stories. The presenter may quite justifiably feel that he or she is the one who appears on the screen before the public and the one to whom all the faults as well as the positive features of the documentary will inevitably be ascribed. Presenters therefore need to be handled with great care. An often quoted show-business adage has it that if you want an artist to appear on screen like a star, you must treat him or her like a star. Of course presenters are not necessarily stars at all—though many may think of themselves as such—and do not usually require the chauffeur-driven limousines and luxury hotel rooms expected by prominent film actors or stage performers. Nonetheless, it usually pays documentary makers working with presenters to look on their artists as important investments, whose well-being and good humour are essential to the success of the film. Patience and tact may be needed to persuade a presenter that, though theirs may be the face which fronts the production, they are not best placed to make informed judgements about the overall appearance or content of the documentary. This is essentially a question of trust. The documentarist must be able to trust the presenter to give of his or her best for the film, the presenter must be able to trust the film-maker to make the best of his or her performance.

Preparation

A well known saying in the television industry states that an hour's preparation saves a day on location. The exact ratio may be questionable, but there is no doubt that a film-maker who goes on a shoot fully prepared is likely to come home with more material, better suited to the documentary's needs than the one who turns up on the day and busks it all the way through. That is not to say that a director should operate on a shoot with a closed mind, impervious to any new thoughts or unexpected discoveries. It is exactly the opposite: only if the day's filming is well prepared and well thought out, will it be possible to take full advantage of the unforeseen eventuality. A director flying by the seat of his pants is likely to be blinkered and unobservant as he struggles to work out what to do next. A film-maker who knows exactly what are the likely consequences of changing her plans will be much more able to respond to serendipity.

Preparation for filming means conceiving of a schedule for the day, allowing for setting-up time, preparing time, lighting time, shooting time, wrapping-up time and, possibly, time for travelling to the next location. Unless the film-maker is working alone and shooting the material him or herself, making best use of the day means taking account of the fact that while some of the tasks can only happen in sequence, one after another, there are things which can be going on in parallel. One cannot shoot before setting up the lights, nor record before the microphone has been connected. But a documentarist can spend necessary time with an interviewee while the camera and microphone are being put in place.

Developing the schedule for a shooting day involves changing the mental focus brought to bear on the enterprise from the images and sounds that the film-maker hopes to capture, to the process of capturing them. Clearly an accurate estimate of how long each set-up will take depends on the film-maker's experience of the shooting process itself—shooting, that is, to accomplish a particular result—as well as having an idea of the kind of team which will be engaged in the task. With experience will come the recognition that one particular kind of image—perhaps needing elaborate choreography to get a number of different actions to happen on the screen at the same time—is likely to need many retakes, with a lot of resetting required to get ready for the next attempt. Another kind of shot—maybe a series of hand-held close-ups among a crowd—should be relatively easy and quick to realize. Yet another—possibly an intimate interview with a sensitive contributor—can only be tried once, though it may take much of the day to prepare for.

One useful way to reckon the timing of a filming set-up, as well as to make oneself fully prepared for the shooting day, is to conduct an imaginary rehearsal of the entire sequence of events from start to finish. Rather than dismissing any task with the thought that it should only take a minute or two, it is worth stepping right through it, carrying it out in full—foreshortened in the mind of course: it doesn't have to be done in real time. A mental run-through will help give an idea of how long each stage is likely to take. And having made the estimate, experience says: double it.

If the documentarist is not working alone, the technical requirements of the shoot and of the time needed for it will be most accurately assessed by the film photographer, the director of photography, who is effectively the leader of the technical crew. The best assurance of success in the shooting enterprise is to go with the photographer and, if at all possible, the sound recordist, on a preliminary survey visit, a recce, of the location. Sometimes, if an extremely complex and large lighting set-up is necessary, it is important to take the film lighting electrician along too. If it can be managed, the recce should include previewing any events which are to be shot or recorded. Of course, there are many events which only take place only the once and the crew will have to depend on description and prediction. But many are regularly repeated, rush hour at a railway station, for example. In some cases a useful equivalent can be found. If the documentary is to contain footage of a school play or concert, for instance, the recce could be done during the dress rehearsal.

On the recce the film-maker, in the rôle now of director, will suggest the shots that the film will need and the crew members will investigate how these results can best be achieved. Sometimes compromises will have be struck between what is ideal and what is feasible. Sometimes a last-minute decision may have to be made about cost. The electrician, for example, may find that the amount of light the photographer needs in order to realize the director's idea, cannot be powered from available sources and that a generator vehicle would be essential. At other times, the crew may suggest possibilities that the documentarist may have missed, or dismissed—an unusual angle, perhaps, or a simple way to achieve what the director had believed to be impossible. On occasion, crew members may pick up a detail that will affect the time of the shooting. The photographer may realize that a shot will only work with the sun at a particular position in the sky, the sound recordist may be the only one aware of the time the demolition crew on the next block breaks for tea. More mundane, practical details will also be noted, parking facilities for the crew's vehicles, for example, or the distance to the nearest pub for lunch.

Quite separate from the recce with the crew is the preparation of contributors to the film. All will have to know what their involvement entails, not only such details as what time to be where and for how long they will be needed, but also the nature of their contribution to the film. As previously mentioned, in TV journalism, particularly investigative journalism, contributors and interviewees are often kept in the dark about the use which will be made of their contribution. But in documentary film making, even with a political subject, it is counterproductive to hide the aims of the film from an interviewee, thus rejecting a possible source of interesting ideas. When a documentarist engages the contributors' commitment and understanding, they are likely to give more and better of themselves. They may also make helpful suggestions which improve the end result. After all, they know themselves best, and will often suggest details of their life of which the film-maker was unaware, but images of which would greatly contribute to the overall effect of the sequence.

The recce is the last opportunity the director will have for putting the final touches to the treatment or shooting script—even if these are only ever kept in the head rather than on paper. Visiting the location may well have brought new thoughts to mind, revealed further discoveries. These may affect not just the particular sequence under consideration, but possibly also the overall shape of the documentary. A key sequence at the beginning of the film, theoretically simple to shoot, which sets up an important element of the story, may turn out, even at this late stage, to be unexpectedly unachievable.

Chapter 16

The Shoot

Eventually the thinking must end and the doing begin. The preparation is over, complete or not, and now comes the actual shooting. The person in overall charge, both artistically and managerially, is the director. The director may sometimes also be the photographer—a number of well known film-makers always shoot their own material, but this works best on observational documentaries where the main task is to capture the world as it goes by. In other circumstances, where the world has to be stopped to have its picture taken, the two jobs of director and photographer are more often than not done by two separate people.

There are only two jobs. There is no room for a third. In many productions, particularly those commissioned by large production companies or broadcasting organisations, the producer of a documentary may not be the director of the shoot. Under these circumstances, the producer may wish to attend the filming. If so, it is the producer's obligation not to tangle the lines of communication and divide the leadership of the team by chipping in with instructions. When this happens, everyone gets confused and angry, not knowing whether to listen to the director or the producer. It is not unheard of for a director to walk out and leave the location under such circumstances, an action which has been regarded—at least by other film-makers—as justified. It has also been known for the photographer to refuse to continue work until producer and director decide which is to be in charge. Of course, particularly if there is a lot at stake, the producer may equally have the contractual right to send the director packing and take over the reins. None of these outcomes will improve the quality of the work. The proper course of action is for the producer to give notes to the director, who will then convey any necessary instructions to the person concerned.

If preparing for a shoot is a bit like organising a military campaign, directing the shoot itself is like a cross between managing a football team and conducting an orchestra. Neither manager nor conductor play. The director shoots no images, records no sounds, does not appear in front of the camera. Like the football manager, the director of a shoot is responsible for running the enterprise from the smallest detail to the overall strategy. At the same time, like the orchestral conductor, the director's success is judged not by the excellence of the administration, but by the artistry of the result. This artistry is the product of the director's vision, which must be transmitted to everyone at the location, the director's enthusiasm, with which everyone present must be infected, and the director's perfectionism, which must be coaxed, cajoled, or commandeered out of those who are actually doing the work.

There may be times, especially while shooting an ongoing event, when the director may feel that he or she is contributing so little, that the photographer is having to make so many of the decisions, that the value of being on location at all seems questionable. Though a natural feeling, this is an error. The director is the one with the vision of what is to be achieved and who will follow the work through after the filming. The photographer can respond only to the here and now. If the filming can take place successfully and the desired result can be achieved without the director's constant intervention, it is merely a tribute to the degree to which the team has been persuaded to share the director's vision, enthusiasm and perfectionism—as well as the luck of having nothing go wrong, having nothing unexpectedly change, and having nothing new turn up out of the blue.

The director is the one who carries the movie in his or her head, calling for and controlling the shots which will fit together, jigsaw-puzzle fashion, into the imagined sequences. This is a continuous and mentally quite strenuous process which never stops from first arrival on location to the wrapping up at the end: fitting the shots into the puzzle as they are achieved, changing the puzzle-picture to allow for pieces which don't turn out exactly the right shape, adding new pieces and removing others in response to the picture's changes. By carrying a mental image of the sequence, part filled in, part blank, the director will know from looking at it at any stage what has been achieved and what remains to be done.

Some film-makers protest that when they arrive on location they truly do not know what is going to happen. In pure observational work this may sometimes be true, war film photography would be an example—though those who shoot fighting footage usually know perfectly well what they are looking for. In other cases the director who says 'I never know what the next shot is going to be' is a director who is depending on luck and chance to make the film. It is not a very good bet.

The director is also the only person working on the shoot who is able to see the job from every angle. So that other members of the team can concentrate on their own tasks exclusively, the director must help to balance the needs and wishes of all the craft workers and contributors. A wise director will make sure that the preferences of someone being filmed are allowed for as far as possible without detriment to the image, that the quality of the sound is not compromised by the needs of the picture or vice versa, that all members of the team feel that their particular speciality is being taken account of. Maintaining the corresponding level of respect and authority will cost the director an effort. It requires the director to be the first to arrive at the location, the first to have an answer to every question, the first to give a response to every problem. It obliges the director to listen to every difficulty and suggestion and to respond to them all seriously and with care. It means that the director really must have complete mastery of the shooting day's events and that he or she communicates the plan effectively to everyone working on the shoot.

The overall aim of the shooting day is to make it as easy as possible for all to do their jobs to the very highest standard. And, more importantly, for it to look that way on the screen. Problems of the filming process intruding into the shot material confuse the audience. Film, both for cinema and television, is an art-form in which the struggle of the artist for expression is not normally part of the content of the work—unless the struggle takes over and becomes the content. Documentaries have been made showing the fight of a film-maker or group to make a documentary about a person or institution which is opposed to the project and which puts every possible difficulty in the film-maker's path. It can make a good story, but is usually not what the documentarist set out to achieve.

A film is always, in a sense, a record of a performance—a performance as much by those behind the camera as by those on the screen. For a performance to be convincing, it must seem natural, even inevitable, as if it could be no other way. The audience must forget the sweaty pain-racked dancer and believe in the dying swan. The actual achievement of the performance should therefore seem to be effortless. As a performance art, the documentary film adheres to similar ideals.

The amount of effort by the film-makers shown on the screen will reflect the context of the narrative. A shot from a hand-held camera jostled by demonstrators may be a positive contribution to the film, adding realism by relating the image-taking process to the event being shown. A jerky panning shot, caused by the irrelevant and unexplained fact that the photographer had to balance on a narrow ledge to get it, is not. Most film-makers try to keep the intensity and difficulty of their efforts off the screen and to make the resulting images seem effortless and natural, agreeing with Gene Kelly's dictum: 'If the audience can see how hard you're working, then you ain't working hard enough.'

The shooting day

The start of the shooting day will usually involve a quick look over the location to make sure that nothing has changed since it was last seen. Contributors sometimes believe that they can help the filming by making surprise alterations at the last moment. Tactful intervention can sometimes rescue the situation, like the huge, awful and distracting painting which has suddenly materialised on the wall just behind the planned interviewing position. Sometimes the change is irreversible, as when the large colourful shrubs in the garden which were going to make such an attractive background to the shot have been cut hard back 'because they looked untidy'. Sometimes discretion is the better part of valour. Interviewing Prime Minister (now Lady) Thatcher, one director carefully placed a vase of flowers in the background, to help soften the PM's image. Mrs Thatcher asked to see the shot in the monitor and proceeded firmly to remove the set decoration herself.

If the filming team comprises more than director, photographer and sound recordist, many directors begin the day by bringing everyone together: contributors, crew, production, to allow those who have not met before to say hello, for each to understand the other's role, and to make sure that everyone knows the plan for the day and the aims of the filming. Only then does the real work begin.

Shooting will take place, shot by shot, throughout the day, with the director keeping the work going at a steady and methodical pace. At the very start of the day, the principal task is to bring everyone up to working speed as soon as possible; everyone always begins a new job relatively slowly. This is not best done by arbitrary command, but by letting everyone understand the director's schedule for the day from the start, and by ensuring that it has collective assent. It is important for the director to be seen to be in control of the time factor, both at the start as well as subsequently through the day. Ideally the director needs to keep in mind an internal representation of the day's progress, rather than to respond to events as they happen. It does not benefit the end product of the filming for the day to alternate between periods of lethargy and moments of panic. It may sometimes be hard to stimulate a tired team into renewed activity, but the attempt is preferable to the alternative: a mad rush to get shots in at the end.

Where the documentary is purely observational, a record of an ongoing event or situation, the film-maker's intervention in the shooting process may be minimal. Director and photographer may effectively be the same person. In other circumstances, a more formal style of filming may be called for. The director will propose the camera position, the style of shot, and the action to be filmed. The photographer will then set up the shot in consultation with the sound recordist and any other crew members involved.

It is important for the director to allow the photographer and the sound recordist enough time to do their work. Impatience is natural when there is a lot to do and limited time to do it in. But, in spite of the temptation, the situation is usually not improved by constant anxious enquiries and urgings to speed things up. As long as everyone knows and understands the constraints on the time available for filming, an occasional reminder of the passing of the minutes is all that should be needed. Even more importantly, a thoughtful director will not constantly change his or her mind, altering the set-up before it is complete. Film photographers say that they find the greatest difficulty in working with directors who are not sure what they want. Sometimes, of course, change is unavoidable, but such cases should be rare exceptions.

When the shot has been set up, the director will want to know exactly what it is going to look and sound like. Some directors, working with a crew they know well, leave the details of the shot to the photographer's and recordist's judgement. Others prefer to look through the camera and listen on the headphones themselves, before the shot begins. Now that separate video displays are available for both video and film cameras, some directors prefer to monitor the image themselves directly, though there is always the danger that depriving a craft worker of autonomy may be interpreted as devaluing that person's artistic contribution and may result in losing their motivation. One cameraman has said 'It's like having somebody else staring through your eyeballs.'

If the acoustic quality of the sound recording is crucial to the sequence, as it often is, most sound recordists are happy to let the director listen to the take itself on headphones. Many sound recordists feel undervalued during filming and ignored even afterwards. While the photography of a documentary often receives public critical acclaim, the quality of the sound recording almost never. This is perhaps a legacy of television's ultimate origins in the silent cinema. Whatever the reason, it is certainly in strong contrast to the other major medium of popular culture, the recording industry, where producers and recording engineers are recognised as important artists in their own right. Yet film sound recordists know that without the right high quality sound, many kinds of images are valueless. A wise director takes the trouble to make sure that the sound is as carefully crafted as the picture.

That means making an effort over microphone placement, particularly when working in stereo, as is now often the case, as stereo demands much more forethought about the way in which the shots are intended to be used.

Industry ritual is for the shot to be started by the director saying 'turn over' or its equivalent. When working with film, sound-vision synchronization is then established either with the traditional clapper board or with an electronic device. This records an identifiable moment which can subsequently be used to bring to the picture and sound into alignment. If a film shot must be started in a hurry, synchronization is often left to the end of the shot, where its unorthodox position is indicated to whoever will later do the synchronizing of sound and vision, by holding the clapper board upside down. This is known as an 'end board'—and is often forgotten in the heat of the moment by even the most experienced director who will find his call of 'cut' overridden by the photographer's call of 'end board.' Video requires no such marker as the sound and picture are recorded onto the same tape and the time relationship between them never changes. However, many directors find it useful to mark the beginning of each video shot with some kind of identification.

The director then waits for an indication that the camera and recorder are ready and running to speed—the photographer may call 'speed' or 'ready'—before giving the cue for the action to begin. At the beginning of the day there may well be a few false starts as one or other member of the team jumps the gun and starts before everything is ready.

While the shot is being taken, the director will keep a careful eye on exactly what is happening in front of the lens, making a mental note of any continuity details which may be needed later. Often another member of the team—an assistant director perhaps, or the production co-ordinator—may take responsibility for this task. Whoever does this job, it is an essential one. If, for instance, a contributor is handling a prop, there must be somebody whose job it is to be able to recall afterwards exactly which hand did what, so that any further shot which needs to match can be sure to do so. When working with a video camera, continuity notes are perhaps not quite as crucial, since it is technically possible to run the tape back and look at the previous take. This wastes time, however, and many video-photographers are reluctant to wind the tape back, firstly to minimize wear on the master tape, and secondly because of the danger of allowing ridges to form in the flat side of the tape roll, exposing the tape edge to the danger of transport damage and consequent image or sound degradation. Where the shot is part of an interview, the aim may be to shoot the interviewer's questions separately later, to simulate a two-camera set-up. In this case, careful note will also need to be taken of each question so that it can be repeated accurately later on.

If the filming is of an event or an unstoppable happening of some kind, at the same time as observing the current take, the director will also need to keep an eye open for what else is going on in the vicinity, so that the crew can quickly move on to the next shot. The photographer cannot be expected to know what is going on outside the limits of the camera viewfinder. Even under more relaxed circumstances, the director will constantly be alert to significant details in the scene—those details which can tell a whole story by themselves—for later use in building up the sequence. The aim is to avoid wasting time standing around while the director decides what the next shot is to be. The next shot should already be in the director's mind as the previous one finishes. However, the director must resist the temptation, however strong, to urge the photographer on to the next shot before the last one is completed.

It is not always the end of the shot when the camera stops running. It may also be necessary to record a minute or so of the location's sound atmosphere—free of action or dialogue. Such a track is usually needed in the editing process. The recording of an 'atmos' or 'buzz' track is often forgotten by directors but, luckily, most professional sound recordists will raise the issue themselves and ask for a minute's silence on the set.

At the end of the shot, the director, by tradition, will call 'cut' or 'end board'—ideally allowing at least ten seconds' pause between the end of the action and the shut-down of the camera. The camera and sound recorder will stop and the photographer and recordist will check their equipment. If shooting on film, the camera will also be checked for 'hairs in the gate'—black spider-like defects on the edge of the frame, sometimes moving sometimes stationary, which are not usually hairs at all, but tiny slivers of celluloid produced in the course of slitting large sheets into narrow 16mm or 35mm rolls of film. Such a blemish usually demands a retake.

The shot will then be logged. This may be done by the director or, more usually, by an assistant. On film, the shot and take number will be noted, with a précis of the shot's content. On video, the start and end time-codes will be included. Some film-makers who work only with video leave the shot listing until later. If delayed for too long—until the return to base from a foreign filming trip, for instance—this has the great disadvantage that important details, even the name of a contributor perhaps, may have been forgotten. If the shot listing is not done at the time of shooting, it is preferable to catch up with the work at the end of the shooting day, when events are still fresh in the mind. This necessarily involves replaying and viewing the shot material from the master tape, perhaps even through the camera, with all the drawbacks previously noted. It also considerably extends the working day for whoever is doing the logging as the only way to carry out the task properly is to run the video in real time. In general it is quicker and easier to make the record at the time of shooting.

Every shot will then be given a quick post-mortem—how was it for you?—from the photographer, the sound recordist and the contributors. The director will then decide whether to go for another take or accept the shot as it is. Many things can go wrong in taking a shot: there can be equipment problems, operational difficulties. Even if the shot is technically perfect, there can be failures in the content: something that was supposed to happen didn't or something that was not supposed to happen did. The important thing is now to work out exactly why the shot didn't work. Sometimes simply trying again will be enough to achieve what is wanted. Sometimes it may be necessary to change some of the parameters: the camera position perhaps, or the exact action required.

There is no point in plugging on bone-headedly with an impossible task. But equally, some shots do need three or four attempts before all the elements come together perfectly. When working with a presenter, it is not uncommon for a retake to be demanded to perfect some bit of action, or even to get the words out right without stumbling or forgetting. Some presenters are very quick at grasping what is needed of them and managing a perfect performance from the very first attempt. Others—and they include some household names—need a great deal longer. It has been known for one very experienced, very well-known presenter to need twenty-eight takes before words and actions all flow smoothly.

It goes without saying that most critical comments should be communicated by taking members of the team aside, rather than publicly announcing them. Directors' notes to members of the technical team may often be given to the photographer, as leader of the film crew, rather than directly the individual concerned. Though it seems an inappropriately military metaphor for a peaceful enterprise like filming, many documentarists find that maintaining a 'chain of command' in a larger team can help the smoothness and effectiveness of the operation.

At the end of the shooting day, the creative part of the work over, the director reverts to the role of manager once again. Though it may be tempting to rush off immediately and relax after the continuous strain of the day, there are still a number of important jobs to be done.

Firstly written permission should be obtained from all those who have been filmed that the shot footage may be used by the programme maker for public showing. This is confirmation of what would otherwise be a purely verbal agreement, which must be in place for filming to happen at all, and helps to protect the film-maker from contributors who decide, late in the day, that they do not wish their contribution to be used. Naturally, at this stage it is impossible to tell precisely which contributors will be included in the finished work, so permissions should be sought from everyone who has featured in any significant way in the filming. The law is changing constantly, particularly in Europe, and there is a question over the extent to which people can claim the copyright in their own appearance. In theory it might be possible in some parts of the world for someone filmed coincidentally in the street to claim that using the shot is an infringement of copyright. But it is not reasonable to try to get permission from everyone present in a crowd scene, for example, so film-makers usually restrict themselves to the main players.

The permission is in the form of a short document: a 'release form' otherwise known in Britain as a 'blood chit'. This gives the name and address of the contributor, the date and time of filming, the name of the produce or director and the working title of the film, and includes a declaration that the signatory agrees to the use of the shot footage for the purposes of documentary making. In some countries, the USA for example, a nominal sum of money has to change hands before the document has legal validity.

The next task is to make sure that the shot material is properly packaged up and prepared for sending to the right destination. If the shooting has been on film, this means arranging for the exposed footage to be sent to the laboratory for processing, with whatever special instructions are necessary for its treatment. For example, in difficult, low light conditions, film is sometimes shot knowingly underexposed with the aim of forcing it to a higher speed in the course of development. If this has been done, the rolls of exposed film will need to be carefully sorted with clear instructions to the laboratory included in each can. If shooting on tape, it may first be necessary to send the cassettes for duplication, viewing copies with visible time-code may have to be made from the master material, as may sound cassettes, if interviews or other sections of dialogue are to be transcribed.

Over and above these administrative details, however, there is the management task of bringing the filming enterprise to a satisfying end. This needs the same care and concern for the collectivity of the team as at the beginning of shooting. Like with a golf drive, or a tennis service, the conclusion of the stroke, the follow-through, is nearly as important as the preparation, as it exerts its influence back in time to affect the memory of the action itself as well as forward to affect the next occasion. The filming day may well have been an emotional as well as a physical strain on everyone concerned. There may well have been a great deal of pressure on all the participants. Tempers may have become frayed, antagonisms ever less carefully hidden. The director's task now is to bring everyone down to an emotional even keel as gently as possible.

This is not just a matter of thanking everyone for their contribution, though most directors would be unhappy to let the day end without expressing their appreciation of everyone's effort and skill. Nor is the end of the filming day a suitable occasion for an extensive post-mortem, even less for a barrage of recrimination. But it is worth looking to see whether any immediate lessons have been learned in the course of the work, both about technical matters and personal style. This consideration applies as much to the director's performance as to the contribution of the technical crew. If there are things about the director's style that makes it difficult to achieve the best results, it is as well for him or her to know it.

This is not just a philanthropic requirement, a gesture of goodwill to the workers. If the filming is to continue with the same team on the following day, the benefit of leaving the group with a positive attitude is obvious. Even if this is the last day, or perhaps the only one, there are good reasons for trying to bring the work to a close in a satisfactory way. The film-maker may have occasion to work with the same crew at another time in the future. Even if not, the television industry being relatively small and certainly incestuous, personal gossip is rife and reputations, justified or not, spread rapidly. Just as most film photographers would probably wish to be thought of as fast, stylish and co-operative, so would most documentary directors most likely hope to be considered efficient, pleasant and fulfilling to work with.

Section C
Post-production

Chapter 17

Editing

There is a major divide between the film making process so far—the pre-production and the production, the gathering of information, knowledge and understanding, the filming of locations and people—and the post-production, the stage which now begins. In collecting together the material needed to make the documentary, the concentration has been on the exterior world of reality, as well as on the documentary maker's interior world of the imagination. The documentarist has dreamed a film and has gathered its components. Post-production begins a completely new stage of the enterprise, with a completely new approach to the work. From now on the film will, in a sense, be made all over again from the beginning.

The second time the documentary is made, it will be in a different way, with a different approach, using different criteria. The preceding stages have put an emphasis on invention and innovation; the documentarist has been encouraged to imagine the impossible and then to try and achieve it. To this end, the efforts of many people have been contributing to the work, researchers, photographers, sound recordists, contributors, consultants. All have been putting in ideas, suggesting novel approaches. The concept will have grown from small beginnings—the basic notion—to an elaborate constructions of ideas, images and sounds.

All this has now been condensed into a pile of film cans or video cassettes. For this second film-making, that pile is the material that is to be worked with, nothing else. The possibilities are no longer endless. The resources are limited to what is in those film cans or on those videotapes. The project changes from an imaginative open-ended dream into a concrete, closed intellectual exercise: we have a collections of images and sounds—our job is to make the best documentary possible from them.

The task is more like putting together a model out of Meccano, with a limited number of pieces which can only be assembled in certain ways due to their individual design and construction. It is no good dreaming of building a replica of the Forth Bridge, when all you have is twenty slotted strips, four angled corner pieces and half-a-dozen assorted cogwheels. Yet the different permutations of the pieces, the number of ways in which the materials which are at hand can be put together, the number of different models which can be built from them, is still dauntingly large. The trick with Meccano pieces is to work out what is the very best, the most elegant, working model which can be assembled from them. The task when editing is to discover the very best film—one or perhaps more than one—which is concealed in the material, ready to be brought out in the editing process.

To approach the task of editing in this way, the documentarist must cultivate forgetfulness. The director must ignore the story which lies behind every shot, the difficulty of getting it, the cost of setting it up, the funny incident associated with it. None of these factors are relevant now. In fact, remembering them can prove positively detrimental to the assembly of the film. The only questions that count now are: what does the shot show, how does it look, how does it start and end. In short, does it work? No matter if the expedition to capture the view from the top of the mountain took three days and cost half the budget. If the shot wobbles all over the place, or does not reveal what it was intended to, then it will not be used. No matter if the contributor is a living witness to the events that led the Honourable Elijah Mahomed to found the Nation of Islam, if he can't keep his false teeth in his mouth without holding them there with his fingers as he speaks, his interview will not be included. Editing is a stern business, best approached with a cold eye.

There will be content faults, and defects will be discovered in the realization of the material. These may be physical or they may be functional. The main centre of interest in the image, or even the whole image, may be out of focus; or the focus may change over time, never resting for long enough with any of the elements of the picture. The lighting may be uneven, under-lit or over-lit, significant parts of the image falling to opaque black, or areas burnt out to whiteness.. The framing may be bad, with the edge cutting off an important feature just in the wrong place; or—proverbial error this, but it does happen—with an object appearing to grow out of somebody's head or, better yet, a chandelier in the background giving a male cabinet minister a pair of elaborate crystal ear-rings. Movement may be uneven and jerky; or the camera may never rest in one place long enough for there to be a stable beginning and end to the shot.

Shots which are in themselves unblemished may look quite wrong when joined together. Two panning shots intended to cut together are found to have been filmed at different speeds; a pair of matching shots of a conversation turn out not to match; in close-up, a character handles an object with the right hand, in a wider shot with the left; a minor but noticeable change of costume makes it impossible to chequerboard two shots into a single sequence.

Conversely there may also be unexpected blessings. A character who will later prove to be important in the narrative, happens by chance to have been caught strolling across a wide shot of the location; an interviewee makes an unexpectedly revealing gesture; a spot of bright colour at the end of one shot matches perfectly in both hue and position the patch of bright colour at the start of the next; a lens flare from the sun mimics a halo over the head of the open-air preacher.

Such pluses and minuses in the shooting will be the controlling factors in making the film for the second time. The originally envisaged film will have to be subtly or not so subtly, changed. This does not, of course, invalidate all the effort the documentarist has put into its pre-production, the devising of the story, the writing of treatments and scripts, the painstaking selection of the contributors. Nor does it devalue the hard work of production, tenaciously sticking to the task until the required shots are achieved. In fact it underlines the importance of all the preceding work. For only by meticulous preparation and single-minded execution can the documentary maker be in any way hopeful that the pile of rushes now awaiting attention in the editing room contains the film he or she intends to assemble—that film and that film only. The whole aim of the director's work is to shoot material in so tightly controlled a fashion, in a manner so carefully related to the subject, that it demands to be assembled in only the one way. Of course no directors ever achieve one hundred per cent of their aims. But only by pitching for one hundred and fifty per cent, is there any likelihood of actually scoring in the high eighties.

The editor

Just as the director may also take the role of cine-photographer when shooting, so the documentarist may also be the editor of the film. The advantages are clear: direct control over the work, no arguments about intentions or realization, no time wasted in having to explain what is in the director's mind, in having to persuade another person that the proposal is the best idea on offer. There are indeed documentary makers who act as complete one-man bands, entirely independent of anyone else, undertaking all the necessary tasks—research, shooting, editing—from the beginning of the project to its end. But such solo artists remain few. The disadvantage is apparent. It is that no other sensibility is available to contribute to the enterprise: no other point of view, no other source of ideas, no other angle or handle on the subject, no other style or creative approach. Whether this limitation is damaging or not depends on the genius of the film-maker. In some cases it gives the work a continuity and unity of vision which raises the result high above the quality level of the average. In other cases it can prove damaging. Composers are not always the best conductors of their own music, playwrights not necessarily the best stagers of their own dramas. Sometimes a new eye sees things the creator didn't know were there. So directors are not inevitably the best editors of their own shot material—they are too close and too involved with the memory of the reality and what they meant to shoot, when all there is to make the film with is what appears starkly in the frames.

At their best, editors edit in two senses of the word: they edit the material physically of course. But they also act as editors in the literary sense: as a second pair of eyes to judge and constructively criticize the work as it develops. And just as even the most successful and able of writers can benefit from the opinions and suggestions of a publisher's editor, so can a documentary maker's work be improved by the contributions of a sensitive and supportive film or video editor.

The relations between a director and an editor are those of a partnership. In the inevitable arguments both need to have their say and listen to the other's opinion. The first thing some editors give a director on the first day of working together is an invitation to: 'go away and let me watch the rushes, and then *I* will tell *you* what the film is that you have shot.' Some directors stand over the editor's shoulder throughout, giving instructions on which shot to cut to which other, and where to cut it. Neither makes for the best documentary at the end. Directors are often reluctant to give up a cherished sequence even long after it is obvious that it won't work as imagined. Editors are often tempted to believe, and sometimes openly make clear to anyone who will listen, that they could have shot the film much better than the director has. But though some film-makers routinely edit their own work with great success, most others would do better to accept an experienced editor's judgement of what works and does not. And though there are a number of examples of film editors leaving the cutting room and becoming well respected documentary makers in their own right, most are professionally in the habit of working alone with only the footage to argue back, and often turn out to be temperamentally unsuited to dealing with imperfect human beings and to accepting the difficulties and compromises which are inevitable when interacting with the real world.

There are occasions when an editor's fresh and uninvolved point of view can be very welcome. Filming is an uncertain business, and it is not rare for a documentarist to enter the cutting room in the depths of despair at the failure of the shooting to capture anything like what was originally intended. Many editors will recall times when they have been able to console the director: 'It may not be possible to make the film you originally wanted, but there is another film in this material which may be as interesting and as valid, perhaps even more so, than the documentary you set out to make.'

Editing technologies

Three technologies are currently in use for editing television documentaries. They belong, roughly, to the past, the present and the future.

The past belonged to 16mm film: prints of the shots culled from the rushes, viewed on an industrial machine, physically cut, put in order and stuck together with joining tape, the sound on magnetic track, edited separately from but in parallel with the picture. The present belongs—just—to off-line videotape editing: sections of shots from time-coded video-cassettes transferred from the master recordings, copied in sequence onto a programme tape using cheap and cheerful electro-mechanical equipment, the sound edited together with the vision. The future will belong to virtual editing: vision and sound, separate but linked, converted to binary codes, manipulated with total freedom and great ease within the electronic memory of a computer system.

The sheer physicality of 16mm film editing its both its greatest advantage as well as its greatest drawback. For many editors who developed their skills on 16mm film, nothing can replace being able to pick up a piece of film, look at the frames against the light, judge the running time from the length in the hands, even the ritual movements of the film joiner giving a feeling of pleasurable satisfaction. Yet the inconvenience of the medium is considerable. It generates a large number of physical clips of every possible length from long sections to individual frames—the trims—which must be carefully preserved and filed; keeping the sound and the picture synchronized is a constant headache; after frequent making and remaking, the physical joins tend to come unstuck. Much time is spent looking for lost trims, trying to discover exactly where the sound goes out of synch, remaking cuts when they fall apart. Many hours are spent spooling backwards and forwards through rolls of film looking for particular images, and then rewinding them afterwards. No kind of junction other than the direct cut can be previewed. But editing on film is extremely flexible, since there is no restriction on the kinds of edit which can be made, and sections of the assembled footage can be removed from anywhere and inserted anywhere else.

Off-line video editing was never more than a stop-gap technique, devised as a cheap imitation of the high-tech means used to edit television studio recordings but using consumer quality videotape recorders and players, usually VHS. The assembly is built up by recording shots from the rushes tapes one after another onto the programme tape. Off-line editing is a self-contained operation which, unlike film, does not need extensive filing and storage facilities; only the cassette copies of the master tapes and the programme cassette itself are needed. But the disadvantages are many. Off-line edit controllers are usually not accurate to the frame. Sections cannot be removed or inserted without remaking the whole assembly from the editing point to the end. To overcome the difficulty, assembled material may have to be copied and recopied up to many generations from the original, becoming, in the end, almost completely indecipherable on the screen. The treatment of the sound is a particular problem as edits can only be identified by the picture. Should sound and vision not cut at the same place, no record of the exact location of the sound edit remains. However, because of its extremely low cost, convenience and general availability, as well as a simplicity of use that requires little experience, off-line editing has been and still is, at the time of writing, the most common technique in use for video documentary making.

It is certain that virtual, or 'non-linear', editing will soon replace the off-line editing of video altogether, as it is already supplanting the physical editing of 16mm film. The development of affordable virtual editing equipment has had to wait until recently for computer power and memory storage capacity to become sufficiently inexpensive. This is now already the case, and costs are still falling steeply; it is hard to guess how low they will fall in the end. By transferring everything from the master material, film or tape, to the virtual memory inside a computer, all the convenience and economy of electronics are added to the flexibility and intuitiveness of physically editing on film. Editing is, of course, accurate to the frame. All possible varieties of picture and sound junctions, cuts, fades, dissolves, wipes, superimpositions, can be previewed and instantly changed if necessary. However many times the cutting order is altered or shots put in and taken out, there can be no damage to the source material in the computer, as all editing is non-destructive; that is, the original shots remain untouched, only a listing of the order in which sections are to be played back is changed. The editing and mixing of the sound is carried out on the same machine and with the same flexibility as the editing of the picture.

When using the virtual editing equipment currently most commonly available, the final production of the programme master is done separately by a technique called conforming. The appropriate sections of the camera cassettes are copied to the required position on the final master tape in a process automatically controlled through an edit decision list (EDL) compiled by the virtual editing system. This is also likely to be an interim solution. The next stage is already in sight. When storage costs have plummeted still further and when techniques of compressing the picture information in the computer's memory have become even more sophisticated than at present, the material will be stored, not as now in a somewhat simplified, low-definition form, but at full broadcast quality. As a result the virtual editing computer will itself be able to export the entire final film and sound to a mastering video recorder. The whole process, linking the camera-shot cassettes to the final master tape, will take place inside a single piece of equipment.

These developments will certainly affect the ways in which editing is carried out. It remains debatable whether they will strongly influence the appearance of the documentaries which are editing's end result. This is an art which depends far more on an intuitive understanding of human perception and on sensitivity to the viewer's response to the material, rather than to the technical possibilities inherent in the means at hand. If anything, simplifying the process can enhance the quality of the product. While trendy styles and flashy tricks will no doubt be taken up by some just because they were never before possible, all-electronic editing is in the end more likely to relieve film-makers of their concern with the technicalities of the process, and direct their concentration instead on the problems of the film making itself. Such a development can only be an advantage.

Viewing the rushes

The first job in editing is to view the rushes. The director may well have already seen them before. In the past, film rushes, returned from overnight processing, were regularly viewed without sound on the morning after the shoot. Video has quickly outdated this tradition, though the director may have had to go through the material in order to compile a shot list.

Even if the footage has been seen before, viewing the rushes at the start of the edit is undertaken in a different spirit. The aim is to get the measure of the material and come to some overall feeling about the potential of the finished documentary. As the shots unfold, the director and editor will be making notes about what they see, *aides memoires* to help them recall particular moments later on in the process when they may be needed. It is surprising what will be remembered later of this great swathe of material. Presumably it is because film-makers are visually oriented that our memory for images and sequences of images is so strong.

By the end of the viewing, both editor and director will have an overall view of what material is available to make their documentary with. They will have an idea of the strengths of the material as well as its weaknesses. They will know the parts which are likely to be hard to make work and the parts which should fall easily into place. They will have recognized the shots and scenes needed to bring out the theme, the thread of the production.

The rough cut

Now the construction can begin. The target of the first stage is the rough cut, an approximate assembly of shots and sequences into the envisaged order and, the film-maker hopes, at roughly the projected length. There will be passages which are missing—a graphics sequence or two, perhaps, or some long awaited archive material—and there will probably be many awkward places and junctions which don't work. But at this early stage, as with a painter's first rough under-drawing, the initial am is to create no more than a framework, a first view of the shape of the whole.

The rough cut may be delineated by discussion and mutual agreement between director and editor. More often, the director initially takes the lead and provides the editor with a suggested cutting order, a list on paper of shots and sequences and the order in which it is proposed that they go together. This cutting order is not to be thought of as engraved on stone; editors will often find it necessary to make changes when converting fine theory into messy practice, particularly where the director's cutting list is derived from notes on paper rather than directly from images on the screen. In any case, a cutting order is generally only the opening move, a place to start, a suggestion to get the work going. It is put forward in full expectation that a response will come from the material itself, which frequently makes its own demands on the way it is to be assembled.

The assembly doesn't have to start at the beginning, go on unto the end and then stop. In fact, it is often helps to work in a different order. Many film-makers and editors begin with the key scenes, the formative sequences, the passages which give the film its structure and its high points, like peaks standing among plains giving shape to a landscape, or perhaps like the principal gemstones in a piece of jewellery around which the setting will later be constructed.

The nature of the key scenes will be different in different kinds of documentary work. Where observation of the world is the major motive, the key sequences are likely to be those on which the dramatic narrative hinges. Where a documentary is built around an idea, the key scenes may be those through which the argument moves forward. Where the retelling of history is the principal aim, the key scenes may be the testimony of outstanding witnesses. The key scenes may not necessarily work as designed on paper. The material may have to be manipulated in ways not entirely foreseen in the shooting. But at this stage it is not necessary to perfect any of the sequences. All that is needed is sufficient assurance that, perhaps with some further effort, the key moments in the documentary will do the job they were intended for.

By first constructing a framework from the key scenes, the film-makers, director and editor, will be able to evaluate the flow of the film and the test the balance between the different elements. They will be able to tell whether the order and position of the scenes is appropriate to their content and their function. Moreover they will know where scenes will need to be prepared for by including extra material before they begin, and where sequences will need conclusions to be drawn out or need tensions to be relaxed by adding further footage afterwards.

With the key scenes in place, and the flow of images and ideas thus determined, the matrix in which they are set can now be filled in piece by piece. As with the key scenes, there may be secondary sequences or linking shots which don't do what they were intended to. The editor and director will work on them, trying different ways of using them, changing them where necessary, until they fulfil their task: carrying the film's narrative thread from what went before to what comes after.

The key scenes together with the secondary sequences now for the first time make up a complete film: the rough cut, which can be watched and analysed in its entirety. At this stage, the sound will be for the most part that which was recorded with the vision, though there may already be some passages in which synchronous dialogue from one scene is laid over the images of another. Sequences to be accompanied by music are also frequently envisaged early on, the music thought of as a support for, or replacement of, the footage's synchronous sound.

Most documentary makers do not rely on a commentary to make the flow of scenes in the rough cut work. Commentary is an easy a way to avoid confronting problems in the film which are better faced up to and solved. When the scenes in a documentary story have been knitted together well enough not to need verbal explanation, any commentary recorded later can be devoted to its proper task: adding what the images can't show, rather than lamely having to explain the meaning of the pictures.

The rough cut will usually be rather longer than is intended for the completed documentary. In part this will be because the transitions and junctions have not yet been worked on and fully perfected, but also because at this stage most material which is in any way relevant will have been included. Sometimes the length will be as much as half as long again as the target duration. Most film-makers would agree that at this stage it is far better to have too much in the assembly, which can later be pared down to only the most successful and most essential scenes, rather than too little, in which case the work may have to be inflated by a number of at best flawed, and at worst irrelevant, sequences.

Like all artistic constructions, documentary films have a natural length, determined by their content and the manner of their realization. But only if the documentarist is totally independent will he or she have the luxury of working to a length dictated solely by the material. Broadcasting institutions work with rigid time slots, designed to permit simultaneous junctions between programmes on different channels, and allow little leeway on either side of the commissioned length. Even private commissions will usually dictate a particular length for the production, related to the purposes for which it is to be used, though a minute or two either way will mostly not be a problem. This target duration will have been in the film-maker's sights from the very start of the project, and will have been borne in mind throughout the research, the development and the shooting. But the uncertainties of filming can make the target hard to hit. Only at this rough-cut stage will the documentarist know for sure how hard it will be to edit the film as shot to a length which coincides with the demands of the commissioning organization. If there is going to be a difficulty with the length, it is best to recognize it now, while a plea to the client for clemency is still possible, or more likely while a radical rethink of the documentary's structure is still—just—manageable.

The rough cut will give the film-makers not only an idea of the length of the completed work, but also a first sight of the film's overall significance and its message. As with other artistic constructions, the whole of a documentary is often greater than— or at least different from—the sum of its parts. Up to the point at which an analogue of the film has been assembled, no matter how roughly, the film-makers have just been working with individual pieces. Now they have an opportunity to look at the work as a whole. Surprise at what they find is not uncommon. The ideas in the mind of the documentarist, when mediated through the appearance of people, events and locations, may turn out to be quite other than expected. Synergy between the different characters who appear on the screen, between the associations, implications and suggestions of different scenes, when seen as now 'in the round', sometimes creates an entirely new and unexpected meaning.

This can be difficult for a film-maker, who may be tempted to manipulate and massage the material until it conforms more closely to some originally envisaged pattern. But such disloyalty to the shot footage is more likely to damage a documentary's integrity than to improve its quality. Documentarists must sometimes simply grit their teeth and follow the dictates of the material, just like the novelist whose characters escape from their predetermined fate and take on a life of their own. Sometimes, the choice is hard. There can be difficulties if the work has been commissioned for a particular purpose by a particular organization. A critical look at management style may not go down too well when rousing encouragement of the workers was ordered—though it was the poisoned relations in the factory which turned the attempt at encouragement into a critique. In such cases it may not be up to the film-maker to decide whether contractual liability or artistic integrity should have priority.

Mostly the disappointments will be more personal: the film-maker set out to depict a certain man as a hero, the documentary turns out to portray him in a less than flattering light; the film-maker intended to tell the story through the eyes and thoughts of one particular woman, the documentary proves to direct the viewer's attention towards a different woman altogether; the film-maker aimed to fill in the background to a particular scientific development, the documentary reveals an imminent ecological disaster.

Yet, in keeping with the doctrine of cultivating film-maker's forgetfulness, the documentarist's original intention belongs to history. A film has been brought to the rough cut stage and now the task becomes one of making sure that the completed work is not only as effective, economical and elegant but also as true to itself as possible.

The fine cut

The completion of the visual side of the documentary is achieved in the fine cut. Decisions over the precise length of the shots, the definitive position of the dissolves, the exact places to cut, have been postponed in the interests of building a complete film structure. Having reviewed the rough cut and made any needed alterations—sometimes trying things in a number of different ways—now is the turn for the finer judgements to be made. In the process, every detail of the documentary will be examined and as far as possible perfected and polished. The aim is to create a flow of images with no gaps, no glitches, no infelicities, the shots trimmed to the right length, the sequences built up to the proper emphasis, the sections shaped to their appropriate value. This is work for an editor rather than a director. The concern will no longer be with the content or overall meaning and shape of the film but only with its technical surface features. If director and editor are the same person, from now on he or she will have to forget being the former and concentrate solely on being the latter, avoiding the temptation to keep tinkering with the content and concentrating on the presentation alone.

The fine cut operates principally on the visual elements of the film. At the end of the rough cut stage, picture and sound begin to go their own ways. Though they can never be considered entirely in isolation from each other, the two require rather different treatment as their technical needs relate to the special characteristics of their particular medium. The fine cut both specifies and puts into effect the final pattern of the images. It also specifies the sound, but postpones its physical assembly to a further stage.

Every cut will be considered. If it is to be an action cut, the question is: does the action flow smoothly and continuously across it, both without a hint of a jump from one position to the next and with no suggestion of either repeated action or a tendency to stall at the moment of change of image? Does the centre of interest have the same screen position in both outgoing and incoming shots, so that the viewer's eye is not required to move between the two? Moving the position of the cut can mean choosing a different frame at which to leave the outgoing shot or selecting a different frame at which to join the incoming shot, or both together. The judgement will be made by running backwards and forwards across the cut, perhaps moving the position a frame at a time, until the junction has been rendered as near to perfect as can be achieved—perfection in this context meaning that the cut is effectively unnoticeable and invisible to the innocent eye.

If the cut marks the end of one scene and the beginning of

another, the editor will make sure that the moment of leaving the outgoing shot gives the right feel of finality, of action completed, of business concluded, while the incoming shot will be timed clearly to imply the start of something new. When making such non-continuity cuts, from one scene to another for example, the editor will ensure that there is enough time available at the commencement of the incoming shot for the viewer's eye to search the screen and identify a new focus of interest. Quite a few frames can effectively be lost to sight in this way and the editor will wish to ensure that nothing essential is missed by kicking off with the action too soon.

Dissolves will also be carefully timed, both for their length and their position. Here the technology being used for the editing makes a great difference, for only with the computer-based virtual editing technique will it be possible to preview the mixes and judge their effect. If editing on 16mm film, the dissolve is represented by a cut, with a diagonal wax-pencil mark made on the film itself on either side. As the marks move through the mechanism they appear to sweep across the screen. This gives the editor at least a symbolic representation of the dissolve effect. Off-line video editing has no way of simulating a dissolve.

Just as with a straight cut, any action that continues across a dissolve should maintain its speed, flow—and usually direction too—as smoothly as possible. By moving the centre point of the dissolve, the editor will try to ensure that location of the focus of interest on the screen coincides in both outgoing and incoming shots.

The preferred length of a dissolve is related to the tempo of the film at that point, the pace of the sequences it joins, the picture quality of both outgoing and incoming shots, as well as to the individual needs of the pictures being mixed. Fast moving sequences demand shorter dissolves than those which are slower and more dreamily paced. Sometimes interviews are edited with very swift dissolves between different sections—softened cuts really—to make an honest declaration to the viewers that material has been omitted. Sometimes, however, the length of the dissolve is determined not so much by aesthetic ideals but by practical limitations. There must be sufficient length of shot available to mix. This means that for a slow, sixty-four frame dissolve, not only must there be a minimum of sixty-four frames of the shot remaining after the start of the mix, but nothing must happen in the course of those sixty-four frames which would disturb the dissolve effect. A new action beginning in the outgoing shot just before the end of the dissolve, even if perceived only very faintly, can be sensed as a blip, a disruption of the smooth flow from one scene to another. The editor may have to adjust the length of a dissolve to make sure that no extraneous movements are caught in the dissolve unintentionally. Exactly the same constraints apply to fades out to black or fades up from black. As far as possible when such visual devices are used, the frames which are overlapped or faded should approximate to a still picture. If the length available for a fade or dissolve is insufficient, it is sometimes possible to extend the shot by freezing it. As long as a freeze occurs in the course of mixing or fading, it is unlikely to be noticeable.

Sound editing

In the process of perfecting the visual half of the documentary, the fine cut will necessarily establish the precise relationship between picture and sound, where each begins and ends, where they need to coincide and where they need to run unconnected but in parallel. Most sequences in most documentaries have their own synchronous sounds: sounds directly related to things happening on the screen. Actions take place—a person speaks, a hammer hits a nail, a car drives off—which the viewer expects to be accompanied by its particular sound. It goes without saying that in such cases, the vision and the sound should be synchronous, 'in synch', with each other.

In certain places, however, the close association between images and their sounds makes difficult decisions necessary. The start or completion of an action, a door closing, for example, is often used to motivate a cut from one scene to another. Such an action will have an associated sound. But there are a number of differences between images and sounds which complicate the matter. A visual moment is instantaneous while sound is spread over time. The sound of a door slamming only begins at the moment the action, the door striking its frame, is complete. Thus if the shot of a slamming door ends as it should visually, at the moment of closure, the sound will have not yet have begun. But if the shot continues long enough for the sound to be fully heard, the picture cut may seem to come too late, some frames after the preferred moment. It is often hard to find the best solution to this problem. Many editors will allow the sound to continue to its completion after the cut in the picture to another scene.

Visual and auditory stimuli seem to take different lengths of time for the brain to assimilate. Pictures are noticeably faster to recognize than sounds. It is as if visual images are directly and instantly decoded by the brain, while sounds go through a two-stage process: the sound being first stored in a raw state, the brain then 'replaying' the raw memory to analyse what the ears have heard. We often remember telephone numbers by memorizing the raw sound of the words and only decoding them into numbers later. Most of us know the experience of failing to understand something somebody has said, perhaps in an unfamiliar dialect, and 'replaying' it in the head to try to interpret the unrecognized words. The consequence of this double sensing of a sound in contrast to the immediate recognition of an image is that where sounds need to be related to pictures in a film, the sound may need to begin before the image. If a scene or a shot begins with a noisy action, many editors will let the sound start some fractions of a second before making the cut to the new picture.

Music

In the fine cut, sound is usually accommodated to picture, the montage submitting to the demands of the visual material. But there are some places in which the vision will need to take account of the sound. In those sequences where music underlies the pictures, the sound will play an important part in determining exactly how the visuals are cut together.

There are two kinds of music sequences: those where the music is incidental to the visual sequence, running along underneath to add emotional and atmospheric depth; and those where the music is the main sound associated with the pictures. The first needs little special treatment. Assuming that the music has been chosen, or composed, with proper sympathy to the pattern of images and is not the most prominent audible feature, the visuals can generally be fine cut without constant reference to the musical accompaniment. But where the music is the main sound, it must be treated almost as if it were a form of speech. For like speech, throughout which a continuous thread of meaning must be maintained, music cannot be cut and joined with the freedom of pictures. Instead, the pictures have to be carefully tailored to work in synch with the sound. Such a visual sequence will be timed to, and cut to, the music.

The music will determine the exact length of the sequence, which will end where the music rather than the vision dictates; simply fading or cutting the music off at the end, with no proper musical conclusion, is disturbing and crass. The music will also indicate where the cuts from one shot to the next should be made. This is not a simple mechanical process. Always cutting to the next shot on the main beat of the musical bar has an overly predictable and pedestrian effect. As with other forms of rhythm, cutting to music involves picking out an ordered deviation from the steady pulse. The cuts will make reference to the musical background without slavishly following it. The content of the images will be only one of the determining factors in choosing exactly at which point in the musical bar each cut should fall. The other will be a feeling for the rhythm, the beat, the swing.

The cuts in a music sequence need to be made in time with the music because of an unexpected equivalence of sound and vision. Rhythm in film terms is established by events. A change of picture is perceived as a film event and so is a sound. A cut from one shot to another is felt by the viewer as the same class of phenomenon as the beat of a drum. Thus a rhythm can be marked or filled in by picture cuts as well as by sounds. In a musical phrase such as a bar of note-note-rest-note (|♩♩𝄽♩ |) a picture cut at the moment of the musical rest (𝄽) can be used to complete the rhythm and satisfy audience expectation, just as a sound event can replace an expected visual moment. (Take the idea yet further and imagine that the musical accompaniment consists entirely of rests and no notes at all. What remains to supply the rhythm are the visual events. Hence the sense of rhythm that editors strive for in the visual montage of all sequences.)

Music which is secondary to other accompanying sounds, where the score is incidental to a sequence rather than its driving force, gives the editor more liberty in its use. When released from the burden of giving a sequence structure and form, it can contribute more of what the pictures cannot: non-verbal suggestions of association, emotion and meaning. Music is used to help the audience recognize where a scene starts and where it ends, to introduce atmosphere, to suggest mood, to give emphasis to particular moments, to make comments. The editor will try to place the music so that the musical logic matches that of the action. Some subtlety is called for when placing the music so as to get the wanted effect. A musical running commentary, such as TV melodrama depends on—a drumbeat for every footstep, a glissando for every fall—is a form of authorial voice and is perceived as such by the audience, who may not welcome constant instruction in how to interpret what they see. In documentaries, musical reference rather than illustration is often more successful.

Music which underscores a scene may begin before the scene or with it. If before, it acts as a bridge linking the one to the other, emphasizing continuity. If music and scene start together, the implication is more of beginning something new, a break from what came before. If the score has been especially composed for film, there will be specified points at which it is designed to fit. The end of the music will usually match some screen event, a panning shot reaching its destination perhaps, or somebody entering into vision. This will have the side-effect of drawing the audience's attention away from the music's disappearance. When music is well placed and timed, its ending often goes unnoticed by the audience. Its beginning, however, even if faded up gradually, can't help raising audience expectations for some parallel change in the screen world.

Track laying and dubbing

Throughout the processes of rough and fine cutting, the editor will have been identifying and collecting the sounds which are intended to go with the sequences. By the end of the fine cut, a full specification of the required sound will have been made. Some of the sound will come from what was synchronously recorded on location, some will come from sound effects disks, some it may be necessary to go out and record.

The sound specification is physically realized in the process of track laying. The phrase refers to the magnetic tapes used to carry sound when editing 16mm or 35mm film. Track laying involves selecting the sections of required sound and connecting them together in proper time relationship with the picture and with each other. The end product is a number of rolls of magnetic tape which all play together in synchronization as they are mixed down to the final complete sound track in a dubbing theatre. The same results are now more often achieved with virtual tape tracks on computer-based sound editing systems.

This is the time when the sound world of the film is created. Many tracks may be needed to build up the wanted atmosphere, beginning with the synchronous location sound, joining sections together, substituting new sounds for on-screen events where the location sound is inadequate, mixing in other sounds to enrich the ambience, sometimes underscoring with a music track, sometimes overlaying with a commentary track, sometimes both at once. Thirty-six tracks is not an unusually high number.

It is not that there are necessarily so many different sound sources to add together at the same time. Working in stereo, as many productions now do, automatically takes twice the number of tracks as monaural sound. But in addition the nature of sound and the response of the human ear make clearly audible any instantaneous change from one sound to another, or from one acoustic to another, or from one sound atmosphere to another, even though the two may seem identical when heard separately. So most sound cuts are executed as fast mixes, which also doubles the number of tracks needed. Dialogue, for example, is almost always prepared as two separate tracks, an 'A' roll and a 'B' roll, one to each alternate speaker, for mixing from one to the other between speeches.

Such doubling can demand considerable preparation. To allow for the chequerboarding there must be enough spare sound available on the tape before the moment of change to accommodate the time needed for the mix. It may be necessary to edit extra passages of location atmosphere onto the beginning and end of many sections of speech, for example, to make mixing in and out possible. (It is here that the film-maker will bless the foresight of the sound recordist in ensuring the provision of an 'atmos' track from the location.)

Film sound mixing, dubbing, was traditionally undertaken in a dubbing theatre, where a projector ran in synch with a battery of magnetic track replay machines, which delivered their sound through a multitrack mixing console. To change the timing relationship of any one track required the sound engineer to get up, go to another room, and move the track physically backwards or forwards on the player. Today, sound dubbing is increasingly being undertaken on computer. The old style film dubbing theatre will soon only be found in museums of film technology.

The mix, or dub, is usually done in a number of stages. There might first be a premix of a selected number of tracks, if a good balance of levels and adjustments between them is difficult to achieve. The sound engineer will try to give all the elements the best possible sound by 'equalizing' them—filtering the frequencies to achieve the most realistic and ear-pleasing effect—both separately and in combination. Using today's digital technology there should be no degradation in quality between generations of copies. In the United States, this process is usually called 'sweetening', though sweetness is not necessarily the sought-after effect. To the premix are then added other tracks to create the music and effects track, the 'M and E'. This carries the entire sound of the production with the exception of the commentary.

The commentary is frequently recorded and added last of all in a separate process, as there may later be occasion to provide a different commentary—in another language, for example. The existence of an M and E makes this possible without having to recreate the entire sound from scratch, hence the alternative name: 'international sound track'. Though it may seem that leaving the commentary recording to the end forfeits the possibility of fine adjustment in the cutting room, in fact the flexibility of a live human performer, who can speed up, slow down, change intonation and pause at will, more than makes up for it. Commentaries are recorded with the voice artist watching the picture and listening to the final mix through earphones. This

allows for the most exact control of timing and tone of voice. Just
as with effects and music, however, the delay in assimilating the
spoken word, compared with the near instantaneous recognition
of a picture suggests that words which are linked to particular
moments in the film should normally precede them by some
fractions of a second.

Such adjustments, like others made in the course of post-
production, will not necessarily be obvious to the audience. And
perhaps they should not be. The many accommodations a film-
maker has to make with human psychology each influence the
overall effect of the work, each making its own small unrecognized
contribution to a whole which is far greater than the sum of its
parts.

Chapter 18

The Review

To gain an impression of the whole film is the purpose of the film-maker's final procedure: the review. The later stages of editing and dubbing have been so concerned with the technical minutiae of film construction that it is all too easy to lose sight of the wood and see only the trees, to forget the appearance and function of the building while concentrating on the precise way the bricks fit together. So it is important to have the opportunity to sit back and watch the documentary from start to finish, seeing it for the first time as the audience will.

This is not merely to check for faults and errors. There should not really be any by this stage, though it must be admitted that on occasion mistakes do only now come to light. One television producer woke in a cold sweat at three in the morning, suddenly realising that the wrong cameraman's name had appeared in the credits of the film he had been reviewing ten hours before. Even now it should not be too late to correct gaffes of that kind. The schedule should allow for last-minute corrections. Other faults will not be so easy to correct and a judgement will have to be made over whether their seriousness warrants unpicking the film and reassembling parts of it, with the resulting impact on cost. Budgets rarely allow for over-meticulous perfectionists to have their way.

The aim of the review is, in any case, not merely to allow a film-maker to make sure that the work is ready for delivery to the client. To see one's own work as the viewer does is the only way to appreciate exactly what one has made—good points and bad. This is an essential part of learning and growing as a film-maker. It is true that watching a documentary in a viewing theatre is not the same experience as seeing the same production when broadcast on television or when played to its target corporate audience. The environment in which the film is shown—home or office—the events that precede and succeed it on the screen, all have a strong effect on the way the documentary is perceived. But the review is an opportunity to take time out to concentrate on viewing the work in the round, to judge pace, flow, balance, variety, intelligibility, interest and all the other qualities upon which the impact and elegance of a documentary depend. It is an opportunity to think about what worked well and what could have been done better.

A modern novelist has said that the aim of constantly rewriting his drafts is to detect 'false notes' in the text—those moments which, like a cracked bell, somehow don't ring true. When reviewing a film, a documentarist has similar aims. But the workings of film are less mysterious than those of prose. A film-maker will usually be able to say with considerable precision why something in the documentary isn't quite right. And most documentarists find something they dislike in almost every example of their work. Some of these antipathies are reasonable: when shots don't quite reveal what they were supposed to, or show more than they should; when sequences don't quite convey the information or the emotion intended, when interviewees don't quite express the thoughts or feelings they were chosen to expose.

But equally film-makers often cringe and groan at moments in their work that nobody else notices or finds exceptional. We all carry engraved on our memories, like Calais on Queen Bloody Mary's heart, moments that we would give almost anything to be able to change. There is a sound edit towards the start of *The Last Exodus*, where the president of the Jewish community of Odessa is describing the mass emigration of the city's remaining Jews. 'This really is,' he says, 'the Last Exodus.' Because the statement came in the midst of an unstoppably rapid flow of words, isolating the thought left the end of the sentence audibly cut off and hanging in the air. Audibly maybe, but only to a fluent speaker of Russian with a particularly good ear for intonation. British and American viewers reading the subtitles have been completely oblivious to what still seems to me a less than elegant truncation.

When I was executive producer of one particular BBC documentary, I noticed that whenever the film-maker was showing me the current state of progress of the production, she would always go into paroxysms of coughing at one particular point in the film. Guessing that she was trying to distract me from noticing some fault in the assembly, I cajoled her into admitting what the problem was. It was that in one of the key images of the documentary, the film-maker herself could be seen lurking in the background of the picture. Of course only those who knew her well would have recognised the tiny blurred figure, but that didn't prevent her embarrassment and bitter dislike of the shot, which was, nevertheless, too important to be omitted. Until she pointed it out, I hadn't even noticed.

Such responses to one's own work are inevitable. Edna St Vincent Millay said of writing: 'A person who publishes a book wilfully appears before the populace with his pants down. If it is a good book, nothing can hurt him. If it is a bad book, nothing can help him.' Exactly the same can be said of a documentary film.

And, as with a book, the principal difficulty is than one never quite knows whether one's work is good or bad. The temptation is to suspect the latter. Even Mario Puzo said of his stunningly successful novel *The Godfather* 'I wish I had written it better.'

Whether a documentarist's negative response to moments in his or her own work is well-founded or irrational, coming to terms with it is an essential part of the film-making process. An error is only an unmitigated disaster if nothing is learned from it. One might go even further: it could be claimed that when a documentarist, like any other artist, is always totally satisfied with what he or she makes, it means that growth and development have ceased and that now is probably the time to stop and take up another profession.

What's it all for?

For most film-makers the aim of the editing process, maybe even the entire production process, is to achieve an impression of unquestioned inevitability. The intention is to make the viewer feel that the film could not have been constructed and perfected in any other way. This is just an alternative formulation of the traditional notion that a product of the creative imagination should be accepted 'as is', that its technique and means of realization should be hidden from and left unexamined by its audience. For the arts in general that can be called a pre-modern attitude. Today's creators no longer take such a view for granted. Much of the history of art in the twentieth century has been about confronting the audience with the artificiality and arbitrariness of the techniques by which artists convey their vision to their public. And as we have noted, some of the devices of the television documentary of today's 'post-modernist' times are concerned, not with the content, the 'meaning', of the images, but with their appearance.

Every documentarist will make his or her own decision on whether to follow the path of the nineteenth century naturalistic novelist, that of the twentieth century iconoclast, or that of the new-age net-surfer. The decision will depend on the film-maker's ultimate purpose and will have its consequences. The new 'multimedia' style, which a British television channel controller once described as having 'a heavily worked surface', as if film were a kind of painting, is specifically designed to attract the young. It may also repel the not-so-young. The traditional still has considerably more immediate general public appeal than the avant-garde—how revealing that one still refers to the 'modern' movement even after almost a hundred years, and that it has been necessary to invent the self-contradictory term 'post-modern'. It took a towering protean genius of modernism like Picasso to break through to recognition by the man and woman in the street. In a recent poll for the nation's favourite poem, the British public firmly endorsed 'If' by Rudyard Kipling. Eliot's 'The Waste Land' may be a greater work of art but many fewer people have ever read it, let alone know it by heart, let alone derive wisdom and comfort from it.

That may of course not matter. It all depends on what one wants the result of one's work to be. Many documentary makers just wish to make a living by serving the needs of others. That is a perfectly respectable purpose. Some are above all concerned to speak to, and entertain, as large an audience as possible. Some are more interested in exploring a subject in serious depth, no matter how small the number of viewers prepared to follow. Some are involved in the creation of art-works, whose *raison d'être* is simply to exist. Yet others wish their films to do something in the world— to have an impact on society or politics. This is no different from artists working in any other medium. P G Wodehouse said that there were two ways of writing novels: 'One is mine, making a sort of musical comedy without music and ignoring real life altogether; the other is going right deep down into life and not caring a damn.' Remove the phrase 'ignoring real life' and much the same can be said of the television documentary.

The greatness of our medium is that it can accommodate all these aims.

The documentary has been through many stages in its time. The very first moving film of all was a documentary—workers leaving the Lumière brothers' factory. In its cinema days it became first an art form, then a movement, predominantly of the liberal left. When broadcast television became the principal mass medium of the age and the chief source of public information, documentary films gained political power. As journalism, television document-aries have often contributed to the public debating agenda. Social documentaries broadcast on tv have often changed society's self-perception in important ways. Television documentaries have even had an impact on national developments in technology. *Now the Chips Are Down*,[1] a film in the BBC's science strand *Horizon*, led to questions in Parliament, the setting up of a select committee to report to the House on the future for information technology in Britain, and the establishment with public money of INMOS, a company to manufacture silicon chip microprocessors (long since—alas—sold abroad). *The Computer Programme*,[2] from BBC Education, broadcast in more than twenty countries, resulted in a generation of British school students growing up familiar with the BBC Micro, one of the earliest affordable personal computers,

[1] BBC 1979
[2] BBC 1980

making Britain at the time the most computer-literate country in the world.

There are those who question whether any television production could have the same impact today. Until the mid-1980s, there were few channels available and it was possible for a single powerful programme to become the subject of conversation the next day in what seemed at the time to be a majority of homes, workplaces, pubs and clubs. Now that the number of channels is increasing and satellite, cable transmission and videotape players are poised to fragment the viewing audience, a television documentary may have to work harder to arouse a similar level of general interest. Yet the changes now under way have their compensations. As suggested at the very beginning, the new technological era has opened up the possibility of documentary making to all, and particularly to those who have previously been mute, to those whose place in life it always was to be the subject of documentaries rather than to make them—people, as one might say, more filmed against than filming. Many channels now carry documentaries shot on high-end consumer equipment. The BBC Community Programmes Unit has shown that productions created by ordinary people about their own lives can have great public impact.

The effect on our society of the advent of television has often been compared to that of the introduction of printing. Though the time-scales are dramatically different, there are indeed some similarities. An original Gutenberg Bible cost about the same as a small landed estate. When television broadcasting first began, buying a receiver was a considerable investment. In both cases more and more people could afford to become engaged with the new medium as the technology cheapened and spread. Ultimately the printing press lead to mass literacy, and even more importantly, mass access to printing technology and therefore to a mass readership. By our own times, anyone from any walk of life can write and be published—as long as, that is, he or she has something to communicate.

It is clear that a similar development is now beginning to take place in the film—or rather, the video—medium. As suggested at the beginning, the time will soon come when all who wish to do so will be able to make documentaries about their own particular ideas, beliefs, perceptions, interests and obsessions.

Unquestionably this will introduce into the public arena a chorus of new voices, original thoughts, and unfamiliar experiences, greatly enriching our culture and our civilization.

But learning to make films is not quite the same as learning to write. Writing is in effect no more than permanently petrified speech. Written text originally developed as a kind of low-tech recording device. The speech was encoded into symbols; when later read again—aloud—the sound of the original words was reproduced. When we read, we still recreate the sounds of the words inside our heads and then listen to what they say. (It is not just those with learning difficulties who move their lips when they read; we all do, though most of us unconsciously suppress it.) That is why writing can use stylistic devices like onomatopoeia, assonance, alliteration and rhyme, that depend for their effect on the actual sounds of the words.

Thus once the coding system has been learned, for anyone who can speak, writing comes more or less naturally. This appears to be very different from film-making technique, which seems non-intuitive and must be painstakingly learned and carefully studied. Or is it and must it?

In any literary or visual medium, artistry and style can only be acquired by effort, practice and experience. But what of the fundamental principles? One of the aims of this book has been to suggest that the basics of film-making are almost as natural and as closely related to our everyday perceptions as writing is to speech. The technology used may change—just as letterpress printing has given way to offset litho—but the fundamental idea remains the same. The documentary technique is an attempt to put the viewers into a situation as if they themselves were there, to show them what they themselves would see and let them hear what they themselves would hear if they were really present. The model for the viewer is, and can only be, the film-maker him- or herself. So to work on putting a documentary film together is, in a sense, to study the way we ourselves see and hear the world, and how we respond to it. To make a documentary film is in essence a form of self-exploration and self-discovery. What is principally demanded of you, as a television documentary maker, is not so much the mastery of principles and the understanding of technology but a desire, perhaps even a passion, to show to others what you have seen yourself, and in the way that you have seen it. Like great portraiture in painting, the truthfulness of a documentary depends not so much on its likeness to the external reality of its subject, but more to its expression of the documentarist's response to that reality. As has been said about writing books, a film-maker is not 'a person who wants to say something, but a person who has something to say.'

Index